A Legacy in Brick and Stone

American Coastal Defense Forts
of the Third System, 1816 – 1867

by

John R. Weaver II

**Pictorial Histories
Publishing Company**

Redoubt Press

LIBRARY OF CONGRESS
CATALOG CARD NUMBER 00-130485
IBSN 1-57510-069-X
First Printing: July 2001

COVER: Fort Jefferson National Monument, The Dry Tortugas, Florida, June, 1996. Photograph by author.

This book is dedicated to my wife, Jan, and my children, Rick and Susan, who have patiently supported my trips to forts around the country, and who may never understand the enjoyment of spending a large portion of my free time sitting in libraries or climbing around old masonry.

This book is also dedicated to my parents, John and Margaret Weaver, who first dragged a five-year-old boy through the Castillo de San Marcos in St. Augustine, Florida, thus beginning a lifelong interest in military history in general and forts in particular.

PICTORIAL HISTORIES PUBLISHING COMPANY
713 SOUTH THIRD STREET WEST
MISSOULA, MONTANA 59801
406/549-8488
406/728-9280
WWW.PICTORIALHISTORIESPUBLISHING.COM

Redoubt Press
A Division of McGovern Publishing

REDOUBT PRESS
1717 FOREST LANE
MCLEAN, VIRGINIA
703/538-5403
703/538-5171 (FAX)
TCMCGOVERN@ATT.NET

Table of Contents

v

Table of Figures

Acknowledgements

First and foremost, I must acknowledge the support of my family in this venture. For nineteen years of research, writing, photographing and manuscript preparation they provided a very high level of support. They supported me emotionally, financially, and physically through this period.

Second, the reviewers of the manuscript, technical and non-technical, deserve a very large amount of credit. They inspired me, kept me honest and grounded in fact, and provided a high level of constructive criticism for the manuscript. It would be of significantly lesser quality had they not made their several contributions. I would like to give a special thanks to William Stokinger and William Allcorn who devoted a tremendous amount of time and energy to improve the quality of this book.

Technical Reviewers		Non-Technical Reviewers
William Allcorn	Terrance McGovern	Sally Frye
Michael Bailey	David Ogden	Barbara Graves
Mark Berhow	Bolling Smith	Fred Kerby
Blanton Blankenship	William Stokinger	David Swinehart
Dale Floyd	Robert Zink	Al and Audrey Wald
		Janet Weaver

Third, the local experts at each of the forts provided information, direction, and inspiration. They work long hours for little pay, maintaining the legacy that this book documents. Without their dedication this legacy would be lost, and the valuable information they provide to those visiting these sites would not be disseminated. The many hours of discussion with these historians, site managers, curators, and fort supporters were invaluable. Their willingness to unlock otherwise locked doors and gates, and in some cases even to use bolt cutters to provide my access into closed areas have helped to unravel mysteries and debunk fort mythology.

Fourth, I owe a great deal to two organizations that have provided me with inspiration, camaraderie, information, contacts, and enjoyable trips through fortifications of all periods. They are the Coast Defense Study Group (WWW.CDSG.ORG) and the Council on America's Military Past (WWW.CAMPJAMP.ORG). B. W. Smith, former CDSG chairman and current editor of the Journal of the CDSG, has been a delightful companion on these quests and has supplied me with invaluable information from the National Archives, his second home!

Fifth, I would like to thank the two people who provided the inspiration and impetus for this project. The inspiration was provided by Emmanuel Raymond Lewis, author of my first book on coastal fortifications, Seacoast Fortifications of the United States, An Introductory History. Ray's book set me off on a quest that ultimately resulted in this book. The impetus for the book came from the late Richard Weinert. Through his pushing an cajoling, this project was born and in his memory this project has been completed.

Finally, my publishers, Terry McGovern and Stan Cohen, deserve a great deal of credit for the completion of this project. They have provided inspiration, kept me on task, and arranged for the final reviews of the work.

Above all, this work could never have been completed without the grace and blessings of God the Father, Son, and Holy Spirit.

John R. Weaver 3709 Sugar Lane Kokomo, Indiana 46902 John@WeaverHome.com

Preface

The Third System of American coastal fortifications was truly a system – individual components making up a whole that was much more than the sum of the parts. As described in Part I, the system consisted of the Navy, the Army and militia, the system of communications, and fortifications. This book deals with the fortifications that were built as a part of the system.

The heart of these fortifications was a group of forty-two forts that were newly constructed for the defense of the coasts. Supporting these new forts were a series of batteries, towers, and other "works" that are smaller than a fort. These structures were also newly constructed for the system, and played an important role in the defense of the harbors they guarded.

Also in support of the newly constructed forts were the forts built in previous projects. One of these forts, Fort Marion (Castillo de San Marcos), dates back to the early Spanish colonial period. Other forts, such as Fort Mifflin near Philadelphia, date back to America's first years as a nation. Finally, forts such as Fort Washington just south of Washington D.C., were built immediately prior to the Third System. These forts were modified during the Third System, and were truly part of the system.

This book deals with the Third System as a whole, but gives emphasis to the newly constructed forts. They are the most dramatic representation of America's theories of coastal defense in this period, and the modifications to the older structures are adaptations of these theories. The smaller supporting structures are also made up of the elements used to create the larger forts.

Forts designed and constructed to defend the northern frontier are a special case. Some of these forts are contemporary to the Third System, but are not part of the system. The first chapter of Part II discusses these forts, and explains their relation ship to the Third System.

A further limitation to the scope of the project concerns the specific information about the Third System forts included. Several books have been written about individual forts of the system. Further attempts to provide material covering the life of each fort was considered impractical. The scope is limited to primarily include the architecture, engineering, and construction of the forts, with little emphasis on their histories. An exception to this is Chapter Four, which covers the effectiveness of several forts during the Civil War. This is included as a necessary element for determining the efficacy of the design of the forts.

There is some controversy among military historians and fort buffs as to the proper names to use for the forts of the Third System. The naming conventions used in the text are described in Appendix C, which also gives a cross-reference of fort names. The author has taken liberty to use a name for each fort in the system. For the reasons a particular name of a fort was used, please see the section dedicated to that fort in Part II of the book.

Fort Alcatraz
Fort Point

New Construction Forts

1816 - 18

Fort Mackinac

Fort Montgomery

Fort Knox
Fort Popham
Fort Gorges
Fort Preble
Fort Scammel
Fort Constitution
Fort McClary
Fort Winthrop
Fort Independence
Fort Warren

Fort Ontario

Fort Niagara
Fort Porter

Fort Schuyler
Fort Totten

Fort Taber
Fort Adams
Fort Trumbull

Fort Wayne

Fort Tompkins
Fort Richmond

Fort Hamilton

Fort Hancock

Fort Delaware
Fort Carroll

Fort Monroe
Fort Calhoun

Fort Macon

Fort Caswell

Fort Sumter

Fort Pulaski

Fort Gaines
Fort Morgan

Fort Clinch

Fort Massachusetts

Fort Pike
Fort Wood

Fort Barrancas
Fort Pickens
Fort McRee

Fort Livingston   Fort Jackson

Fort Jefferson   Fort Taylor

of the Third System
867

Prologue:

Why the Third System?

Questions that are often asked by visitors to the magnificent brick and stone forts that dot the coastline of the United States are "Why is this fort here?" and "Why was it built the way it was?" This book attempts to provide answers to these questions. But before doing that, it is helpful to understand a bit about the history of the periods surrounding their construction.

The period covered in this book, the Third System, was so named because of its place in history relative to other programs to fortify America's shores. Following is a brief discussion of how this period fits into the history of America's coastal defense.

Seven years after the ratification of the Federal Constitution, it became evident that some type of nationalized defense was needed to protect the harbors of our major cities. It was considered a strong possibility that England might muster an attempt to win back her colonies, and the turmoil in Europe was such that several other countries might try to intimidate or subdue the potentially profitable new nation.

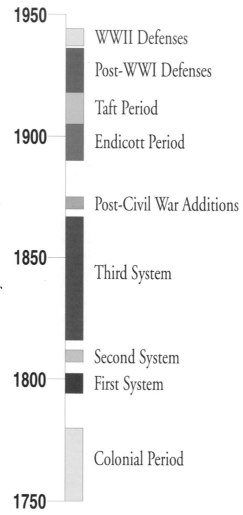

1950 — WWII Defenses

Post-WWI Defenses

Taft Period

1900 — Endicott Period

Post-Civil War Additions

1850 — Third System

Second System

1800 — First System

Colonial Period

1750 —

At the time, the Federal Government had little money and the army had no expertise in the construction of fortifications beyond rather primitive earth-works. As a result of these limited resources and the need for outside expertise, the task of defense became a cooperative effort between individual states and the Federal Government. Congress outlined an overall plan, appropriated some of the required funding, and arranged for employment of European engineers. The states provided (and often maintained possession of) the land, provided additional funds and a substantial amount of the armament, and held "right of approval" of designs and construction.[1]

The results of this effort at coastal defense were varied. Early forts were generally of wood-and-earth construction, and were neither durable nor provided adequate defense.[2] Several of the later forts, however, were of masonry-and-earth construction and are still in existence. Some displayed highly innovative designs (e.g., Fort Mifflin outside Philadelphia) and are well placed (e.g., Fort McHenry in

Baltimore harbor; Fort Moultrie in Charleston harbor). This agglomeration of individual works is known as the First System of American coastal fortifications. It covered the period from 1794 through 1807.

After the turn of the century, peace was the byword and little threat existed to the United States. The First System forts fell into disrepair and were largely forgotten. By the middle of the first decade, however, Europe again had fallen into turmoil. France and England were both considered threats to the new nation, and yet *French* engineers designed the existing coastal fortifications! To address the lack of skills in fort design, the government had appropriated funds to create a national military academy[3] in 1802, and the first graduates of West Point were adding to the ranks of the Corps of Engineers.

In late 1807, following the Chesapeake Affair,[4] Congress appropriated a substantial amount of money to construct what would be referred to as the Second System of American coastal fortifications. Early works followed the pattern of the First System works, but later in the Second System some all-masonry fortifications were constructed. These forts were the first American application of arched gunrooms, or casemates, which would become the pattern for Third System works.[5] Castle Williams, on Governor's Island in New York Harbor, is the most impressive of these casemated forts, mounting 102 guns on four tiers.

A few forts begun during the War of 1812, or immediately following it, fall into the category of Transitional Forts, fitting in neither the Second nor Third System. Most impressive of these forts was Fort Lafayette, which stood on Hendrick's Reef in New York Harbor and mounted 72 cannon.[6] This fort was demolished to provide the eastern base for the Verrazano Narrows Bridge in 1964, with no remnants remaining. A noteworthy Transitional Fort that still exists is Fort Washington, directly across the Potomac River from Mount Vernon. With a reasonable amount of scrutiny the two phases of its masonry construction, Transitional and Third System, can be discerned.[7]

These forts led the way for the development of a third period of fortifications, the Third System, the history of which is described in detail in Chapter One.

Following the period of the Third System, it became clear that the importance of artillery defense surpassed the importance of infantry defense in controlling coastal strongpoints. In the 1870s, money was appropriated for brick-revetted outworks, generally located near Third System forts. These works were designed to mount large-bore cannon at minimal cost, and to make use of the ability of earthen embankments to absorb the energy of enemy shot.

This marked a philosophical change that altered fortification development. The weapon became the item of primary importance in seacoast defense, rather than the fortification that housed the weapon. This philosophy led the transition into the next period of coastal defense.

The 1880s saw the development of steel artillery – large, breech-loading rifles. Masonry was no match for these guns, nor would they fit into the current forts or revetments.

In parallel to this development was the development of Portland cement. The ability to construct gun emplacements with earthen embankments and massive concrete foundations and reinforcement evolved, and a new system of fortifications was born.

Named for Secretary of War William Endicott, the Endicott System consisted of concrete emplacements with little or no defense against infantry assault. These massive concrete emplacements, containing underground magazines and designed with earthen and concrete parapets, provided the platforms for these formidable new guns.

The guns were dispersed over a large area in these widely separated emplacements that were designed to blend with their surroundings. Supplementing these guns were large seacoast mortars and a system of electrically controlled submarine mines.

The Endicott System evolved into the Taft System, which provided for evolutionary changes in artillery development, logistics, and provision for the defense of off-shore locations.

The defensive periods following World War I and during World War II saw further development of concrete fortifications. The use of movable artillery, such as truck-mounted and railroad-mounted guns, began. Aircraft had to now be considered, resulting in the mounting of small-bore rapid-fire antiaircraft artillery. Also, overhead protection was provided for fixed artillery – the casemate had returned. These modern casemates, however, were extremely strong structures with layers of reinforced concrete separated by energy-absorbing earthen layers.

By 1950, the use of artillery for coastal defense was no longer considered viable in the United States. Weapons development had moved the role of defending the coasts to aircraft and missiles, and the Coast Artillery was dissolved. Our shores still show the remnants, however, of this bygone era.

––––––––––––

Notes:

[1] Lewis, E.R., *Seacoast Fortifications of the United States, An Introductory History*, Presidio, 1970, pp. 21-25.

[2] Hinds, J.R., and Fitzgerald, E., *Bulwark and Bastion: A Look at Musket Era Fortification With a Glance at Period Siegecraft*, Las Vegas, 1981.

[3] Prior to this, Washington had established an engineer school for members of the Corps of Artillerists and Gyneers. This school, founded in 1794, was also located at West Point. See Weigler, History of the United States Army, 1967.

[4] The Chesapeake Affair refers to the attack on the U.S.S. Chesapeake by H.M.S. Leopard, in an attempt to recover British and previously-impressed American deserters. The episode nearly began a war between the United States and Britain.

[5] Lewis, pp. 25-32.

[6] *American State Papers, Military Affairs*, Washington: Gales and Seaton, (subsequently ASP-MA), Vol. I, p. 628.

[7] The upper portion of the masonry was added during the Third System. The lines of demarcation between the upper masonry and lower masonry are quite clear. The design of the fort, originally completed by L'Enfant, was greatly modified during construction. How much of the existing "lower masonry" is the product of L'Enfant's design or the construction modifications is not clear.

Part I:

Overview of the Third System

The Coastal Fortifications Board

The Organization of the Board of Engineers

In 1816, the country was reeling in the aftermath of the War of 1812. Having been humiliated by the unsuccessful invasion of Canada, several major defeats, and especially by the burning of the capitol, our military competence and national security were in question. As a counterpoint, however, the spirit of chauvinism that has so characterized our nation was sparked with the victory at New Orleans and the "winning" of the war. Stories of American heroism and the "victorious underdog" syndrome fueled the feelings of national superiority. This ambivalence did not, however, cloud the perception of the need for national protection. The price that had been paid over the previous years was firmly in mind.

The military, above all, understood the piti-ful state of our defenses. Operating from bases in Canada, Bermuda, and Jamaica, the British had landed at will on our shores, ravaged several seaports, and successfully dominated the coast-line. Several existing fortifications were destroyed — either in battle or to avoid capture — although a few properly garrisoned forts had proven adequate. Additionally, the war had proven that a naval power could sustain a fleet in battle some two thousand miles from her shores. Most of our military leadership understood that the true reason for our "victory" was Britain's inability to sustain two wars simultaneously, with Napoleon's exploits in Europe taking precedence.

Post-war fiscal and political attitudes in Congress assured that a standing army of any size would not be maintained; indeed, the existing army had been reduced in size immediately following the war.[1] It appeared that a repetition

Figure 3: Fort McHenry, in Baltimore, Maryland, held the British fleet at bay during the War of 1812, thus demonstrating the importance of fortifications to the leadership of the young nation. The development of the Third System can be attributed, in part, to the battle that provided the United States with its National Anthem. *(Photo by author)*

of the British invasion could occur at any time (since the Napoleonic Wars had ended) and our defenses would be even less able to repel them than they had been in 1812. It was clear that action was required to secure American shores, but what method would be most effective was being hotly debated in Congress.

Recent martial events had led our military leadership to the conclusion that a system of coastal fortifications was required. Several battles in the Napoleonic Wars involved small coastal forts that were attacked by large fleets. With few exceptions — some military leaders claimed NO exceptions — these forts prevented invasion by far superior forces.[2] It was clear that even a small fort with emplaced guns could repel the warships of the day.

Here in America, Fort McHenry, supplemented by channel obstructions, prevented the entry of the British fleet into Baltimore harbor and prevented the capture of the city. With their fleet held at bay, the British could not support a land-based invasion of Baltimore, and the location of the fort precluded a ready siege against its works. Consequently, the British recalled their troops and the city was not attacked. In New York City, the very presence of the several forts guarding the harbor precluded a British attack. In this case, the forts provided a tacit deterrent to the invading enemy.

The single exception to the impregnability of masonry forts during the war involved the nation's capital. Fort Washington, guarding the Potomac approach to Washington City, should have held off the attacking British warships, but the desertion of the garrison after minor bombardment (and virtually no damage to the fort) allowed the British to capture the fort. A court-martial of the fort commander ensued.[3]

These events convinced the military, but Congress was and is the keeper of the finances for such projects. While they had been sporadic in the funding of masonry defenses in the past, the Congressmen now had a different perspective. Many had fled for their lives during the British invasion, and some had lost their homes. They were meeting in temporary quarters as a result of the burning of the Capitol, and had a clear vision of the importance of national defense. President James Madison and his logical successor Secretary of State James Monroe, long-time supporters of coastal fortifications, were able to obtain support for the development of a true system of coastal defense.

Madison worked with his friend James Barbour, Chairman of the Senate Committee on Military Affairs, to obtain an outside expert on coastal defense. With Barbour's guidance, Congress appropriated money for the Corps of Engineers to employ a "skilled assistant" for the planning of a coastal defense system.[4] Through the recommendation of the Marquis de Lafayette, they obtained the services of Simon Bernard, former aide-de-camp to Napoleon, for the position.[5]

Bernard was a recognized expert in fortifications. He had studied at the prestigious École Polytechnique and was the designer of several European forts and fortresses, most notably the defenses of Antwerp. He was available by virtue of having fallen into political disfavor in France for twice having supported Napoleon over the victorious King.[6] Now being *persona non grata* in France, Bernard was open to opportunities to apply his special skills. The fact that he was a dedicated Anglophobe — and that America considered Britain as her principal enemy — made the opportunity which Madison was offering all the more attractive.

From Madison and Monroe's viewpoints, the young Frenchman provided many advantages. By bringing in an engineer of Bernard's caliber, Madison had obtained an *expert* view of our coastal defense needs. He knew that any program presented by Bernard would have more credibility than one developed by the *biased* sources who would control the projects, our own military. He had thus obtained a useful lever to use with Congress in obtaining funding for the coastal fortifications project.

Figure 4: Simon Bernard was a Brigadier in the French Army who was hired by the United States government as a "skilled assistant" to the Corps of Engineers. His leadership was instrumental in the development of the Third System and the presentation of that system to Congress. *(Photo of bust on display at the Casemate Museum in Fort Monroe, Virginia)*

Madison gave Bernard the honorary rank of Brevet Brigadier General, the equivalent rank to the one he held in the French Army, and assigned him to the Corps of Engineers. The acting Secretary of War, George Graham, immediately formed a Board of Engineers to survey our defenses and set in place an overall strategy for defense of our frontiers. Bernard assumed the role of president of this board, but without official acknowledgment of the position.

At that point, the problems began. First, Bernard's rank was the same as the Chief of Engineers, J. G. Swift. With the two men holding equal rank, the reporting structure was unclear.

It was also implicit that the President and Congress had more confidence in *a foreigner* than in their own Corps of Engineers, or they would not have hired Bernard. The leaders of the Corps had been the designers of most of the Second System fortifications, in which they took great pride. Also, they had commanded troops in victorious battles during the War of 1812. Both General Swift and General McRee, members of the Board of Engineers, took great exception to what they considered a reflection on their professional credibility, as well as a personal insult.

Swift and McRee argued that the trusting of our coastal defenses to a foreigner with obvious allegiance outside of the United States was a breach of national security. Swift was the first graduate of West Point, and he had designed some of the fortifications of New York City, which had successfully deterred a British invasion. Swift and McRee were both filled with the patriotic zeal of the post-war Army.

Additionally, there was the professional jealousy of the West Point graduates. They were painfully aware that their young school did not enjoy the reputation of Bernard's École Polytechnique, and that the defenses of New York were less prestigious than the defenses of Antwerp. The very traits that Madison found desirable in Bernard were those that caused the greatest conflict with his peers. Coupled with these professional issues, Bernard did not speak English and had to be accompanied by an interpreter.

Interestingly enough, this jealousy and lack of acceptance of Bernard appeared only in the upper ranks. The young engineers in the Corps enjoyed serving with someone of such a reputation and readily accepted the Frenchman. Charles Gratiot, a young engineer who would go on to head the Corps in the 1830s, became both a close personal friend and working colleague of Bernard. Joseph Totten, destined to be a reigning figure in the history of the Corps, worked closely with Bernard during his entire tenure in this country, though not without conflict[7].

The Navy also accepted Bernard immediately. There was neither consideration of professional jealousy nor any competition for credibility or stature. As well as reportedly being personable,[8] Bernard held the Navy in high esteem and sold the system of fortifications as a supplement to our Naval forces.[9] Also involved in its attitude, no doubt, was the rivalry of the sister service, which had not accepted Bernard.

Amid this confusion and antagonism, the original Fortifications Board was convened in 1816 with Swift (ex officio), Bernard, McRee, and Totten.[10] Swift and McRee, both senior officers with significant reputations and egos, grew bitter with the favoring of Bernard's opinions over their own. Swift attempted to have Bernard transferred to the leadership of the Military Academy, but that attempt failed. At length, both Swift and McRee resigned from the Army in protest in 1818, leaving Totten and Bernard to comprise the Board. Captain J. D. Elliot of the Navy was officially on the Board as well, but played a much less significant role than did the engineers. Totten was also reported to favor resignation, following in his superiors' footsteps, but claimed that personal finances precluded that decision.

Even with these stresses at work, the board began to function immediately after it was chartered. Of first order was the defense of several coastal areas that appeared highly vulnerable and needed to have construction begin immediately.

The two areas first targeted for construction were the approaches to the city of New Orleans and Hampton Roads, the anchorage off Hampton, Virginia. The strategic value of New Orleans had been confirmed in the late war, and it was extremely vulnerable to attack. Hampton commanded a prime strategic location at the entrance to both the James River and the Chesapeake Bay, and its vulnerability had also been shown when the British burned the city during the war.

Design and construction of forts at these locations was followed by surveys of other major harbors and a systematic study of the nation's coastal defense needs. This study concentrated on the location of fortifications, but also proposed a system of interior roads and canals for communication and for transportation of reinforcements.

The First Report of the Board of Engineers

In 1818 the Board submitted a preliminary report that was primarily a status of current projects. In 1821 it submitted its first full report.[11] This report was signed by "Bernard, Brigadier General./J. D. Elliot, Captain U. S. Navy./Joseph G. Totten, Major of Engineers, Brevet Lieut. Col." It is interesting to note that while Totten indicated his rank was brevetted, Bernard simply listed himself as a Brigadier General.

The report began with an analysis of the methods of defense. It then espoused a philosophy that was to carry through the next forty years and which, in many ways, would provide the foundation of our coastal defenses until 1950. Finally, it systematically addressed all areas of the coastline, grouping proposed fortifications into three classes, according to priority.

In defining the philosophy of what was to become the Third System, four elements of national defense were outlined. The strength of

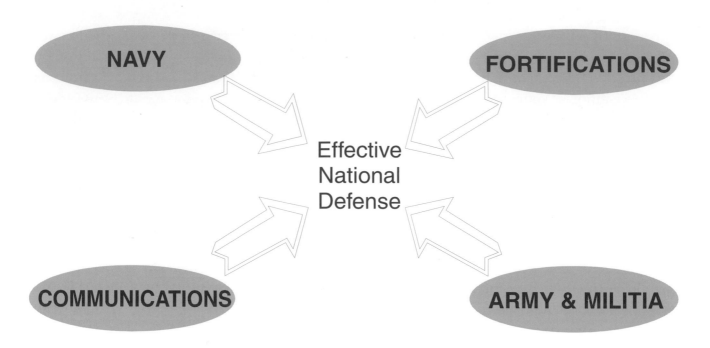

Figure 5: The Coastal Fortifications Board described an encompassing program for the defense of the vast American coastline. Four major elements were to work together to provide defense: a strong navy, well placed fortifications, a system of communications by land and water, and a standing army with a reserve militia. Bernard used significant political skill in addition to his military skills in defining this program, plying into the political power of the Navy and using preconceived notions that would be suitable to Congressional leadership. The Congress readily embraced the program, and the fort-building program was funded.

these elements lay not in their individual values, but in the synergistic combining of all four. No element had priority over another; the elimination of any one would have left the effectiveness of the whole disproportionately diminished.

The first element listed in the report was the Navy. The importance of a strong fleet was affirmed, as well as the components required to support this fleet. These components were defined as four types of locations that must be provided and secured:

1) Establishments for construction and repair

2) Harbors of rendezvous

3) Stations (bases)

4) Ports of refuge

The first recommendation of the board was the identification of proper sites for each of these purposes, and the relocation of existing facilities to these sites.

Significant detail went into the selection of these sites, with criteria such as defensibility, accessibility to sailing ships in various wind conditions, protection provided by the harbor in severe weather situations, and the size and depth of the available harbors. The selection of these sites was a precursor to the implementation of the other elements of the defensive system.

The second element listed by the Board was fortifications. The fortifications were for one or more of the following purposes:

A. To close important harbors to an enemy, and secure them to the navy of the country.

B. To deprive an enemy of strong positions, where, protected by his naval superiority, he might fix permanent quarters in our territory, maintain himself during the war, and keep the whole frontier in perpetual alarm.

C. To cover our great cities against attack.

D. To prevent as much as possible the great avenues of interior navigation from being blockaded by a naval force, at their entrance to the ocean.

E. To cover the coastwise and interior navigation, and give to our Navy the means necessary for protecting this navigation.

F. To cover the great naval establishments.

First Class - To be erected during the first period	
Proposed	Built
Fort St. Philip	Repair of old fort
Fort at Plaquemines	Fort Jackson, Louisiana
Fort at Chef Menteur	Fort Wood, Louisiana
Fort at Rigolets	Fort Pike, Louisiana
Fort at Bayou Bienvenue	Works only, Louisiana
Fort at Old Point Comfort	Fort Monroe, Virginia
Fort at the Rip Raps	Fort Calhoun, Virginia
Fort at Pea Patch Island	Fort Delaware, Delaware
Fort at New Utrecht Point	Fort Hamilton, New York
Fort at Tompkins's Point	Fort Tompkins, New York
Fort at Wilkins's Point	Fort Totten, New York
Fort at Throgg's Point	Fort Schuyler, New York
Fort at Brenton's Point	Fort Adams, Rhode Island
Fort at Dumpling's Point	Works only, Rhode Island
Fort at Rose Island	Works only, Rhode Island
Fort on the channel of Boston Harbor	Fort Warren, Massachusetts
Fort at Portsmouth	Fort Constitution, New Hampshire

Table 1: Forts of the *First Class* according to the 1821 Report. These forts were considered to be the highest priority for construction, the points most vulnerable to attack. The column on the right shows what was actually constructed at the location indicated. "Works only" refers to the construction of batteries and other structures, but not a fort.

Multiple forts were projected at major sites, and single forts, sometimes with supporting works,[12] at the less-critical locations.

These principles were the guiding force behind the fortification projects, and were carried through in the almost annual revisions in the number and location of forts and works. While the importance of the cities and harbors changed, the reasons for choosing particular locations remained constant.

The third element was a system of internal communications "by land and water" for the purpose of moving information and military strength to the points where they were required. It was well understood that fortifications were not invulnerable to siege, but that properly designed forts would cause significant delays to an enemy. Bernard's goal was to design forts that would be able to withstand a siege for 14 days, ample time for reinforcements to relieve the besieged forces. Thus the goal of the internal communications system was to allow the transportation of a sizable army to any point on the frontier within 14 days.

Finally, the Board listed as its fourth element a "regular army and well organized militia." The entire fortification strategy hinged on small peacetime garrisons in the coastal forts, to be supplemented by trained militia artillery in time of war. The posture of Congress regarding the maintenance of a standing army of significant size precluded full garrisoning of the fortifications. Therefore, a small "caretaker" garrison was planned for each fort, with a full wartime garrison many times larger provided should action against our shores occur.

After defining the entire system of defense, the report turned its attention almost entirely to

Second Class - To be erected during the second period	
Proposed	Built
Fort at Mobile Point	Fort Morgan, Louisiana
Fort at Dauphin Island	Fort Gaines, Louisiana
Fort at Savannah	Fort Pulaski, Georgia
Fort at Charleston	Fort Sumter, South Carolina
Fort at Smithville	Fort Caswell, North Carolina
Fort at Beaufort	Fort Macon, North Carolina
Fort at Soller's Point Flat	Fort Carroll, Maryland (nearby)
Fort at Hawkins's Point	Works only, Maryland
Batteries opposite the Pea Patch Island fort	Works only, Delaware
Fort Hale	Repairs to old fort, Connecticut
Fort Wooster	Repairs to old fort, Connecticut
Fort at Marblehead	Works only, Massachusetts
Fort at Salem	Works only, Massachusetts
Fort at Portland	Forts Gorges, Preble, Scammel

Table 2: Forts of the Second Class according to the 1821 Report. These forts were of a lesser priority, but were still considered to be very important to the System. As in the previous table, "works only" indicates that no fort was constructed, only batteries and appurtenances.

fortifications, the first project to be addressed that was under the control of the board. Some mention was made of the road and canal system, but this was always stated in the context of a future project. While the proposed forts were mentioned only in generalities, their functions and some justification for the selection of a given harbor were stated.

The size of each fortification took into account the population proximal to it that could be drawn upon to supplement the peacetime garrison; i.e., the militia. The Board's strategy assumed that sufficient notice of an invasion would be given to muster local troops to man the forts, but that time would be insufficient to transport Federal troops from central concentrations. It was further assumed that an alarm of invasion would likely be nonspecific, so that numerous forts would have to be fully (wartime) garrisoned simultaneously. This, along with the Congressional constraints regarding a peacetime army, eliminated the possibility of fully manning the forts with Federal troops.

In addition to the philosophy and strategy, the Board spent many words justifying the development of the system, especially the forti-

fications. In flowery language they described several worst-case scenarios of the tragedies that would befall the land if the system of defense were not implemented. This narrative culminated with a detailed example of the destruction of Philadelphia if only Fort Mifflin were present for the city's protection, and the way the city would be spared from all harm should the proposed forts be constructed, properly equipped, and manned.

In addition to the descriptive narrative justifications, the Board also provided financial justification for the forts. The costs of building the forts were weighed against the costs of maintaining sufficient troops in each location to defend against a possible aggressor. While this argument could be considered specious due to the restrictions applied by Congress, they did allow a dollar-value to be placed on the fortifications. Also mentioned was the cost of no defense, in terms of the loss of commerce from the harbor

Third Class - Forts to be erected during the third period	
Proposed	Built
Fort at Grand Terre	Fort Livingston, Louisiana
Tower at Pass aux Herons	Not constructed, Alabama
Tower at Bayou Dupré	Tower only, Louisiana
Fort at St. Mary's river	Fort Clinch, Florida
Fort at Beaufort	Works only, South Carolina
Fort at Georgetown	Works only, South Carolina
Fort at St. Mary's	None, Maryland
Fort at Annapolis	Works only, Maryland
Fort on the Middle Ground	Fort Hancock, New York
Fort on the East Bank	Fort Hancock, New York
Fort Trumbull	Fort Trumbull, Connecticut
Fort Griswold	Works only, Connecticut
Battery at Plymouth	Works only, Massachusetts
Battery at Provincetown	Works only, Massachusetts
Fort on the Kennebeck	Fort Knox, Maine
Fort on Wiscasset	Works only, Maine
Fort on Penobscot	Fort Popham, Maine
Fort on Mount Desert Bay	Works only, Maine

Table 3: Forts designated as Third Class in the 1821 Report. These forts had the lowest priority for construction, but were considered necessary to fill out the defenses of the coast. As in the previous tables, "works only" indicates that no fort was constructed, only batteries and appurtenances.

cities. These, of course, were expressed in the most pessimistic terms, but the damage inflicted on several harbor cities during the previous war did provide some justification for the assumed losses.

The Board concluded its report with a prioritized listing of the required fortifications, dividing them into three "periods" of construction. The first period, forts "indispensable to the defense assigned to that class[13]," consisted of the construction of sixteen forts and the repair and improvement of one fort. This group of forts included those that previously had been commenced, plus seven forts for the defense of New Orleans, Hampton Roads, and Mobile Bay. As a supplement to their listing, the board prioritized these seventeen forts into ten sub-classes, ranking the priority of construction, should "the treasury.... not permit their simultaneous commencement."

The second period consisted of thirteen forts and a group of batteries, and the third period consisted of fourteen forts, two towers, and two batteries. The total cost of the fortifications projected was $17,795,055, with some $8 million to be spent in the first period.

Thus, the Third System of American coastal fortifications was launched. Subsequent years would show a significant expansion of the program, to 115[14] works in 1851, but only 42 forts, one short of the 43 originally projected, were ever constructed, and several of these were not completed. Nevertheless, this system of forts was a landmark undertaking and provided us with a legacy, in brick and stone, of our coastal defense policies.

Evolution of the Board of Engineers

As the Board progressed on the surveys of the coast, the number of projects grew along with the number of sites that needed specific atten-tion to develop a project. The priority list grew to four categories from the previous three, and each of the categories seemed to contain more projects annually. The list was allowed to grow subtly through the commencement of construction of the first-priority forts. When construction of a fort began, it was removed from the priority list for fort planning. This left a vacancy on the first-priority list, and forts from the second-priority list were moved up to fill that vacancy. Third priority forts were now moved to the second-priority list, leaving the third-priority list and the newly created fourth-priority list for new projects.

Bernard listed the fortification of Dauphin Island and Mobile Point, the two points controlling the entrance to Mobile Bay, among the top-priority projects, and actually began construction of Fort Gaines and Fort Morgan prior to the 1821 report. Construction began in 1818 on both forts, but problems ensued at Fort Gaines. A contractor had been hired to begin construction of the fort, but at that time no representative of the Corps of Engineers had been assigned to the site. Construction of the fort had begun, but the quality of workmanship was poor and there was a scandal related to missing funds. With Fort Gaines falling "under the microscope," two changes took place that had a very significant impact on the construction of the Third System.

First, the Corps of Engineers became aware that they needed an officer present at each construction site to watch out for the interests of the government. This decision required an increased staffing of the Corps, but it also provided a tremendous training ground for new engineers. From that point on, no construction began on a fort until an engineer had been assigned and had traveled to the site.[15]

The role played by these engineers varied greatly. Some, such as William Chase, showed great initiative in the projects and made innumerable contributions to the forts built under his superintendence. Others acted more as a liaison between the contractor and the Corps of Engineers in Washington, D.C.

The second change related to the Fort Gaines controversy was the role Congress began to play in fort planning. With the close scrutiny of the Fort Gaines project, Congress began second-guessing the proposal. Even though such an expert as Bernard had been chosen to provide strategic guidance, some congressmen felt that they had a better understanding of the military's needs. Additionally, the economic climate was pushing for a reduced military budget and, since spending on fortifications was very large compared to other Federal budget items, it was an obvious target.

Congress argued that Fort Morgan and Fort Gaines were not both necessary to protect the bay. The water off Dauphin Island was too shallow to allow the large ships-of-the-line to enter the western side of the channel, and the congressmen argued that Fort Morgan was adequate to guard the entrance to the bay. They overruled Bernard and cut off the funds for the construction of Fort Gaines.[16]

While Bernard protested, he was astute enough to move the fort on Dauphin Island to his Priority Two list, assuring that it was not ahead of the projects for which he sought immediate funding. Meanwhile, a partially constructed Fort Gaines sat uselessly beside the entrance to Mobile Bay. Eventually, the use of steam-powered, and therefore shallow-draft, warships opened up the western entrance of Mobile Bay and Congress thereupon allowed the construction of Fort Gaines. A new design was developed and construction resumed. It was completed during the Civil War and played a role in the famous Battle of Mobile Bay.

From this point on, Congress appropriated funds by fortification rather than as a general appropriation to be disbursed by the Corps. Congressmen became very active in the decisions on which forts should go forward and which should be delayed, and "pork-barrel" politics was in its heyday. As can be imagined, the influx of money and jobs to the site of a new fort was similar to the planning of locations of military bases today. Whether or not it was strategically justified, congressmen wanted forts built in their state.

Although problems such as the Dauphin Island controversy arose, the fortification project flourished through the 1820s. During this decade, ten forts were begun and three were completed. Funding was very consistent, growing from $300,000 in 1821 to well over $1,000,000 in 1830. Bernard maintained both his interest and his personal touch on the projects during the early portion of that time period.

During the middle 1820s, however, Bernard became interested in canals. The original 1821 report gave significant importance to the development of a system of internal communications, and in 1824 a Board of Engineers for Internal Improvement was commissioned. Bernard, Totten, and John L. Sullivan constituted the Board —Totten and Bernard having surveyed the Mississippi and Ohio rivers in 1822, and Sullivan having superintended the operations of the Middlesex Canal[17]. More surveys were done, and construction of several canals and the Delaware Breakwater followed. Bernard was also involved was the planning of a second National Road to supplement the National Road then under construction. Bernard's greatest project was the planning of the Chesapeake and Ohio Canal, a mammoth undertaking that dwarfed all canal projects before or since.[18]

This project was the beginning of the end for Bernard's role in American engineering. Many professionals ridiculed Bernard's estimates for the cost of the canal, stating that it could be built for far less money. They stated that the

Frenchman did not understand the American way of doing business and the greatly reduced costs gained from American labor. He was overruled on the project, and was wont to find support from any quarter. He gave up his role in the project and returned to his coastal fortification work, his ego certainly bruised.

History, however, vindicated Bernard. The actual construction cost for the first section of the canal stretching to the Appalachian Mountains was remarkably close to his estimates, and it far exceeded the estimates of his domestic contemporaries. By the time this was known, however, Bernard had returned to France and was engrossed in pressing projects there.

Bernard's return to France in 1830 proved fortuitous. A small revolution had overturned the Bourbon dynasty for the final time, and an Orleans king came to power out of the rising middle class (the bourgeoisie). With Louis XVIII gone, Bernard's previous "sins" had been forgotten, and his mother country needed his talents. The latter, to Bernard, was an irresistible draw. Making the decision easier, it can be assumed, was the cancellation of his American canal projects and the scrapping of the project for the second National Road.

Once home, he finished an already illustrious career with even more contributions, but fell into political disfavor. Ironically, he was made a Baron of France on September 4, 1839, and died the next day. His greatest legacy was the founding and initial establishment of the Third System of American Coastal Defense — he was truly its founding father.

The Totten Years

On Bernard's departure, Totten took over the reins of the Fortifications Board. Charles Gratiot, friend and colleague of Totten for almost 20 years, was Chief of Engineers and Totten flourished under his administration. Totten's

Figure 6: General Joseph Totten was the longest-standing member of the Coastal Fortifications Board. From his role as a young understudy to Bernard in 1816, he progressed to chairman of the Board, then to Chief of Engineers. He died while Chief of Engineers during the Civil War, leaving the Third System as his legacy. *(Photo courtesy of NARA)*

years of close association with Bernard and a prominent role in the design of virtually all of the Third System forts allowed him to succeed Gratiot as Chief of Engineers in 1838, holding that post (as well as being President of the Fortifications Board) for almost 25 years.

While Totten had always been in the forefront of the designs and the planning of the system, he was now in charge. With Bernard no longer present to challenge and overrule his designs, he began to put his mark on the system of fortifications to an even larger degree.[19] Totten involved himself in the details of the fort designs, giving little latitude to his engineers in the field. Gratiot was very strict regarding the financial aspects of the fort construction, and Totten continued the scrutiny. He scrupulously allocated the monies according to the directives he received.[20]

It is ironic that Totten tolerated little questioning of his designs from any of his field engineers. Totten was infuriated in instances when Bernard interfered with the work he was doing in the field, Fort Pickens being a prime example of this frustration. This tendency appears to have worsened as Totten aged, and in his work on the Pacific forts he actually removed engineers for questioning his designs.[21]

During the Mexican War, Totten retained his position of Chief of Engineers, but he also took on the responsibilities of the Chief Engineer of the Army in the field. Living away from his office in Washington, he was forced to leave administration of the Third System projects to his more junior officers. Following the Mexican War, his prestige well established by the successful siege of Vera Cruz, he returned his attentions to the Third System. Programs moved along during this postwar period, and the system was really taking shape. Funding throughout the 1840s was sporadic, but several forts were completed.

The 1851 Report

On November 1, 1851, Totten responded to a request from Congress to review the progress of the coastal fortification project and to answer some specific questions related to fortifications.[22] This report, analogous to Bernard's report (in which Totten participated) of thirty years earlier, detailed the entire project of coastal defense, restated the purposes of the system, and argued convincingly for the continuation of the project.

The report was Totten's masterpiece. He began with a review of the four ways an enemy could wage war against us:

1) At sea, not to be considered in the report

2) With a combined naval and military attack on one or more important points on the coast

3) By a naval attack on our principal commercial cities and naval yards

4) By attacks on our small coastal towns.

He then reviewed the reality of our enemies and the idea that war was a very real possibility.

Next, Totten addressed the specific questions of Congress. The first question was, "How far the invention and extension of railroads have superseded or diminished the necessity of fortifications on the sea-board?" This he addressed with an introduction followed by a systematic review of portions of the coast, providing sound arguments for the continued necessity of coastal forts. Of particular note, however, was that the necessity of the forts to protect against land-based siege was greatly diminished by the railroads. This had a major effect on fort design in the latter half of the Third System.

The second and third questions regarded the effect of steam vessels on forts, and the possibility of using steam batteries in lieu of permanent fortifications. Here Totten argued that steam vessels heightened the importance of the coastal forts, and that steam batteries were a valuable supplement to the forts but were useless without them.

It was at this point in the report that Totten gave the Third System its name. He reviewed the periods of fortification up to that time, dividing the forts into three distinct systems — the "permanent system" that was underway being designated as the Third System. He also designated its starting point as 1816.

Finally, Totten reviewed all works to be utilized in the Third System, both the repaired and modernized First and Second System works, and the new works of the Third System. His review involved text supplemented by tables, giving justification of the site, manpower and armament required, and costs incurred or to be incurred for each fort.

The last point in Totten's summary was the bottom line of the report. With it he justified what had been done in the past as well as what would be continued over the remainder of his career. It also was the implicit justification of his reference to the Third System as a "permanent" system of fortifications. He said:

"No improvements or inventions of modern times, tend, in any degree, to lessen the efficiency of fortifications as means of coast defence; while the principal one, namely, the firing of shells[23] from guns, unquestionably augments their relative power."

In his statement, Totten debunks the myth that exploding shells will lessen the importance of masonry fortifications. On the contrary, exploding shells have less penetrating power than solid shot. The inherent protection of the gunners in casemated fortifications becomes more important, and the importance of masonry works grows rather than diminishing. Thus Totten brushes aside the criticisms of fixed fortifications and the Third System continues its growth.

The Fortifications Board through the Civil War

Major William Chase, Totten's senior engineer on the Gulf Coast, fell afoul of Totten. In 1853, he led a major opposition to the entire philosophy embodied in Third System forts, suggesting that floating batteries were of more value and cost less than fortifications. This is ironic, as Chase had played a key role in the construction of several of these very forts.[24] Chase attempted to find support in Congress, but Totten thwarted the effort very effectively. Current affairs also came to Totten's aid — in the Crimean War, the importance and effectiveness of fixed fortifications was being proven.

Nonetheless, Totten kept Chase active, banishing him to Key West to superintend the construction of Fort Taylor. Chase unsuccessfully attempted to have his orders changed, and in 1856 Totten attempted to move him out of the way in a similar manner that Swift attempted with Bernard forty years previously — he had Chase appointed to the Superintendence of the Military Academy. In this case, however, the tactic was successful. Chase refused the appointment and resigned shortly thereafter.

This incident and its resolution were very important in the progress of the Third System. A victory by Chase in his support of floating batteries could have ended Third System construction, leaving many of the most impressive forts of the period unbuilt. With Totten resolving the issue in favor of permanent fortifications, financial support from Congress was forthcoming and the program continued.

Immediately prior to the Civil War, the emphasis in completing Third System forts changed direction. Priority was given to the Federal fortifications located in the South, with an eye to keeping the Southern states in line during the current political turmoil. In the aftermath of Lincoln's election, feelings reached and surpassed the critical point. A minor skirmish erupted at one of these Third System forts, Fort Barrancas in Pensacola, Florida. The Federal garrison, moved into the fort only days before, fired on a group that approached the fort and refused to respond to the challenge from the guard. The group retreated, and the fort was held.[25] Some time later, shots were exchanged at yet another Third System fort, Fort Sumter, in Charleston harbor, thus marking the beginning of the Civil War.

As the war began, the Corps of Engineers was given three tasks:

1) Establish the defenses of the capital
2) Complete and arm strategic Third System forts still in Federal hands
3) Support army activities on the battlefield

13

The critical nature of these activities caused a large surge in the funds and manpower available to Totten and the fortifications board. Additional manpower was immediately added to Third System forts in locations that were considered most important to the war effort, with the emphasis on readying these forts to receive their armament.

Also at this time, an additional series of coastal defense forts were constructed. These forts were not part of the Third System, as they were considered *temporary* rather than *permanent* works. While using plans and profiles that were also found in Third System forts, these works were generally wood-revetted earthworks, and contained little or no masonry.

In most cases, these forts were much smaller in trace than Third System forts, and mounted many fewer cannon. Since these were earthworks, they had no casemates and mounted all guns en barbette. In many cases the guns were mounted to fire over the parapet, but in some cases wooden open-toped embrasures were used.

Many of these earthworks had bombproof structures for magazines and places of refuge for the soldiers, but no cannon were mounted within these bombproof structures. Fort Fisher, at the mouth of the Cape Fear River in North Carolina, and Fort Foote, on the Potomac River just south of Washington, D.C., are classic examples of this type of fortification.

With the large amount of labor required for the increased construction efforts, it is interesting to note the continued use of slaves for labor in the construction of Federal forts. Until the Emancipation Proclamation, the Corps of Engineers used slave labor for fort construction at several sites.[26] After the 1863 Proclamation, it was illegal to use slaves on Federal property and the superintending engineers were faced with a major problem. It was next to impossible to persuade white workers to do many of the heavy manual tasks the black slaves had been performing. Attempts were made to hire the former slaves, but this met with only marginal success.

Finally, these tasks were relegated to military prisoners. Soldiers sentenced to "hard labor" began to appear at numerous fort sites, setting a precedent of major consequence to the history of Third System forts. The ease of conversion of casemates to cells, the construction of detention barracks, the remote locations, and the limited strategic importance of the forts in the post-Civil-War era, caused many forts of the Third System to become prisons. Most dramatic in this trend was the fort on Alcatraces Island in San Francisco Bay, commonly referred to as Fort Alcatraz. Its use evolved from disciplinary labor, to housing of military discipline cases, to the first military prison, and finally to the most famous Federal Prison in the country. In addition, many Third System forts were used to house prisoners of war during the Civil War — and others[27] — with Fort Delaware becoming known as the "Andersonville of the North."

Work continued on many of the forts during the war, some by Federal forces and some by the Confederacy. Emphasis was given, however, to temporary earthen fieldworks because of the rapidity of their construction compared with masonry forts. Many of the permanent forts played major roles in the war, some with great irony. Robert E. Lee put many of the finishing touches on Fort Monroe in Hampton Roads, Virginia, while serving with the Corps of Engineers, only to watch major campaigns launched from that same fort against him while he was commanding Confederate forces.

In 1864, Totten died while still on active duty with the Corps of Engineers. He was the first General Officer to serve as the Chief of Engineers of the Army, adding great prestige to the office. His developments in the design of

Figure 7: Construction of Third System forts was a marvel of the engineering technology of the day. Cranes and narrow-gauge railways supplimented the traditional ramps and blocks and tackle. This period photograph shows the construction of the scarp of Fort Totten, guarding the northern approaches to New York City. *(Photo courtesy NARA)*

forts had implications worldwide, especially his development of strong, small embrasures, his expansion of the angle of fire available to casemate-mounted cannon, and his development of "Totten Shutters" to protect gunners between firings of a casemated cannon. These features are considered in detail in the next section. Additionally, he personally designed, and in some cases personally superintended construction of, many of the Third System works.

Joseph Gilbert Totten is truly a legend in the Corps of Engineers. Many refer to the Third System as the "Totten System," because of the outstanding leadership he provided and his presence during all but the last three years of the system. The bulk of his eulogy, as presented to the Congress, was primarily a political justification for the use of fixed fortifications for coastal defense![28] This seems appropriate, however, with 56 years of his life dedicated to fort building.

The End of an Era

Following Totten's death, Richard Delafield was appointed Brigadier General and Chief Engineer. He had extensive experience in superintending fort construction, and he took over the task of finishing the Third System. However, for all intents, the major work came to a halt by 1867 and many forts were never completed. Principal in the demise of the efforts was the effect of the rifled and very large smoothbore cannon on exposed masonry walls. The breach in Fort Pulaski, Savannah, Georgia, from siege batteries of this type supported these opinions. Congress and other forces in the Corps of Engineers took the advice put forth in the reports of both Gillmore,[29] the artillery commander responsible for the sieges of the southern Third System forts late in the Civil War, and von Scheliha,[30] a German officer who served with the Confederacy. They believed that exposed masonry was

Fort Name	Defending	Location (at or near)
Fort Knox	Penobscot River	Bucksport, ME
Fort Popham	Kennebeck River	Popham Beach, ME
Fort Gorges	Portland Harbor	Portland, ME
Fort Scammel	Portland Harbor	Portland, ME
Fort Preble	Portland Harbor	Portland, ME
Fort McClary	Piscataqua River	Portsmough, NH
Fort Constitution	Piscataqua River	Portsmouth, NH
Fort Warren	Boston Harbor	Boston Harbor, MA
Fort Independence	Boston Harbor	Boston Harbor, MA
Fort Taber	Acushnet River	New Bedford, MA
Fort Adams	Narragansett Bay	Newport, RI
Fort Trumbull	Thames River	New London, CT
Fort Schuyler	Hell Gate, New York	New York City, NY
Fort Totten	Hell Gate, New York	New York City, NY
Fort Hamilton	New York Inner Harbor	New York City, NY
Fort Richmond	New York Inner Harbor	New York City, NY
Fort Tompkins	New York Inner Harbor	New York City, NY
Fort Hancock	New York Outer Harbor	Sandy Hook, NJ
Fort Delaware	Philadelphia	Delaware City, DE
Fort Carroll	Baltimore	Baltimore, MD
Fort Monroe	Hampton Roads	Hampton, VA
Fort Wool	Hampton Roads	Hampton, VA
Fort Macon	Pamlico Sound	Morehead City, NC
Fort Caswell	Cape Fear River	Wilmington, NC
Fort Sumter	Charleston Harbor	Charleston, SC
Fort Pulaski	Savannah River	Savannah, GA
Fort Clinch	St. Mary's River	Jacksonville, FL
Fort Taylor	Key West Harbor	Key West, FL
Fort Jefferson	Garden Key Anchorage	Dry Tortugas, FL
Fort Barrancas	Pensacola Bay	Pensacola, FL
Advanced Redoubt	Pensacola Bay	Pensacola, FL
Fort Pickens	Pensacola Bay	Pensacola, FL
Fort McRee	Pensacola Bay	Pensacola, FL
Fort Morgan	Mobile Bay	Mobile Point, AL
Fort Gaines	Mobile Bay	Dauphin Island, AL
Fort Massachusetts	Ship Island Channel	Ship Island, MS
Fort Pike	New Orleans	New Orleans, LA
Fort Wood	New Orleans	New Orleans, LA
Fort Jackson	New Orleans	New Orleans, LA
Fort Livingston	New Orleans	New Orleans, LA
Fort Point	San Francisco Bay	San Francisco, CA
Fort Alcatraz	San Francisco Bay	San Francisco, CA

Figure 8: New construction forts of the Third System. This list of forts contrasts to Bernard's original plan, as the engineer in charge of the Coastal Fortifications Board updated it annually. This list includes all forts that began construction during the Third System. For details regarding fort names and for arguments for inclusion in the list, please see the individual fort descriptions.

no longer safe with the presence of rifled artillery, and that, therefore, masonry works were obsolete.[31]

The Third System thus came to a close. Work progressed on several transitional works, primarily in the modernization of some Third System forts to accept the heavier armament and to construct brick-and-earth works for large Rodman and Parrott guns near existing Third System forts. Politicians declared our shores secure, and our coastal fortification activities became maintenance-oriented. The Third System forts continued to be armed and occupied, and funding was available for maintenance activities, but no funding was appropriated to complete the construction in progress or to initiate new construction. This ending of Congressional appropriations signals the end of the period.

Three years after the end of the Third System, Congress again decided to improve our coastal defenses at selected sites. This program, however, was relatively small and was, in most cases, simply an extension of certain Third System forts. Masonry-revetted earthworks were constructed, and large-bore – generally 10-inch and 15-inch Rodman guns – were emplaced on barbettes behind these earthworks. This short-lived construction effort was not named, although a few historians refer to it as the "Fourth System."

In subsequent years, many of the Third System sites were incorporated into more modern coastal defense systems. Under the Endicott System at the end of the century, concrete emplacements for the breech-loading guns of the Spanish-American War period were constructed at many sites, in some cases directly in the forts themselves. Newer ones constructed during the World War I and II eras in turn superceded many of the Endicott System emplacements. Even following the demise of the U. S. Coast Artillery in 1950, guided missiles found their way to locations near some Third System forts.

Of the forty-two forts newly constructed for the Third System, only one, Fort McRee in Pensacola Harbor, is gone without a trace. The rest provide us with a legacy of coastal defense in an age gone by.

Notes

[1] *ASP-MA*, Vol. I, p.779.

[2] Halleck, Henry Wager, *Elements of Military Art and Science*, Westport, CT, 1846.

[3] There were extenuating circumstances. Local militia did not support the fort, and a land force had already captured Washington City. These factors lowered the morale of the garrison and certainly contributed to Dyson's decision to surrender the fort. *ASP-MA*, Vol. I, p. 588-9.

[4] Peters, Richard, ed., *Public Statutes at Large of the United States of America*, Boston, MA, 1850, Vol. III, p. 342.

[5] Moore, Jamie W., *The Fortifications Board 1816-1828 and the Definition of National Security*, Charleston, SC: 1981

[6] Arthur, R., and Weinert, R., *Defender of the Chesapeake, The Story of Fort Monroe*, Shippensburg, PA, 1989, p24.

[7] Harrison, Joseph H., Jr., The American Middle Period: Essays in Honor of Bernard Mayo, *Simon Bernard, The American System, and the Ghost of the French Alliance*, Charlottesville, VA: 1973.

[8] Ibid.

[9] *ASP-MA*, Vol. II, p. 305.

[10] From the 1820s on, the Board also included the superintending engineer from the area involved. General reports, however, included only regular Board members.

[11] ASP-MA, Vol. II, p.304-312. A preliminary report had been written in 1818, but this was more of a status of current projects. The 1821 report was the first

full discussion of the strategy developed by the Board, and how that strategy was to be implemented.

[12] "Works" is a term used to describe any construction, but in the context of the Third System it is generally used to indicate a structure smaller than a fort. These would include batteries, redoubts, towers, etc.

[13] Bernard used the term "class" to indicate importance or priority. He used the word "period" in much the same way, though its usage implied a chronological sequence. While this sequence was not universally maintained, it did indicate an estimate of the order in which the forts would be built.

[14] This number includes forts, towers, batteries and "works," projected as new construction. It does not include the 29 forts from previous systems that were repaired and updated during this period.

[15] The fortifications-related activities of the Corps of Engineers were not their only task. Additional tasks involved maintenance and improvement of harbors and rivers for transportation and commerce, design and construction of federal roads, and oversight of the Military Academy and its curriculum.

[16] *ASP-MA*, p. 368. For the rebuttal by James Monroe and others, see pages 368-375. While arguments appeared compelling, Congress bought none of them and cut off funding of the fort.

[17] Boles, p. 155.

[18] As constructed, the C&O Canal was smaller than some others, most notably the Erie Canal. The plan, however, was to bring the C&O across the Appalachian Mountains. That project would have been the largest in our history.

[19] As some examples of their style, Forts Monroe and Adams were distinctly Bernard, Fort Pickens was a blending (albeit not without conflict) of Totten's and Bernard's approach, and Sumter and Point were distinctly Totten.

[20] See Coleman, James C., *Fort McRee "A Castle Built on Sand"* for an account of Gratiot's and Totten's "by the book" attitude on the dispersal of funds during McRee's construction.

[21] Bearss, Edwinn C., *Historic Structure Report: Fort Point*, U.S. National Park Service.

[22] House Executive Document No. 5, 32nd Congress, 1st Session, Dec. 8, 1851.

[23] Here Totten refers to exploding shells as opposed to solid shot.

[24] For further information regarding Chase, see: Dibble, Ernest F., *William Chase, Gulf Coast Fort Builder*, Gulf Coast Collection, Wilmington, Delaware.

[25] Coleman, James C. & Irene S., *Pensacola Fortifications 1698-1980: Guardians on the Gulf*, Pensacola Historical Society, 1982. Note that the fort was occupied by the Confederates a short time later when the Federal garrison moved to the more defensible Fort Pickens.

[26] Fort Massachusetts, Fort Zachary Taylor, and Fort Jefferson were all using slave labor during this period; it is likely that other sites were using slaves as well.

[27] Fort Pickens gained fame as the site that held Geronimo during the Indian wars, etc.

[28] Martin, Benjamin Ellis, *Eulogy on the late Brigadier General Joseph Gilbert Totten*, New York, 1866.

[29] Gillmore, Q.A., *Official Report to the United States Engineer Department on the Siege and Reduction of Fort Pulaski*, New York, 1862.

[30] von Scheliha, Viktor E.K.R., *A Treatise of Coast Defense: Based on the Experience Gained by Officers of the Corps of Engineers of the Army of the Confederate States*, London, UK, 1868.

[31] James R. Hinds, in *Bulwark and Bastion*, has a very different viewpoint on the subject. Both arguments will be discussed later.

Architecture of the Third System

The nomenclature applied to the elements of American forts is almost exclusively French. This was not due to Bernard's influence, but predates his coming to the United States by many years. The terminology is derived from the French influence during the infant years of the American military in general, and of fort design in particular. French engineers designed our earliest coastal forts after we became a nation – the First System of coastal defense. In addition, the textbooks on fort design initially used at the United States Military Academy[1] were written in French; it was not until the middle nineteenth century that instructors at West Point translated some of the texts into English and eventually wrote original works based on the French texts.[2] By this time, the French names for most elements of a fort had been ingrained in the minds of the American engineers.

Elements of Nineteenth Century Fortifications

A fort, like any structure, can be viewed three ways: in plan, or as it would be seen when looking straight down on it; in section, or from the side as if a portion had been sliced off; or in elevation, looking at the entire structure from the side. This analysis of military architecture during the Third System will start by analyzing the plan of a fort.

The line that defines the outer wall of a fort is called the **trace** of the fort, also referred to as the magistral line. The trace of a fort is said to be **regular** if it forms a regular (equal-sided) geometric figure, otherwise the trace is irregular. Many times the trace of a fort was a **truncated polygon**, a regular polygon that was "chopped off" at less than the complete figure.

All the structures defined by the trace of the fort are considered the **enceinte**, or body of

the work. All components of the fort outside of the trace are **outworks**. The perimeter of the enceinte is faced by a surrounding wall, known as the **scarp** or **scarp wall**. This wall is considered to be part of the enceinte, and provides the division between the enceinte and the outworks.

Figure 8: Third System forts were often built on the plan of a partial regular polygon. The most common of these geometric forms was the truncated hexagon. Four sides of the fort were on the plan of a regular hexagon, while the fifth side closed the polygon.

The scarp wall of all Third System forts was constructed of either brick, stone, or a combination of the two materials. Some forts in the latter part of the Third System used masonry faces on the scarp wall, and filled the interior with materials such as concrete or ground-shell formulas. The scarp wall was a minimum of five feet thick at its junction with the parapet in early Third System works. This was increased to eight feet thick in later works to compensate for the technological advances that allowed the construction of more powerful artillery.[3] The scarp wall gradually increased in thickness as it progressed down toward the foundation. Near the foundation, it sometimes tapered sharply outward to its thickest point, sometimes more than twenty feet.

In most cases, the mass of the scarp was reinforced with a very thick (approximately 25 feet) arched structure of brick or stone masonry. In several Third System forts, the arched structure behind the landward scarp was replaced with approximately 30 feet of earth to provide additional resistance to siege cannon.

While it is obvious that this formidable barrier was designed for self-protection, that protection addresses two distinct types of opponent. Seaward, the primary purpose of the scarp was to protect against cannon fire from enemy ships; landward, the purpose was to prevent entry of the fort by the enemy, by siege or by storm. For this reason, the scarp wall on the **gorge**, or landward side, was often somewhat different from the scarp wall on the **faces**, or seaward sides of a fort.

It was commonly believed throughout the early and middle nineteenth century that shipboard cannon, due to the movement of the deck of a ship even in relatively calm waters, could not consistently strike the same area of a masonry fort and create a breach in the wall.[4] For this reason, the seaward faces of a fort were generally left as unprotected masonry with the scarp walls placed close to the shoreline and devoid of outworks. This allowed maximum offensive and defensive viability through increased visibility, better angles of fire, and more tiers of guns.

The seaward side of a scarp wall was generally penetrated by openings, called **embrasures**, for cannon to fire on the enemy. These embrasures may be simple openings in the wall, as in early Third System forts, or may be protected by complex mechanisms such as the Totten Shutters used in later Third System forts. Embrasures were tapered inward from both the inner and outer surface of the scarp. The narrowest point of the embrasure is called the **throat**, and provided the smallest opening possible to enemy

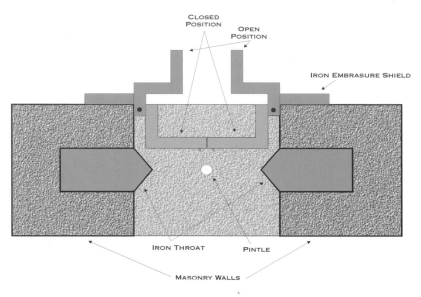

Figure 9: The Totten Embrasure System consisted of iron components inserted into, and attached to the face of, a masonry embrasure. This system protected gunners between firings, and reinforced the most vulnerable portion of the scarp - an embrasure .

fire while still allowing an adequate angle of traverse for the cannon.

The embrasures were the weakest part of the scarp wall. For this reason, a great deal of research was conducted[5] in this area. In the early years, cannon were less powerful, and fewer precautions were required. Granite forts required no special treatment of the embrasure, as the granite provided sufficient strength. Brick forts used either special, hardened brick or granite for the embrasures.

Totten initiated the use of iron in embrasures, using 4-inch-thick pieces of cast iron at

20

the throat and thinner plates around the outer surface of the embrasure to reinforce the stone or brick masonry. These "Totten Embrasures" significantly strengthened the thin portions of the masonry, but created problems due to the vulnerability of iron to the salt air. Not only did the iron weaken when rusted, it expanded and broke loose large masonry sections of the embrasures.[6]

A further innovation by Totten was the development of the so-called Totten Shutters. These iron plates, installed with a complex, self-closing mechanism, were designed to protect cannon and gunners during loading and aiming operations. The shutters automatically opened when the cannon was run out and closed when the cannon recoiled after firing. Their angular shape allowed them to open wide enough to allow the full traverse of the cannon. If not properly maintained, these shutters were vulnerable to the salt air as well. In the worst case, the shutters tended to rust closed. An unsubstantiated tradition has it that attempts to fire through "frozen" Totten shutters caused entire embrasures to be blown from the scarp wall.

On the landward side, the threat was somewhat different. Emplaced siege cannon could consistently strike a small area of the scarp, eventually creating a breach. For this reason, the scarp wall was generally protected from direct cannon fire by outworks. Also of concern was the ability of an attacker to storm the walls. Cannon embrasures were often traded for musketry **loopholes**, or rifle slits. These tapered, narrow openings allowed a rifleman to command a relatively wide field of fire, while enjoying the protection of a relatively small opening. Most forts mixed loopholes with embrasures on the landward side, usually mounting howitzers (short-barreled cannon generally used for antipersonnel missions) in the embrasures. These howitzers acted as large shotguns, firing

Figure 10: To support the incredible weight of a Third System fort and its artillery, the arched form was used. In addition to the magnificent arches seen when touring these forts, hidden arches below the floor distribute the load more evenly on the foundation. This inverted arch is in the seacoast front of Fort Pickens, guarding Pensacola, Florida. *(Photo by author)*

canisters filled with shot varying in size from three-fourths inch to two inches in diameter.

The primary location for howitzer embrasures was in the flank of the bastions, but howitzer embrasures could also be found in the landward curtains of some forts and the faces of the bastions of others. Another favored location was at the junction of two counterscarp walls. Some forts have a howitzer embrasure immediately above the main sally port.

A typical feature found in all Third System forts was the **casemate**. A casemate is an arched

Figure 11: Early Third System forts used long passageways between the gun position and the parade to provide additional protection for the gunners. Shown above is a "tunnel casemate" in Fort Wood, defending New Orleans, Louisiana. *(Photo by author)*

In most cases, embrasures provided the capability for guns to fire out of these protected areas, and in many forts housed a major portion of the fort's armament. In addition to their principal function as a gun room, casemates also served as barracks, kitchens, powder magazines, storage rooms, and for other miscellaneous uses. This minimized the number of separate, freestanding structures required in the fort and provided a more protected location for the fort's supplies and quarters.

An important goal of the casemate was to provide overhead protection for gunners, partially due to the early nineteenth century practice of placing snipers in the rigging of attacking ships. These snipers were charged with the elimination of the gun crews in the fort under attack. Additionally, casemates were considered "bombproof," or resistant to exploding or solid shells hitting their tops.[8]

gunroom or bombproof shelter, generally located along the curtain wall of the fort and set in the flanks – and sometimes faces – of the bastions.[7]

The casemate was developed in Europe, long before the American Third System, and was applied in several Second System forts. Castle Clinton in New York Harbor was the first American fort to make use of the casemate in its design, though casemates had been used extensively in Europe by this time. A most impressive use of the casemate prior to the Third System was Fort Lafayette, also in New York Harbor. It boasted two casemated tiers of cannon with a third tier of barbette guns. This transitional work was completed in 1819, and "modernized" later. Also of note is Castle Williams with 78 guns.

In several instances, casemates were constructed external to the fort. Fort Monroe had a casemated Water Battery immediately across the moat from the fort, and several forts had casemated counterscarp batteries that fired the length of the ditch. A few had casemated caponiers and demilunes, while Fort Adams had a casemated crownwork and tenailles.

To expand this protection to the gunners' rear, casemates of early Third System forts – Forts Jackson, Pike, and Wood defending New Orleans, and Monroe defending Hampton Roads – communicated with the parade through long tunnels. While this was effective in protection, the amount of smoke and noise generated from the firing of the large weapons made life nearly intolerable. Smoke vents were provided in the casemates, but these proved inadequate. Throughout the duration of the system, experimentation continued regarding the placement of these vents. Unfortunately, no adequate solution was forthcoming. Most Third System forts solved the problem through the design of casemates that were relatively shallow, and open to the parade in the rear.[9]

Another major benefit of the casemate, rapidly put into effect, was to provide multiple tiers of guns, greatly increasing the firepower of a fort. As the Third System progressed, this became the primary motivation for building casemated forts.

Powerful forts could be built with smaller traces, and large forts could amass tremendous firepower. Several forts in the later portion of the Third System utilized three tiers of guns, with two forts boasting four tiers.[10]

Casemates were constructed as a masonry web – piers supporting arches in both axes. These arches, constructed without keystones, were masterpieces of brickwork and, in a few cases, granite work. The scarp wall closed the face of a casemate, but the scarp was not structurally joined to the casemate. This architectural separation allowed the destruction of the scarp without bringing down the casemates, and also allowed for differential settling of the casemates and scarp.[11]

The casemates, fronted with the scarp wall, comprised the basic mass of the work, referred to as the **ramparts**. The term ramparts is derived from earthwork forts where the mass of the work was an earthen mound excavated from the ditch. In the Third System, the mass of the work was usually made up of casemates. The top of the casemates contained drainage piping that fed the cisterns of the fort, and the entire area was covered with earth. This earthen area, called the **terreplein**,[12] formed the top of the ramparts.

Some Third System forts had non-casemated walls, usually on a landward face. These walls used an earthen rampart that either sloped to the parade or had a masonry parade wall. This earthen rampart was more resistant to the bombardment of siege cannon, and was used where casemates were not needed.

In all cases, the earthen terreplein provided an inexpensive, easily leveled surface. Being a compressible material, it could absorb the impact of shells striking the rampart and the vibration of the firing of heavy cannon without damaging the masonry below. In some cases this earthen terreplein was paved with brick or slate,[13] but was generally planted with grass.

The front of the terreplein was the **parapet**, the highest part of the defensive structure. In Third System forts, the parapet was revetted with masonry on the rear, and the front was usually made up of two sloped, earthen masses. The

Figure 12: Typical casemates of a Third System fort. Each casemate would hold a seacoast cannon along this curved face of Fort Pike, guarding New Orleans, Louisiana. *(Photo by author)*

entire structure, usually breast high, was often topped with a stone coping. In some forts the parapet was an extension of the scarp, with no sloped surfaces. In others, only one slope ran from the top of the scarp to the coping of the parapet. The classic shape, however, included a steep **exterior slope** joining a flatter **superior slope**.

Immediately behind the parapet, on top of the terreplein, a wide, continuous step, or **ban-**

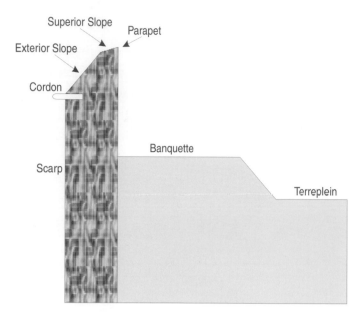

Figure 13: This sketch shows the typical elements in the enciente, or body, of a Third System fort. In the drawing, the attackers would be approaching from the left, with the parade of the fort to the right.

quette, was generally provided. This platform allowed small arms to be fired over the top of the parapet, while a person not standing on the banquette was shielded from enemy fire. Also provided behind the parapet were elevated mounts for cannon, referred to as **barbettes** or barbette platforms. Cannon mounted on this level were said to be mounted *en barbette*. In rare cases, open-topped embrasures called **crenels** penetrated the parapet and provided more protection to the gun crews than the open barbette mounts.[14]

While the scarp wall formed a difficult obstacle to forcing entry into the fort, it also provided shelter for an attacker who came close enough to it. By standing very close to the scarp wall, the attacker was out of the trajectory covered by embrasures and loopholes as well as being masked from view from the parapet. **Bastions**, or projections from the fort walls, were designed to eliminate this avenue of shelter. These bastions, generally — but not exclusively — located at the corners of the fort, provided a view along the straight wall, or **curtain**, of the

fort. The curtain is the portion of the scarp wall between the bastions

When a bastion protruded from only one wall of a fort at a corner, it was called a **demibastion**, or "half bastion." Bastions and demibastions were always casemated, and were designed to mount the small, short-barreled howitzers mentioned previously. These howitzers fired canister shot along the walls to "sweep" them of an enemy who was seeking refuge against the scarp. Canister shot consisted of a container filled with small balls, ranging in size from three-quarters inch to balls about two inches in diameter. On firing, the canister ruptured, discharging the balls in a pattern similar to a shotgun.

The design of the bastions of a fort was a lesson in geometry. The sides of the bastion that attached to the curtain were called the **flanks** of the bastion. These flanks were at an angle of at least 90 degrees to each curtain, depending on the angle formed by the projection of the two curtains.

The **faces** of a bastion were the other two walls, which formed the point or **salient** of the bastion. The intersection of the face and the flank of a bastion is known as the **shoulder** of the bastion. The angle of the face of a bastion, if projected, met the curtain at the flank of the opposite bastion. This ensured that the cannon in the flank of the bastion could sweep the salient of the opposite bastion.

Since a bastion projected outward from the fort, it was the most vulnerable part of a fort. If overrun, it would provide an area for the attacker to assemble that was level with the terreplein. To control this area, a **cavalier** is a wall that divides the bastion from the remainder of the fort. It generally forms a continuation of the parapet as if the bastion were not present. In the Third System, Fort Jackson, on the Mississippi River south of New Orleans, had cavaliers at each bastion.

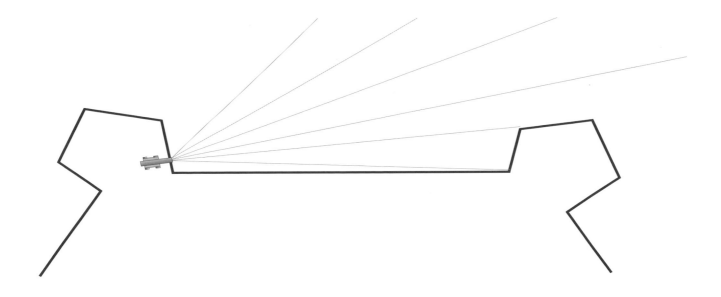

Figure 14: Bastions are designed to eliminate any points of refuge for an attacker, especially against the scarp of the fort. The geometric form of a bastion allows the opposite bastion to sweep its face as well as the curtain that joins the two bastions.

Inside the ramparts was a flat area, generally level with the lowest level of casemates.[15] This area, called the **parade**, was the primary place for the training and assembly of troops. The parade often housed barracks, and sometimes a strong defensive barracks called a **citadel**. These citadels generally had loopholes in the walls, and some were designed to mount cannon on top of them, en barbette. The citadel was considered to be the last line of defense if the remainder of the fort fell.

Around the outside of the scarp was usually a **ditch** or **moat**. While, by technical definition, a ditch can refer to either a dry ditch or a mud- or water-filled ditch, the term ditch generally is applied to a dry ditch, and moat is generally applied to a wet ditch. Both served as a physical obstacle to deter the approach of an attacker to the scarp wall. A dry ditch provided an obstruction to attackers descending into it, provided the scarp additional effective height, and increased the effectiveness of canister shot by providing surfaces from which it could ricochet. A wet moat would prevent

(if deep) or slow (if shallow) an attacker wading across it, giving defenders more time to fire on him. A wet moat also inhibited mining operations against the fort. In both cases, earth from the ditch was used to form the glacis and build the outworks, as well as to level the top of the ramparts.

Some Third System forts immediately adjacent to the water provided a small sea wall

Figure 15: The citadel at Fort Pike, guarding New Orleans, Louisiana, is one of the few remaining citadels in the Third System. Its role as a barracks was less than successful because of the poor ventilation provided by the loopholes, and additional barracks were constructed elsewhere on the site. *(Photo by author)*

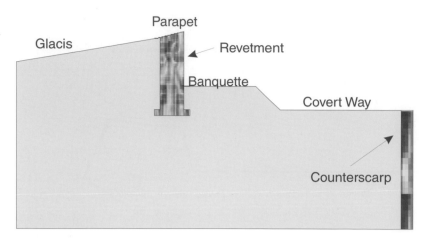

Figure 16: This sketch shows the typical elements in the outworks of a Third System fort. The glacis gently slopes toward the route of attack, while the ditch is to the immediate right of the drawing. Defense of the ditch was provided for by additional outworks, by elements of the main fort, or both.

around the perimeter of the fort to define the perimeter of a wet ditch. This sea wall would also serve the structural function of protecting the fort from wave action. A well-preserved example of such a sea wall is at Fort Jefferson in the Dry Tortugas.[16]

Elements of a fortification in advance of the scarp wall are referred to as **outworks**. These took many forms, from simple earthworks to elaborate earth-and-masonry designs. Outworks had four principal functions: 1) to provide multiple lines of defense and fall-back points for defenders; 2) to provide additional firepower on the seaward side of the fort; 3) to guard the enceinte and ditch from attackers; and, 4) to protect the scarp from direct cannon fire.

The concept of *defense in depth* was strongly supported by most engineers of the smoothbore-artillery period, and was well exemplified by the works of the famous French engineer, the Marquis de Vauban (1633-1707). A major part of his theories involved the principle of multiple lines of defense. He believed that siege warfare was a battle of attrition, and that defenses should consist of progressive lay-

ers of fortification which would have to be overrun one at a time, at a high cost to the attacker. While it was understood at the time of the Third System that **any** fort would eventually fall to a protracted siege, fort designers used progressive layers of fortification as a delaying tactic until the siege could be lifted through outside reinforcements, or the price to the attacker became too high.

The outworks of a fort included all elements from the scarp wall to the structures furthest from the scarp wall. Many of these structures were located in the ditch, others were well beyond the ditch, up to the range of the main guns of the fort.[17] In this treatment, we begin with the outworks located the maximum distance from the fort and proceed toward the scarp wall.

The detached, self-contained works generally located most distant from the enceinte were **redoubts**. A redoubt was simply a small, fortified work that had been constructed in advance

Figure 17: This curved passageway through the outworks shielded the main work from view, but more importantly, from direct fire from artillery. While it is now a mere remnant of its original form, it provides insight into the careful design of the outworks of Fort Wood, guarding New Orleans, Louisiana. *(Photo by author)*

of the main fort. This meant that an attacking force would come under fire from the redoubt before reaching the main fort. Classically, the defense of the redoubt raised the alarm that an attack was imminent. Scouting patrols could not reconnoiter the outworks or the enceinte of the fort without the capture of the redoubt, which would generally require more than a small force. In the Third System, the redoubt generally controlled topographical features – high ground – that could expose the main work. In both cases, a redoubt served as a first line of defense in the "defense in depth" concept. When the attack on the redoubt began, the war of attrition also began. The attacker must expend significant resources in the reduction of the redoubt, but possession of the redoubt does not give him a significant advantage in his assault on the main works.

The redoubt at Fort Adams, in Newport Rhode Island, represents the classic purpose of a redoubt. It was located on high ground on the peninsula that led to the main work, requiring the attacker to first reduce this work before proceeding to the other levels of defense. Two proposed redoubts at Fort Point in San Francisco were designed in a similar manner. They were not constructed.

The Advanced Redoubt at Pensacola Florida was built for an entirely different purpose. The Advanced Redoubt was designed to seal off one end of the land approach to the Navy Yard, with Fort Barrancas designed to seal off the other end. Rather than sitting in advance of the main work, Fort Barrancas, it was to cooperate with it. This factor, as well as it being similar in size to Fort Barrancas, has caused the Advanced Redoubt to be treated as a separate fort in this work.

An important feature in a redoubt was the design of its gorge – the wall facing the main work. To deny the attacker the establishment of a strong point in the captured redoubt, the gorge was designed such that guns could not be mounted on that face. The defenses of the gorge of a redoubt were limited to those that would prevent a coup de main, generally a ditch and demibastions.

The approach to the fortifications, redoubt, outworks, or main work, was the **glacis**, a gentle slope cleared of all trees and obstacles, thus providing a clear area for fire from the fort's guns. The slope of the glacis was carefully calculated to provide maximum protection to the scarp wall while providing an area that was raked by the barbette guns of the fort. A line projected from the top (superior) of the parapet, across the ditch to the crest of the glacis, would generally define the slope of the glacis. From a distance, this would make the earthen parapet of the fort appear to be an extension of the slope of the glacis.

In addition to providing a clear field of fire for the guns of the fort, the glacis also provided a significant amount of protection for the walls of the fort. The earthen slope hid almost the entire scarp of the fort from land-based cannon, making it very difficult for shot to strike the more vulnerable masonry walls. Instead, most of the shot was absorbed in the soft earth of the glacis or parapet.

Immediately toward the fort from the glacis outer slope was the parapet revetment and sometimes a banquette. The revetment was generally masonry, but earth or earth-and-wood construction was also used. Some forts had barbette mounts for cannon in addition to the banquette for small-arms fire. Behind (and lower than) the banquette was a large pathway, called the **covert way** or covered way. This pathway was hidden from the attackers, but covered by the guns of the fort. It allowed communication along the perimeter of the outwork, and often opened into a **place d'armes** or place of arms. A place d'armes was a gathering place for a counterattacking force, and was referred to as a salient place d'armes if at an outward-pointing angle in the outworks or a reentering place

Main Fort

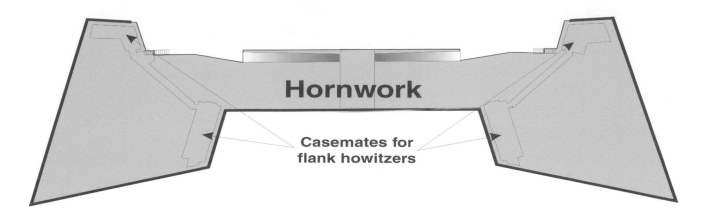

Figure 18: A hornwork is an elaborate land defense that divides the ditch into two distinct parts - an inner ditch and an outer ditch. Its major role is defense in depth, and - because of its massive size - the assault of a hornwork is very similar to the assault of the main work. The above sketch is based on the hornwork at Fort Schuyler, guarding the northern approaches to New York City.

d'armes if at an inward-pointing angle in the outworks. The places d'armes were fronted by the same banquette, parapet, and glacis as the covert way.

Immediately behind the covert way was the **counterscarp wall** or slope that formed the side of the ditch opposite the fort. Communication between the banquette and the ditch was provided by stairways and/or ramps that led from the ditch to the covert way.

While in most Third System forts the ditch was either empty or filled with water, some of the forts provided a further level of defense within the ditch. Large detached **crownworks** or **hornworks** were positioned in advance of the walls of the fort. A crownwork consisted of a central bastion with two flanking demibastions, joined by masonry curtain walls.[18] A hornwork consisted of two demibastions joined by a masonry curtain. Both provided flanking fire as well as forward fire from casemates in the bastions and demibastions. In addition, they often had cannon mounted en barbette for forward fire.

Tenailles, small detached works within

the ditch and between the bastions of a fort, protect the curtain of the fort from direct fire. In the Third System, the only tenailles also provided flanking fire in the ditch and forward fire against an attacker who had crossed the parapet of the

Figure 19: In its pure form, a caponier provided the dual function of a passageway and a defensive structure. Third System caponiers, such as the caponier at Fort Washington, Maryland, shown above, sometimes provided only the latter role. *(Photo by author)*

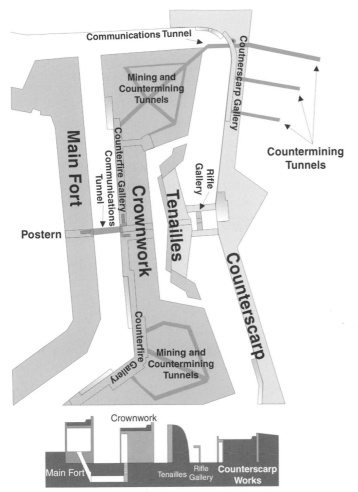

Figure 20: The amazing land defenses of Fort Adams, guarding Newport, Rhode Isand, were the most extensive in the Third System. Most impressive to today's visitor is the network of tunnels that provide communication between defensive elements and provide mining and countermining capability. Also note that each outwork is progressively lower in height, allowing all elements to be used simultaneously.

outworks. These tenailles consisted of two casemated demibastions joined by a masonry-and-earthen curtain. Fort Adams, Newport, Rhode Island, is a classic example of the use of a crownwork with tenailles for land defense, while Fort Schuyler, New York City, has a classic hornwork.

Another type of outwork designed to control the ditch through the use of enfilading (or flanking) fire was the **caponier.** A caponier was a masonry gunroom running perpendicular (or

nearly perpendicular) to the ditch, with loopholes and/or embrasures in each side. It was often a projection from the scarp wall, and could be accessed directly from the fort. Detached caponiers could be accessed either by a tunnel from the fort or by a separate entrance from the ditch. Caponiers were generally used to defend the ditch of unbastioned forts or the unbastioned sides of forts.

The most extensive type of outworks designed to guard the scarp wall and control the ditch was a **counterscarp gallery.** A counterscarp gallery, also called a counterfire room, was a masonry vault behind the counterscarp wall equipped with loopholes and, often, casemates for howitzers. These galleries, completely protected from artillery fire and any other forward fire against the fort, provided a crossfire with the fort on an attacker who has entered the ditch. At the salient angles of the counterscarp were generally casemates with howitzer embrasures, which provided enfilading fire down the ditch.[19] Counterscarp galleries and casemates were entered either from the ditch or from the fort through a tunnel under the ditch.

An additional outwork seen in some Third System forts were **listening galleries** or **countermining tunnels**. These consisted of masonry-revetted tunnels that extended beyond the scarp, and often beyond the ditch. They were designed to allow defenders to detect mining operations by listening. If mining operations were detected, openings in the walls allowed charges to be placed in the direction of the mining operation. These charges would be detonated, bringing down the mine. Additional chambers under the bastions would allow the bastion to be reduced if it fell to the enemy, killing the enemy emplaced there. Fort Adams in Newport Rhode Island and Fort Pickens in Pensacola Florida have excellent examples of these chambers.

29

The **demilune** and **ravelin** are members of another family of outworks that may be located in the ditch or beyond the ditch. In classic fortifications, the terms are synonymous, but Third System engineers distinguished between them. They were both freestanding, open-backed[20] works consisting of a parapet with banquette and/or barbette platforms. The demilune, literally translated as "half moon" from French, was curved while the ravelin was an open-backed triangle.

Third System ravelins were generally constructed opposite a front, with the open end of the ravelin approximating the length of the curtain. They usually had cannon positions on both fronts of the ravelin.

Third System demilunes were generally smaller, with the smallest one consisting of a curved rifle gallery with no cannon positions. Larger demilunes included cannon positions.

Ravelins and demilunes were commonly located opposite the gorge wall of the fort, providing defense of the sally port, but were also on seacoast fronts to provide additional cannon for seacoast defense.[21] Prior to the Third System, ravelins were often as tall as the scarp of the fort, masking a curtain wall. Access to these ravelins was via bridges across the ditch. By the Third System, most ravelins and demilunes were constructed at an elevation even with the parade.

Outside the ditch of a fort were another group of works, constructed on the channel-bearing front and designed entirely for seacoast defense. These works were designed to mount additional seacoast guns to supplement the firepower of a fort. **Water batteries** were freestanding works designed to add additional cannon to the seacoast fronts of a fort, while **coverfaces** were works that protected the scarp of the fort while providing additional cannon emplacements. These works were either of masonry, masonry-revetted earth, or all-earth construction. Two of

these structures remain, the coverface of Fort Warren in Boston Harbor and the water battery of Fort Barrancas in Pensacola, Florida. Unfortunately, the two most unique water batteries have been lost. The fully casemated water battery at Fort Monroe was removed during later periods of construction, and the detached-scarp (Carnot wall) water battery at Fort McRee was lost with the fort due to coastal erosion.

Integration of the Design

During the Third System, basic design elements were integrated in many unique combinations to provide for the defense of particular locations. While the elements themselves evolved during the period, so did the relative importance of the functions that drove their implementation. Each fort of the System, with its specific elements, is explored in Part II, but a discussion of the basic principles of coastal fortifications during the Third System is in order.

Third System coastal fortifications were charged with the six functions outlined in the 1821 Report of the Board of Engineers,[22] but these can be summed up in one goal: to secure a particular harbor or waterway against a hostile naval force. In order to meet this goal, a fort had three basic defensive missions: 1) to guard against attack by ships at sea; 2) to preclude the possibility of a coup de main; and 3) to provide a resistance to a land-based siege. The structural response to these three missions manifested itself in the implementation of the different architectural elements that were described in the previous portion of this chapter.

Since the primary purpose of the Third System forts was to prevent passage of ships into a harbor or near a city, the forts were generally located at a narrows in the channel; this is why so many Third System forts now lie in the shadows of a major bridge.[23] A narrow channel forced ships closer to the guns of the fort where they *literally* had more impact, gave the ships less opportunity to maneuver, and caused the ships to be in the range of the guns of the fort for a longer time. To take full advantage of this effect and therefore maximize their ability to deny passage to ships, the seaward faces of the fort would mount a maximum number of cannon. For most forts, this was achieved through stacking cannon tier over casemated tier, in a similar manner to the way a ship-of-the-line stacks guns deck over deck.

TIERS OF CANNON IN THIRD SYSTEM FORTS

ONE TIER	15 FORTS
TWO TIERS	15 FORTS
THREE TIERS	10 FORTS
FOUR TIERS	2 FORTS

The front of a fort that most directly bore on the channel was referred to as the **primary seacoast front** of the fort. Depending on the location of the channel in relation to the fort — and whether multiple channels were involved — there could be one or more primary seacoast fronts.

Supporting the primary seacoast front were fronts that bore on the channel at a less-ideal angle. These were referred to as **secondary seacoast fronts**. They would generally provide fire on a ship before or after the ship passed the fort, increasing the amount of time that a ship was under fire from the fort.

As the Third System progressed, so did the technology of warship construction. At the beginning of the Third System, capital ships were constructed of wood, powered by sail, and contained multiple decks of light, smoothbore cannon.

By the end of the system, however, all these changed. The wooden ships were armored with iron, sails gave way to steam-driven engines, and multiple tiers of small cannon were replaced by small numbers of large-bore, rifled guns. These were often placed in turrets to allow firing in all directions.

To combat these developments, the designs of the forts also evolved. The number of tiers of guns increased, making it possible to keep a high rate of fire on increasingly faster steam-powered ships. At the beginning of the Third System forts, especially when coupled with floating obstructions and torpedoes (mines), could deny passage through a narrows. The Civil War, however, proved that forts alone could no longer deny passage to fast-moving ships.[24]

Land defenses for Third System forts lessened as the period progressed. It was found that the basic design of the enceinte was sufficient to prevent a coup de main, and that even relatively simple land defenses would require the attackers to mount a protracted siege, and reduce the work through artillery fire. This reduced the need for extensive land defenses designed to repel infantry attacks, requiring only outworks sufficient to shield the scarp from artillery.

The front of the fort that provided the primary land defense of the fort was called the **gorge**. This front, often containing the main sally port, was the most vulnerable front in a siege, and required the most extensive protection of the masonry.

Early Third System land defenses were quite extensive. Defending New Orleans, Forts Pike and Wood[25] both sported two moats, with a glacis, parapet and banquette between them. At Newport, Rhode Island, Fort Adams boasted a major crownwork, with two tenailles, in addition to counterscarp galleries and the conventional glacis, parapet, and banquette. Fort Schuyler, defending the northern approach to New York City, had an impressive hornwork, complete with casemates. Fort Caswell, in North Carolina, had six caponiers, and the original design of Fort Morgan, Mobile, Alabama, included three caponiers in addition to the five bastions of the enceinte, though none were built. Fort Tompkins (Staten Island), Fort Macon (North Carolina), and Fort Barrancas and the Advanced Redoubt (Pensacola, Florida) had full counterscarp galleries, including emplacements for howitzers in the counterscarp. Both Fort Barrancas and the Advanced Redoubt communicated with the galleries through tunnels under the ditch, as did Fort Adams.

A classic, but unique to the Third System, application of separate land and water defenses was at The Narrows in New York Harbor. Topographical limitations drove the fort designers to build separate land-defense and water-defense forts, rather than combine both elements in a single structure.

Fort Lafayette, a transitional work, was a casemated water-defense fort on a shoal in The Narrows, but it had bare masonry walls that would be vulnerable to land-based batteries on the shore. Fort Hamilton was constructed immediately ashore of Fort Lafayette, and while it had several guns which would be used for water defense; it was primarily a land-defense fort in support of Fort Lafayette. Likewise across the channel, Fort Richmond was built as a tower battery with four tiers of cannon to seaward but minimal defense to landward. Fort Tompkins was built on the high ground above Fort Richmond to provide land defense. In this way, two land defense forts and two water defense forts could be designed and constructed with a purity of purpose and not have to compromise their design to a mixed mission.

An interesting note is the counterpoint between the Corps of Engineers and the leadership of the soldiers who were to man the forts. While the Corps of Engineers worked very hard to design structures that were readily defensible, in many cases they did not expend a commensurate effort on living quarters. The garrisons often complained that the citadels[26] and the casemate quarters were very inhospitable. In some cases, the living conditions were blamed for sickness and death among the garrison.[27] While some concessions were made, engineer reports indicated that the Corps lacked interest in dealing with these problems and the troops were frequently forced to construct temporary quarters outside the confines of the fort. These structures were usually wooden, and were to be burned upon attack of the fort by an enemy. Ironically, at Fort Pike these "temporary" buildings got out of hand, with gun emplacements on the ramparts of the fort being taken up by a commandant's quarters, and fields of fire completely blocked by barracks structures.

In some forts however, comfortable and sometimes elaborate barracks buildings were constructed. These engineer-designed buildings, generally masonry, were designed specifically as quarters and served that function well.

Later in the Third System, loopholes were often broken out to form window-like openings that would provide better ventilation. In the citadel of Fort Alcatraz in San Francisco Bay, the openings in the wall were made at full window width, with bricks stockpiled to close them to loopholes should a threat present itself. At Fort Warren, Boston Harbor, and Fort Gorges, Portland Harbor (see descriptions), extensive efforts to reduce dampness were undertaken by constructing double walls of masonry with heat from the fireplace ducted between them. While these efforts made some progress, the healthiest living conditions throughout the period were in separate barracks buildings rather than dual-purpose structures.

Location of Third System Forts

Four general locations were chosen for Third System forts: islands, shoals, shorelines or riverbanks, and hilltops. Which of these locations were used depended on the topography of the land and on the characteristics of the waterway they were designed to secure. Shorelines and riverbanks were the most common locations, and were the site of nearly half of the Third System forts. These twenty forts were divided between six riverbank locations, thirteen shore sites and one inland location.

Of nearly equal proportion were islands. Eighteen Third System forts occupied island locations, with some dominating a small island while others were located at one end of a large island. Shoals came next, with four forts built on moles (artificial islands) in these shallow areas. Finally, only three forts were located on hilltops. Two of these forts were discussed previously, Forts Hamilton and Tompkins, with the third being Fort Knox near Bucksport, Maine. These three forts also meet the shoreline or riverbank criteria, and are therefore double-counted.

There is a tactical reason why Third System forts were usually not located on "high ground." This reason was the practice, common in this period, of skipping cannon balls along the water surface en route to a target. It allowed for significant error in the calculation of the distance to a ship, as the ball would seek the first projection over the water it found. To accomplish this, the cannon had to be fairly close to water level.

A second item in regard to the location of Third System forts is that they were generally some distance from the city they protected. This was due to the desire to allow as much time as possible to muster a secondary defense of the city. The longer a distance an invader had to travel after laying siege to a fort, the more time was allowed for the transportation of more defensive forces and/or the "calling out" of a militia defensive force. This drove the Third System designers to locate the forts farther from the population centers when geography allowed.

An additional factor was that the longer range of the artillery by the time the Third System had begun. A fort had to be located farther from a city for that city to be beyond the range of a ships guns, and the longer-ranged guns of a fort allowed a wider channel to be protected than was previously possible. This wider channel was generally further from a population center and closer to the sea.[28]

Finally, Third System forts were usually located very close to the water. Engineering had sufficiently matured by this time to allow the construction of these massive forts on less-than-ideal soil systems.[29] By taking advantage of this technology, designers were able to maximize the effective range of their cannon to block a passageway, and to provide fire on an attacking vessel for a longer period of time.

The decision of what places needed to be defended on the nation's long coastline was laid out in the 1821 report, but "pork barrel politicize" played a role in modifying this philosophy. The dominant factor, however, was when the Navy was involved. The Navy had significant backing in Congress, and when a fort or series of forts were needed to protect a naval installation, the funds were always forthcoming. Both Bernard and Totten were astute enough to pick up on this fact and were careful to support the desires of the Navy in the formation of projects for forts.

By the close of the Third System, a very distinct "clustering" of new-construction forts could be noted. The coast from just west of the mouth of the Mississippi to Pensacola, Florida, had the largest cluster, with eleven forts filling this rather small area of coastline. Two forts guarded the Florida Strait at Key West and the Dry Tortugas, and forts from the Florida-Georgia border were fairly evenly spaced up the long coastline to New York City. New York had a cluster of six forts in a very small space, with four more filling the relatively short distance between New York and Boston. Five more forts were clustered on the coast of

New Hampshire and Maine, from Portsmouth to Prospect. Finally, two closely spaced forts guarded the harbor at San Francisco.

Note that the forts cited were new construction only. These were supplemented by renovation of existing forts, sometimes very substantial, by defensive towers, and by smaller batteries. Together this formidable line of defense incorporated a set of works that numbered more than 150. These works are discussed in the descriptions of each of the harbor defenses in Part II.

Sizes of Third System Forts

Certainly the size of a fort can be considered proportional to the perceived importance of the harbor that it protected, but many other factors were considered in the sizing of the forts of the Third System.

These forts, as discussed earlier, were to be garrisoned by only small peacetime units until a war was imminent, then the garrisons reinforced with local militia artillery. This meant that fort size would depend on the number of militia artillery available from the populace to garrison the fort in time of war. Forts Monroe, Adams, and Pickens were designed to hold relatively large permanent garrisons. These "headquarters" forts had many functions other than defense that were implemented within the enceinte, and they required a large area to carry out these activities. Additionally, these forts were near significant population centers that could supplement the permanent garrison in time of war.

Also of consideration was the number of guns that would be needed to defend the site.

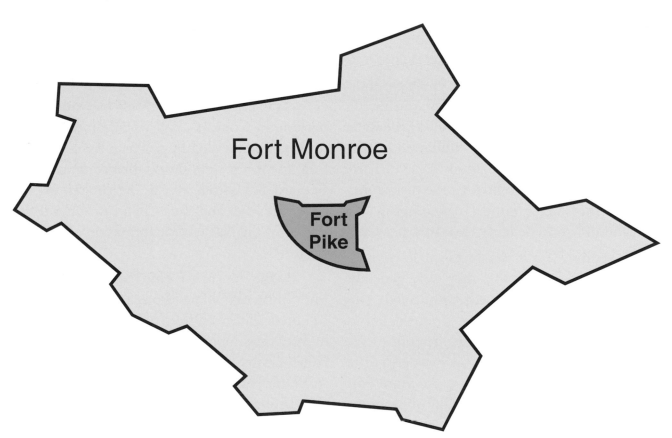

Figure 21: As shown in this scale drawing, the sizes of Third System forts varied dramatically. Fort Monroe, the largest of the system, is shown here with Fort Pike, which began construction in the same year. While most Third System forts fell between these two in size, there was a very wide variety in area, armament, and garrison.

Fort Jefferson, designed to be the most heavily armed fort in the history of the United States, mounted three tiers of cannon around the perimeter of its very large trace. Away from any population centers, it relied on a large permanent garrison to control this crucial location in the Florida Strait.

As construction technology improved through the course of the Third System, multiple levels of casemates were used, allowing forts of smaller trace to mount the same number of guns. Fort Richmond with four tiers of guns and Forts Taber and Popham[30] with three tiers were of relatively small trace, but sported large numbers of cannon. The local soil, however, played a major role in the number of casemates that could be stacked. This was a difficult lesson learned at both Fort Calhoun (located on a shoal) and Fort Pulaski (located on a mud island). Although designed for multiple levels of casemates, neither foundation was able to support more than one casemate tier and one barbette tier of cannon. Many other forts, however, were able to support many tiers of guns through proper foundation design. Fort Delaware, for example, boasted four tiers of cannon on a foundation of timber piles and grillage.[31]

Shapes of Third System Forts

The forts of the Third System were the last closed forts in the United States. Their complex geometrical shapes were the accumulation of fortification knowledge spanning at least two centuries, with contributions from engineers from several countries. Subsequent fortification efforts[32] involved the use of multiple detached batteries, not at all "forts" in the classical sense.

The first consideration involving the design of a fort was the location it was to defend, driving its overall shape. The major factors in this involved the position of the fort in relation to the channel or channels it was to defend, and the maximum arc of the guns mounted *en casemate*. While center-pintled barbette guns had very large angles of rotation, the shape of the embrasure and the relationship of the fore-pintled carriage to that embrasure governed the maximum traverse of a gun. With the goal of the fort to apply as much firepower to the channel as possible, it was desirable to have multiple fronts bearing on a given channel.

A counterpoint to this idea was the size of the fort. The larger the angle between walls, the larger the interior of the fort became, and the area consumed and the cost of construction went up proportionately. Several early Third System forts were built on the trace of a regular pentagon, the classic shape of a fort of the French school. This was a compromise of size and angle of the fort wall. Later, the designs shifted to truncated shapes, with the gorge wall on the landward side treated differently from the seacoast fronts. This changed the rules: in an unrestricted setting, a regular figure of shallower angle could be used without increasing the size of the fort. A 60° angle of traverse of the guns was common, which promoted the use of 120° as the angle between adjacent faces of the fort. This is the angle of a regular hexagon; therefore many Third System forts were built on the trace of a truncated hexagon.

The amount of truncation of the polygon varied according the desired size of the fort and the number and position of channels to defend. A five-sided plan was most common, with a single gorge wall connecting the two secondary seacoast fronts.

In significantly smaller forts, however, a four-sided plan was employed. In this design, one primary front faced the channel and two secondary fronts came off at 120° angles. The gorge wall then connected the ends of these secondary fronts. This left a very small parade, and made the use of conventional bastions guarding

35

the gorge inconvenient. The size and angles of a conventional bastion would be very awkward, and demibastions were used. Also, the importance of a bastion guarding a seacoast front in the latter Third System was much less and may have contributed to the decision to use demibastions. The demibastion would continue the seacoast front beyond the gorge wall, then turn nearly parallel to the gorge. A flank of the demibastion, perpendicular to the gorge wall, would provide defense of the gorge wall and sally port through the use of howitzer emplacements.

In rare cases, a fort was designed with all sides acting as fronts, with no gorge. Fort Jefferson, located on an island with deep water surrounding it, was a classic example of this design, having six faces and no gorge. Other forts, especially those forming a regular geometric figure, would have multiple landward faces. The two regular pentagons, Fort Jackson and Fort Morgan, each had two landward faces.

The true exercise in geometry came about with the design of the bastions and their relationship to the connecting curtain wall. The purpose of a bastion was to provide flanking fire down the length of the curtain and the face of the opposite bastion, thus leaving no area around the perimeter of the fort uncovered. To achieve this purpose, the flank of the bastion was formed at greater than 90° to the curtain[33] and provided embrasures for howitzers and sometimes loopholes for rifles. When constructed, the face of a bastion is on a line that terminates at the point where the flank of the opposite bastion meets the curtain. This geometric exercise assured that no area on the face of a bastion was outside the fire of the howitzers of the opposing bastion.

In Third System forts of very large trace, the design of the bastions changed. In conventional Third System forts, the bastions were closed-back structures with relatively narrow throats protruding from the salient angles of the trace. The bastions were entered from the adjacent casemates or from the parade, but usually with a clear separation from the parade.

In three very large Third System forts, Fort Monroe at Hampton Roads, Virginia, Fort Adams at Newport, Rhode Island, and Fort Warren in Boston harbor, the bastions were open structures with parade-like areas in the middle. These areas were open to the sky, unlike the interior of conventional Third System bastions.

Viewed from the parade, these bastions appeared to be angles in the fort wall. A row of casemates followed the scarp wall along the flank of the bastion. In the case of Fort Adams and Fort Warren, the faces of the bastion also contained casemates and embrasures. In Fort Adams, these embrasures were for seacoast cannon to increase the firepower of the seaward front. Fort Warren had seacoast cannon embrasures in its channel-bearing faces and loopholes in the bastion faces that secured the coverface, ditch, and rear glacis.

Although the appearance of these very large bastions varied from the smaller bastions employed in most Third System forts, the function was the same. The flanks of these bastions were pierced with howitzer embrasures, and Fort Adams actually had howitzers mounted en barbette atop the gorge demibastion. The faces of these bastions also followed the geometric rule mentioned previously, allowing them to be washed by howitzers. They also served as extensions of the curtain wall to increase the complement of barbette guns.[34]

Another major consideration relative to shape of a Third System fort was the available area and its physical features. Fort Point in San Francisco was shaped to fit on the very small amount of land available near the water. In fact, when it was found that shallows existed on either end of the point, the trace of the fort was modified to use these areas as well. Fort Warren in Boston Harbor was designed as a regular pentagon "squashed" to fit on Georges Island. Fort Jefferson on Garden Key in the Dry Tortugas was built in the general shape of the island on which it was located. This resulted in a regular hexagon that was shortened on two parallel sides. Fort McRee, on Foster's Bank near Pensacola, Florida, was built very long and narrow to fit on the narrow island.

Fort Alcatraz was the ultimate in regard to adapting a fort to its physical surroundings. It was built using the physical features of the land, with some blasting to make some cliffs steeper and the addition of masonry walls in some locations, for its enceinte. In this way the island and the fort were inseparable.

Finally, the unknown prevails. Why did some forts have sharp angle between adjoining seaward faces while others where rounded? Why were some forts built as truncated hexagons and others of the same period as truncated octagons?

It is interesting to note that there were two pair of forts with a shared design, and one set of three forts shared a common design.[35] Only two of the three forts sharing the same design were constructed as such, Fort Pike and Fort Wood. Fort Livingston was to be the third of that design, but delays in construction allowed new technologies to be employed, and it was completely redesigned prior to its construction. The two pair of forts coincidentally includes Fort Gaines in both. Originally designed as a twin to Fort Morgan, construction was halted after only foundation work had begun. When construction was resumed many years later, the revised design was the same as the more modern Fort Clinch[36]. They shared a unique design, utilizing the "detached scarp" concept. This resulted in the Third System utilizing 40 individual designs, each with its distinctive touches.

Other Structures

While the heart of the Third System was in the group of 42 newly constructed forts, the success of the system depended on the integration of these forts with other subsidiary structures. These subsidiary structures were used to protect lesser channels, to assist the newly constructed forts in the protection of major channels, and to provide a second line of defense for important harbors.

These structures fell into three primary categories: older forts modernized and/or preserved as part of the system, defensive towers, and masonry-revetted earthen batteries. The size and shape of these structures varied greatly, from very large, relatively modern forts to very small Martello Towers designed to mount one or two cannon. As with the newly constructed forts, their designs were appropriate to their function in the overall protection of a harbor.

The modernization of existing forts consisted of changes needed to accommodate the larger cannon prevalent in the Third System, and the modification of existing designs that were not up to Bernard's (and later Totten's) standards. A classic example of the latter took place at Fort Washington, guarding the Potomac River south of Washington, D. C. This transitional fort had been designed and construction began before Bernard came to the United States. When inspecting the fort, Bernard was concerned about the absence of defenses on the rear of the fort, facing the deep ravine that separated the fort's promontory from the Maryland countryside. To remedy the shortcomings, Bernard modified the trace of the fort to include two bastions and added a caponier at the midpoint between the bastions.

At Fort McHenry, Bernard was concerned about the rather week sally port and the design and locations of the supporting ravelins. He modified the fort with a conventional sally port and rearranged the ravelins and supporting batteries.

Defensive Towers

Defensive Towers became popular following the successful defense of the Mortella Point in Corsica by three small cannon[37] in a defensive tower. It is believed that the popular name Martello Tower is a corruption of the Mortella Tower that held off the British Navy.

Seven defensive towers were constructed during the Third System. Some of these towers, such as Tower Dupré, were very similar in design to classic Martello Towers and were referred to by that name. Other towers, such as Fort Proctor and Fort Winthrop, were much larger structures that reflected the general principles of a Martello Tower but departed from the classic design. These were generally referred to by the more general term *towers* or sometimes *defensive towers*.

The original Castle Pinckney at Charleston, South Carolina, the Martello Tower on Tybee Island, Georgia, and Tower Dupré near New Orleans, were the three towers that approximated the design of the classic Martello Towers of Europe. The towers at Key West were square towers that departed from the design of these classic Martello Towers, but were referred to by that name. They also departed significantly from the Martello Tower concept with the addition of a surrounding scarp, ditch, and external batteries. The large, square tower of Fort Winthrop differed most from the Martello Tower design and concept in size, strength, and the presence of external batteries. Fort Proctor, near New Orleans, was very similar in design to Fort Winthrop, but lacked the external batteries.

Several other towers were planned, and some were designed, but they were not constructed.

Batteries

The general term *batteries* was used to describe a number of structures that differed greatly in size and complexity. The more general term *works* also referred to these structures.

The batteries referred to here are stand-alone defensive structures, not the external batteries under the protection of the main fort. Those batteries were described earlier in this chapter.

Batteries in their simplest form were masonry-revetted earthworks. These consisted of a glacis terminating in a parapet, with barbettes located behind the parapet. These were either linear, or more often V-shaped, essentially designed as a ravelin. The angle of the V was, however, usually much less acute than a ravelin.

Where a battery extended over a projection of land – such as at Lime Point near the northern terminus of the Golden Gate Bridge – it might form a multiple-sided, open-backed structure.

In there most complex form, batteries consisted of closed geometric forms, even incorporating a sally port. A battery at the mouth of the Columbia River, now part of Fort Stevens, was a truncated hexagon with a sally port in the "gorge" wall. It was also protected by a surrounding ditch.

In the Third System, batteries were masonry-revetted earth[38] and were not casemated. Usually, the only interior structures in these batteries were earthen-covered magazines. Battery Bienvenue outside New Orleans – the most impressive Third System battery – had a closed form with barracks inside the enceinte.

Cannon at Third System Forts

While the purpose of this book is to discuss the design and construction of Third System forts, a better understanding of the forts can be achieved by understanding the weapons these forts housed. This is in no way intended to be a detailed look at the artillery of the period, but a brief overview of the cannon typical in Third System forts.

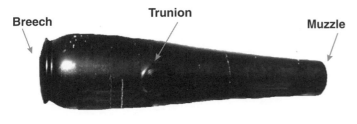

Breech **Trunion** **Muzzle**

Figure 22: The above diagram shows the basic parts of a cannon from this era. The majority of the cannon used in Third System forts were iron - falling between the older brass cannon and the yet-to-be-developed steel cannon. *(Photo by author)*

Seacoast Cannon

The primary armament at Third System forts was the seacoast cannon. These cannon were the weapons called upon to control the waterways adjacent to the fort, to provide a defense against ship borne attack, and to combat a siege. They were cast iron muzzle-loading artillery – both the powder and the ball were loaded through the muzzle of the cannon.

During most of the Third System – until the early 1860s – all cannon were smoothbores. This means that the cannon fired a spherical ball and that the interior of the gun tube had no rifling. The introduction of rifled cannon added lands, or ridges, to the inside of the barrel that caused the projectile – now cylindrical – to spin.

This modification served two purposes. First, the spinning cylindrical projectile had significantly greater accuracy than the spherical ball fired from a smoothbore cannon. Second, the windage – the difference between the diameter of the projectile and the bore of the cannon – was reduced. This caused more of the force of the powder explosion to drive the projectile, increasing both the range of the cannon and the size of the projectile.

About the same time that rifled cannon

were being introduced, Thomas J. Rodman was making a major improvement in the methods of designing and manufacturing smoothbore cannon. The result of his development, the Rodman cannon, was a series of cannon that had larger bores and longer range than the previous generation of seacoast guns.

Rodman's method was essentially the solving of a physics problem. When traditional cannon were cast, the tube cooled from the outside surface to the inside of the casting, thus creating an expansive (outward) stress in the metal. Thus the stress was in the same direction as the forces encountered when firing the cannon. Over time, the metal would fatigue and the gun would explode on firing. Adding additional thickness to the metal increased the amount of stress, providing little benefit.

Rodman developed a method of cooling the bore of the cannon during the casting process, thus creating a compressive (inward) stress. The stresses in the metal were now opposed to the stresses encountered during firing. Less metal fatigue resulted, and made feasible the casting of thicker, and therefore larger bore, cannon.

Figure 23: A Columbiad cannon on a fore-pintle mount. This type of carriage and mount were very common in the Third System, used both en barbette - as shown here - and en casemate. *(Photo by author)*

39

The second step in Rodman's approach was to calculate the force vectors present when the cannon fired. If these vectors were plotted with the base of each vector along the bore of the cannon, the tip of the vector arrows defines a smoothly curved tapered form. This form is the exterior of a Rodman cannon.

Both types of smoothbore cannon – the pre-Rodman design and the Rodman cannon – fired cast iron spherical shot, solid iron balls, and shell, hollow iron balls filled with an explosive charge.

Both types of cannon went under the general name *Columbiad*. The pre-Rodman design was generally classified by the weight of the solid shot fired from the cannon. Rodman cannon were generally classified by the diameter of the bore. Thus the pre-Rodman seacoast cannon present in Third System forts were generally 32-pounder and 42-pounder cannon, and the Rodman cannon were generally 8-inch, 10-inch, and 15-inch cannon. A 32-pounder had a bore just under 6 ½ inches and a 42-pounder had a bore of just over seven inches. An 8-inch shot weighed approximately 45 pounds, a 10-inch shot weighed approximately 90 pounds and a 15-inch shot weighed approximately 300 pounds.

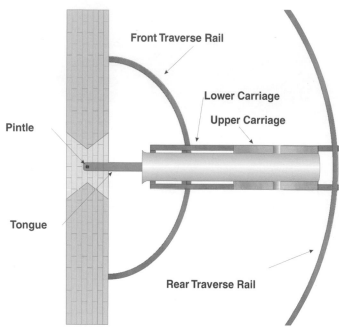

Figure 24: The fore-pintle mount, later referred to as front pintle, was designed to give a maximum angle of traverse in a minimum area. Placing the pivot point at the narrowest point of the embrasure accomplished this goal.

Rifled cannon increased the range and weight of the projectile for a given bore size. An 8-inch Parrott rifle fired a 200-pound shot, more than twice the weight of the shot fired by a 10-inch Rodman gun. A 10-inch Parrott rifle fired a shot approximately the same weight as that fired by a 15-inch Rodman gun.

Howitzers

The primary purpose of howitzers – smoothbore cannon with significantly shorter barrels than other cannon – in Third System forts was for defense against infantry. The workhorse weapon for this purpose was the 24-pounder flank howitzer.

While rated a 24-pounder, these cannon were generally not used for shot or shell, but for canister rounds. A canister consisted of a thin metal casing – similar to a coffee can – that contained a large number of iron balls. On firing, the casing would disinte-

Figure 25: A Parrott Rifle is shown here on a fore-pintle mount, inside a casemate at Fort Sumter, guarding Charleston, South Carolina. *(Photo by author)*

Figure 26: The above photograph shows a 10-inch Rodman cannon on a fore-pintle barbette mount. Note the iron carriage used for this massive gun, as opposed to the wooden carriage on the Columbiad shown previously. *(Photo by author)*

Figure 27: Two of the common types of shot used in howitzers are grapeshot, shown on the left, and solid shot, shown on the right. This round of solid shot is shown attached to a sabot, a wooden "donut" that fixes the position of the shot in the bore of the cannon. *(Photos by author)*

grate spraying the balls in a pattern similar to that of a shotgun.

A 24-pounder flank howitzer would fire a canister with 48 iron balls approximately $1^{1}/_{3}$ inches in diameter. As can be easily imagined, this would be a formidable weapon against massed infantry, especially in a confined area such as a ditch.

Mortars

While not the primary armament at Third System forts, most forts had one or more seacoast mortars assigned.

Mortars were large-bore, short-barreled weapons that would fire shot or shell on a very high trajectory, resulting in what is generally referred to as plunging fire. These had two purposes during this period. First, the high trajectory would allow shot and shell to penetrate the lightly armored decking of a ship. Shot would

Figure 28: The most impressive weapon used in Third System forts was the 15-inch Rodman cannon. Weighing up to 66,000 pounds - not including the massive iron carriage - these weapons were generally mounted on center pintles. This provided maximum flexibility in the use of the weapon by allowing a full 360-degree traverse. *(Photo by author)*

use its heavy mass to cause significant damage below decks, while shell would penetrate the upper deck and explode below decks. Shell could also be fused to explode over the upper deck of a ship, causing significant damage and/ or loss of life on this deck.

The second use of mortars was to hurl shells over obstacles – natural or man-made – that provided cover to besieging troops and artillery.

The most common seacoast mortars used during the Third System were 10-inch and 13-inch models. 10-inch mortars weighed between five- and eight-thousand pounds, and 13=inch mortars weighed over seventeen thousand pounds.

Carriages

The carriage is the often-complex mechanism that supports a cannon or mortar. Car-

riages are designed for particular applications, by function, by location within a fort, and by the size of the cannon being supported.

The carriages used for both seacoast guns and howitzers consisted of two parts – an upper carriage and a lower carriage. The upper carriage was firmly attached to the cannon, and moved with the cannon during recoil. It also provided the mechanism for adjusting the elevation of the cannon.

The lower carriage provided the support on which the upper carriage rode, and provided the traverse – the side-to-side aiming of the cannon.

The most common carriage design is the fore-pintle carriage, later called the front-pintle carriage. Within this category are two types of carriage, a barbette carriage that is designed to allow the gun to fire over a parapet and a casemate carriage that is designed to allow the gun to fire through an embrasure.

Both of these designs use a similar upper carriage – it is the lower carriage that separates the two applications. The upper carriage consisted of a framework – metal, wood, or a combination of both – that supported the gun barrel by the trunions. This framework was supported by two axels, each with two eccentric cams and two wheels.

When the gun was fired, the axel would turn such that it would rotate off the eccentric cam and the bottom of the upper carriage would contact the top of the lower carriage. The friction caused by these two flat surfaces sliding against each other would dissipate the energy of the recoil. To return the gun to its firing position, the axel would be rotated – using long poles placed in holes in the surface of the wheels – such that the upper carriage was supported by the wheels. The upper carriage and gun would then be rolled forward into firing position.

The lower carriage of a fore-pintle casemate cannon consisted of a four-wheel framework that supported the upper platform. The wheels of this framework were mounted transverse to the length of the carriage, allowing the carriage to be rotated left and right. Protruding from the front of this framework was a long metal tongue that extended through a slot beneath the embrasure. This tongue had a circular hole near its front that was engaged by the pintle, a long large-diameter cylinder that extended from the bottom of the embrasure to the floor of the casemate. The pintle was located at the throat – or narrowest part – of the embrasure.

The wheels of the lower carriage rode on two sets of flat, semicircular plates attached to the floor of the casemate, called traverse rails. The angle of traverse of this type of carriage was approximately 120 degrees.

The lower carriage for a barbette mount consisted of a similar framework as the casemate mount, but with only two wheels. The lower front member of the lower carriage rested on a fixed pintle set in a barbette, or gun platform (hence the name barbette mount). The rear wheels again ran on a traverse rail attached to the terreplein.

A center-pintle barbette carriage again used the same upper carriage, but with a unique lower carriage. The lower carriage had wheels fore and aft, and the center member attached to a pintle mounted in the barbette. The traverse rails extended to form a full circle, allowing a full 360-degree rotation of the gun.

The most common center-pintle barbette mounts were for 15-inch Rodman cannon. Because of the weight of these massive cannon –over 50,000 pounds – three pair of wheels on the front and three pair on the rear supported the lower framework. This necessitated three concentric circles of traverse rails.

The carriage for the flank howitzer was much smaller than the carriages for the larger guns, as there was far less weight to support. The upper carriage looked like a miniature version of the seacoast carriage, but the lower carriage was much lighter in design. It consisted of a upper framework that supported the upper carriage. This framework connected directly to a pintle located in the throat of the embrasure. The rear of the framework was supported on a vertical frame that terminated in two wheels at floor level. These wheels rode on a single traverse rail.

Mortars had the simplest carriages of all. They consisted of a framework that connected to the trunions of the mortar and terminated in a sled that was manually turned for right-left movement. Elevation was set by a mechanism built into the framework of the carriage.

While the style of each of these carriages is consistent, the size of the carriages varied greatly. The massive iron carriage of a 15-inch Rodman gun was of a similar design to the wooden carriage of a 32-pounder, but the difference in size is dramatic.

Relative Sizes of Shot

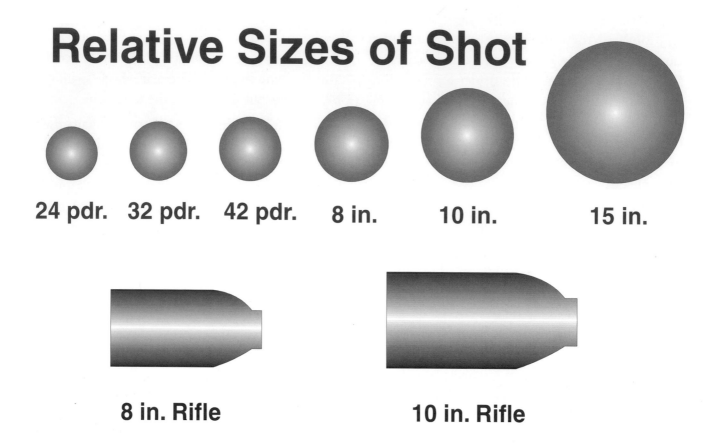

24 pdr.   32 pdr.   42 pdr.   8 in.   10 in.   15 in.

8 in. Rifle   10 in. Rifle

Figure 29: The above scale drawing shows the relative sizes of shot used in the artillery emplaced in Third System forts. The increased mass of a bolt used in a rifled cannon over the round shot used in a smoothbore cannon can be clearly seen in the diagram.

Time and technology were major factors in the manner in which guns were mounted. As with fort design and artillery design, evolutionary changes were taking place in the design of carriages. The early wooden carriages used to mount cannon at Fort Pike in the 1820s looked quite different from the iron carriages in use late in the Third System. Necessity and availability also played a role – identical guns were sometimes mounted on different carriages, depending on what could be allocated to the fort at that time.

In general, one can also identify the size of the gun last mounted in a casemate by looking at the floor of the casemate – providing that the floor has not been altered. A single traverse rail and a pintle located above the sill of the embrasure indicate that a flank howitzer was emplaced at that location. Two traverse rails indicate a seacoast gun, with the distance between the embrasure and the traverse rails in the casemate floor giving an indication of its size.

On the terreplein, a semicircular traverse rail truncated by the scarp is indicative of a fore-pintle mount. A full-circle traverse rail (usually multiple concentric circles) was used for a center-pintle mount.

For a more in-depth review of nineteenth-century artillery, there are many books on the subject.[39] Several forts have artillery emplaced, some actual artillery that has been restored and some replica hardware. In both cases, the emplacements aid the visitor in understanding the appearance of the forts when armed.

Manning the Forts

Private contractors, under the leadership of the Corps of Engineers, performed the construction of the Third System forts. After the debacle at Fort Gaines discussed in Chapter One, a superintending engineer was assigned to each fort-construction site. His role was to watch over the government's interest during the construction process, modify the designs as appropriate, to manage the contracts for materials, and to control the budget for that project.

The engineers who performed this function were some of the best of the Corps of Engineers. Such household names as Joseph Totten, Robert E. Lee, P. G. T. Beauregard, and William Chase served in the role of superintending engineer during the construction of various Third System forts.

The ideal process for the transfer of a fort from the construction phase to the operational phase was for the Corps of Engineers to complete the construction, supervise the mounting of the guns, then turn the fort over to the Regular Army unit that was to man it. In the absence of a threat to our shores, that is the procedure that was used. For many of the forts, however, it was necessary to mount some of the guns and man the fort prior to the completion of construction. In these cases, the Engineers were still building the fort while the soldiers were training on the emplaced cannon. Many forts of the Third System were never officially completed, although all of them received armament.

With the arrival of the troops came the materiel to sustain them — quartermaster supplies, individual weapons and ammunition, etc. Information regarding the arming of individual forts is beyond the scope of this work, but is available in the books and guidebooks related to each particular fort.

Notes

[1] The Academy itself was patterned after the École Polytechnique in France.

[2] The first text, Gay de Vernon's *A Treatise on the Science of War and Fortification*, was the standard text at the Military Academy prior to works by Henry Wager Halleck and Dennis Hart Mahan, both professors at the Academy.

[3] These advances included improved methods for casting cannon and the development of rifled cannon. Both increased the size and velocity of the shot and shell that could be brought to bear on the scarp wall.

[4] Following the Civil War, this subject again became a subject of debate, but the majority opinion still held that even rifled cannon mounted on an ironclad ship was not adequate to maintain a prolonged attack on a masonry fort. See Chapter Four.

[5] Totten gained prominence through the studies he conducted at Fort Adams (and elsewhere) regarding the firing of Ordnance against various types of embrasures. This work led to many of the innovations he developed for various latter Third System forts.

[6] Several forts undergoing restoration have had the iron removed to minimize further damage to the fort. If the iron were properly maintained, it would remain free of rust and therefore be sound. The poor maintenance of Third System forts, due primarily to lack of allocated funds and manpower, caused these iron components to become vulnerable to the salt air and the problems, now irreversible, began.

[7] Fort Livingston and twin Forts Gaines and Clinch had interior casemates which served only as bombproof shelters.

[8] Fort Macon did not have casemated cannon emplacements, all cannon were mounted en barbette. When the Union siege of the fort took place, the gunners drove the defenders from the ramparts and forced the surrender of the fort. It can be speculated that casemated cannon positions would have allowed the fort to mount a longer defense.

[9] Many forts had a few casemates that were closed in the rear because of the design of the fort. The casemates in the curved portions of Fort Calhoun were closed, as were the casemates in the bastions and demibastions of most of the forts.

[10]Ten forts had three tiers of guns; Forts Richmond (NYC) and Point (San Francisco) had four tiers.

[11]The separation of the scarp and the casemates at Fort Point in San Francisco is very dramatic. After the 1990 earthquake, the scarp angled outward, leaving a large gap in the upper tiers. Work is planned to stabilize the wall and attempt to draw it back to its previous position.

[12]Many documents of the period used two words, terra plein, to define this area. The single word, terreplein, was coming into use at that time and is used here.

[13] Fort Morgan, at the entrance to Mobile Bay, Alabama, is an excellent example of a fort with a brick-paved terraplein.

[14] In Fort Adams, Newport R.I., and the Advanced Redoubt, Pensacola Florida, crenellated embrasures were used to protect the main sally port.

[15]Fort Adams has a unique "internal ditch" which provides access to the lower-tier casemates on the seaward face. The second level of casemates was at the level of the parade and was accessible from the parade through a series of bridges over this ditch. Fort Warren has an analogous access ditch to the lower level of casemates guarding the gorge. Fort Totten was to have a parade even with the highest level of casemates on the seaward fronts, but this was the level of the only casemates on the remaining sides. The fort was designed this way because of the sloping terrain on which it was constructed. This portion of the fort was not constructed.

[16]Fort Taylor on Key West, and Forts Pike, Wood, and Jackson defending New Orleans had similar seawalls, but these are no longer intact. The absence of the seawall at Fort Pike and on the marina side of Fort Wood demonstrates the devastating effects of marine and riverine erosion on the foundation of a masonry fort. Both forts have suffered structural damage and will eventually be destroyed if the erosion is not abated and the foundation repaired.

[17]In Third System forts, this maximum distance is approximately one mile. While the larger guns of the fort had considerably more range than this, this distance was adopted as the maximum distance to a redoubt in advance of the fort.

[18]Mahan, in his Attack and Defence of Permanent Works defines a crownwork in the more general case. He described it as having "two or more bastioned fronts" rather than the more classical definition used here. Only one crownwork was constructed in the Third System, and that followed the definition in the text. An earthen crownwork was constructed at Yorktown, Virginia during the Revolutionary War and reconstructed during the Civil War. This also followed the definition in the text. The author is not aware of any larger crownworks in the United States.

[19]Fort Adams, Newport, RI, had both counterscarp galleries and counterfire rooms. The counterfire rooms were located in the rear of the crownwork, so cannot be called "counterscarp" galleries though they were identical in design to counterscarp galleries.

[20]While open-topped, open-backed works defines this family of outworks, there are exceptions. The demilune at Fort Warren, Boston Harbor, was a masonry vault with both a roof and a rear wall. A tunnel from the covert way provided access.

[21]Fort Warren, Boston Harbor, had both a demilune and a ravelin. The ravelin was an earthwork seacoast battery, while the demilune was an all-masonry casemated rifle gallery set in an earthen coverface guarding the gate.

[22]See Chapter One for the definition of these six goals.

[23]Fort Point actually lies *below* the Golden Gate Bridge. The architect of the bridge saw the historical significance of the fort and provided a special arch to allow construction of the bridge without demolition of the fort.

[24]At Fort Jackson in the Mississippi River and at Forts Gaines and Morgan in Mobile Bay, Federal ships ran past the guns of the fort to enter the guarded area. These forts, however, had a significantly smaller concentration of armament than the "tower forts" of the latter Third System.

[25]Fort Wood was renamed Fort Macomb, the name it carries today. In this text, however, it is referred to by its original name. The name was changed to minimize confusion with Fort Wood on Bedlow's Island in New York City, now the base of the Statue of Liberty.

[26]A note from J. M. Scarritt to J. G. Totten on 20 March 1849 states "...in time of peace the citadel be not used as quarters for officers & men. In summer the rooms were warm, damp, and wanting in ventilation. We have also myriads of mosquitoes and it requires a thorough draft of air and

that moving with all the force of the sea breeze to make the rooms habitable. The soldiers & laborers I have here are forced to sleep on top of the parapets."

[27]See especially the construction and early garrison records of the Louisiana forts of the Third System. Fort Jackson had special problems in this regard, but the other Louisiana forts had near-mutinies of the garrison due to living conditions inside the fort.

[28] Lewis, p. 12.

[29]The major exception to this progress in engineering is the ever-sinking Fort Calhoun. This fort was never completed due to the constant settling of its foundations into the bottom of Hampton Roads. Only one and one-half tiers of what was to be a three-tiered fort were ever completed. The fort site is still sinking today.

[30]Fort Popham was planned for three tiers, but only the first casemated tier was completed and the second tier partially completed.

[31]*The District: A History of the Philadelphia District, U. S. Army Corps of Engineers 1866-1971*, Snyder and Guss, 1974: p.46-51.

[32]These efforts began even before the close of the Third System. The subsequent work, sometimes referred to as the Fourth System, began with masonry-revetted earthworks built from 1866-1876. In 1885, the Endicott System used structural concrete for detached batteries, a practice that, with refinements, continued through World War II.

[33]This angle varied from 90° to 135°, though rarely did it hit the larger figure. Using a larger angle between the flank and the curtain made the bastion much smaller, a necessity if the curtain wall was relatively short or the enceinte angle relatively small.

[34]There was a tendency to reduce the size of the bastions in Third System forts as the period progressed. This was not a strong trend, however, as Fort Totten was designed late in the system with very large bastions. Fort Hancock, also a later fort, also was designed with large bastions. As a general trend, however, smaller bastions and even the unbastioned shoal forts like Carroll and Sumter became prevalent.

[35]Fort Pike and Fort Wood were of nearly identical design, with Fort Wood being slightly smaller than Fort Pike. An additional difference in the two was due to the fact that they were both constructed by the same team. Lessons learned in the construction of the former had an impact on the way the latter was finally built.

[36]In actuality, Fort Clinch was an insignificant 25 feet shorter than Fort Gaines on each of its curtains. The bastions were the same size and all other proportions of the fort were identical.

[37] The armament of the tower consisted of one six-pounder and two eighteen-pounder cannon.

[38] Fort Stevens, at the mouth of the Columbia River, was wood-revetted earth. This causes a controversy on whether it was part of the "permanent" system.

[39] Works by Edwin Olmstead and Wayne Stark are highly recommend, as is a very nice web page by Chuck TenBrink at www.cwartillery.org .

Development of the Third System

The Third System spanned a fifty-one-year period, from 1816, when the War Department created the Board of Engineers and brought Bernard from France, until 1867, when construction on major forts was halted in the aftermath of the Civil War. It was inescapable that changes would occur in fort designs during that long period of technological development. This section explores those changes through a review of forts built during the various decades comprising the Third System.

The remaining two fronts were gorge walls, protected by demibastions at the front and a full bastion at the junction of the gorges. These gorge walls were protected by a large, complicated series of outworks that included two ditches with earthworks between.

Bernard applied this design to three remote, sparsely populated locations guarding New Orleans. The small trace was compatible with the smaller number of people available as militia in these remote areas. Forts Pike and Wood were

Figure 30: Fort Wood, guarding a passage between Lake Borgne and Lake Ponchartrain north of New Orleans, sported a curved masonry front and a barbette tier of guns above. While the seacoast front was unprotected masonry, the landward fronts had extensive outworks. *(Photo by author)*

The First Decade, 1818-1827

Bernard's first efforts at fort design consisted of two very conventional designs and one very large work of irregular trace. The first design used by Bernard was for a fort with a very small trace protecting a narrow, river-like passage. For this application he chose a single, curved front facing the channel. This shape provided a maximum number of cannon to bear on the channel simultaneously.

constructed using this design, but Fort Livingston was built on a later Totten design.

The second design was the traditional regular pentagon, with full bastions at all corners. The design sported three seacoast fronts and two gorge walls with a significantly larger trace. The outworks were not as extensive as those of the smaller forts, but were still formidable. One of the forts using this design, Fort Morgan, was unique in having a sally port through the outworks followed by a second sally port into the fort.

Bernard applied this design to three forts, Forts Morgan and Gaines guarding the entrance to Mobile Bay in Alabama, and to Fort Jackson guarding the Mississippi River south of New Orleans.[1]

Bernard's third design at the beginning of the Third System was for an extremely large fort, built with an irregular six-sided trace customized for the chosen site. The 63-acre parade was lined with casemates in select areas, and with flank howitzer embrasures in only some bastions. Extensive outworks, including a redoubt, guarded the approaches to the fort and the landward-facing curtains. This design was applied to Fort Monroe, which was to be the headquarters fort for the coastal defense system. The work was so massive that it was considered nearly impregnable.

Although very different in configuration, these forts had several elements in common. First, only a single level of casemates was used in each fort, and then the casemates were used sparingly. All heavy guns were to be mounted en barbette, with only smaller ordnance mounted inside the casemates.[2]

Forts Pike and Wood had even fewer casemates: except for the howitzers mounted to protect the fort walls and a couple of forward-facing howitzer positions, the only casemates were located on the seaward sides of the forts. Fort Monroe used casemates in the secondary seacoast fronts, and a casemated battery in advance of the primary front.

This served two purposes. The primary threat of damage to a fort was from land-based cannon, and by minimizing the number of casemates on the landward side of the fort more earth could be used in construction. This made the fort less vulnerable to damage from these cannon, as the earth would absorb the impact of the shells.

It also provided more firepower for the amount of money spent on construction. Casemate construction was expensive, and the greater number of cannon was needed on seacoast fronts, not on landward fronts. Using earth on landward-facing fronts rather than casemates reduced the cost of a fort without reducing the seacoast firepower.

The similarities extended to inside the fort walls. Forts Pike, Wood, Jackson, and Morgan had defensive citadels on the parade as a "last line of defense" against an attacker, while the bastions of Fort Jackson and Fort Monroe were independently defensible. Select bastions of Fort Monroe even had loopholes opening to the parade of the fort to allow for their defense.

A significant difference in the forts regarded placement of the channel-bearing batteries. The seacoast batteries of Forts Pike and Wood were contained in the casemates and barbette tier of the curved face that fronted the channel. Fort Morgan had a similar casemated front with barbette battery. Fort Monroe, on the other hand, had a unique design. The main channel batteries consisted of a tier of barbette guns atop the fort, and a casemated water battery external to the ditch. The walls beneath the barbette guns were earth-backed. Flanking the main battery, casemated batteries within the fort and the barbette guns above them bore on secondary areas of the channel. These provided oblique fire on ships approaching the fort and passing beyond the fort. This oblique fire was far less effective than perpendicular fire on a ship opposite the fort, where the primary batteries were located.

Fort Calhoun, designed as a complement to Fort Monroe, was constructed on a man-made island immediately across the channel in Hampton Roads. This fort, known as the "castle of the rip raps," was designed for an impressive amount of armament ¾ 232 cannon ¾ given its relatively modest perimeter. This was to be achieved through multiple tiers of casemates, crowned by a barbette tier. This was to be the Third System's first venture into more than one tier of casemates. Nature, however, had other ideas and it seemed that no matter how much stone was put in the "rip raps" the foundation continued to sink. Ultimately Fort Calhoun (renamed Fort Wool) was left with one completed casemate tier and one incomplete tier with guns mounted en barbette. This precluded mounting large numbers of cannon, but Fort Monroe was armed heavily enough to adequately control the channel.

Monroe, and it stands today as a well-preserved archetype of an early-Third-System fort.

In the final years of the decade, three forts were begun: Fort Hamilton guarding the lower approach to New York Harbor, Fort Caswell guarding the passageway to Wilmington, North Carolina and the Cape Fear River, and Fort Macon, guarding Bogue Sound, North Carolina.

Fort Hamilton was the first Third System

Figure 31: Fort Adams, protecting the main channel of Narragansett Bay and Newport Harbor, boasted two casemated tiers and a barbette tier of cannon. Again, this long seacoast front was of unprotected masonry, while all landward-facing fronts had outworks for protection. *(Photo by author)*

Next in the chronology came Fort Adams, a truly unique work that fully utilized the shape of the land on which it was built. A masterpiece of combining multiple layers of land defense toward the neck of the peninsula with three tiers of seacoast cannon on the channel side, this irregular fort was designed for 468 cannon. Its perimeter of 1793 yards is second only to Fort

fort whose primary purpose was land defense. Built on the hill overlooking casemated Fort Lafayette, Fort Hamilton prevented an attacker from mounting a siege of the island fort and closed the land route across the southern portion of Long Island. Mounting an impressive 130 cannon, Fort Hamilton could provide significant fire on approaching ships, but also was well designed and well armed against a landward assault. Unlike most other Third System forts, Fort Hamilton's sally port was on the seaward face, not on the traditional gorge wall. This placement provided a more secure gorge and had the added advantage that the face was well guarded by Fort Lafayette.

Forts Caswell and Macon had land defenses integrated into their design. Fort Macon used counterscarp galleries and a large ditch, while Fort Caswell used six caponiers to guard a wet and a dry ditch. Only barbette guns provided coastal defense on both works, a factor contributing to the defeat of Fort Macon during the Civil War.

Thus ended the first decade of construction, with eleven forts begun in the ten-year period. Only two of the forts, Forts Pike and Wood, were finished during this decade and those were the two smallest designs. Peace still prevailed, however, and the coastal fortification project was allowed to continue at a steady pace without the pressures of preparing for war.

The Second Decade, 1828-1837

The second decade of construction opened in controversy. Totten had designed Fort Pickens, guarding the entrance to Pensacola Bay, and had begun construction without Bernard's approval of the plans. Asserting his authority without wasting the effort that had already been expended, Bernard approved the plans for the two faces that had been started, but modified the landward side of the fort, reducing both the size of the bastions and the overall size of the fort. He intended to use the money saved in this way to construct a previously unforecasted fort on the opposite side of the channel, Fort McRee.

Even with the reduction in size, Fort Pickens was a substantial work. About half the perimeter of Fort Adams, it was designed for 252 cannon and had a 7-acre parade. McRee, on the other hand, had a very small trace, only slightly larger than Pike and Macomb, but was to mount three tiers of cannon to Pickens' two. The result was a tall fort designed to mount 144 cannon in a very compact design. Most unusual were the "folded wing" design of McRee and the absence of any integral land-defense capability.

Pickens and McRee each had unusual casemate designs, undoubtedly devised as further experimentation in fort designs. Pickens had wide, sweeping arches above casemates designed to mount two cannon each.[3] McRee had both tall and wide casemates, with a timber floor halfway up the height. This allowed four cannon to be mounted in each casemate.

Also during this decade, work began on the first of the "tall forts," those multiple-tiered forts that invoke the awe of those who walk through them today. Fort Sumter, guarding Charleston Harbor, had a combination of height and a moderately large trace, allowing a tremendous number of cannon to be mounted. It was looked on as impregnable to naval assault when constructed, and its shortage of armament tempted the South Carolinians to open fire on this impressive structure at the beginning of the Civil War.[4] It was, in fact, the fear that a reinforced Fort Sumter could never be taken that prompted the initial shots to be fired.[5]

Although first of the tall forts, Fort Sumter is no longer the awesome sight it was when constructed. The Union bombardments late in the Civil War shattered the top two tiers of the fort, and modifications in the late nineteenth century finished the emasculation of this formidable work. One can appreciate its former height, though not its area, by visiting Fort Point in San Francisco. This California work is a well-preserved fort of the latter Third System, and used a casemate arrangement very similar to that of Fort Sumter. Fort Point, however, had a significantly smaller trace.

Figure 32: Fort Richmond, guarding the approaches to New York's Inner Harbor, boasted four tiers of cannon. This massive fort supplied an incredible number of cannon in a very small trace. *(Photo by author)*

A unique fort during this period was the redesigned Fort Livingston, south of New Orleans. This fort was designed as a seacoast defense fort, but its location required elaborate land defenses. To accomplish this, large counterscarp galleries were constructed on the two landward fronts. Seacoast cannon were mounted en barbette, with the casemates pierced by loopholes rather than cannon embrasures. Its small trace was to be surmounted by 60 cannon, and possessed the most well developed living provisions of any Third System forts up to that time.

The remaining three forts in this period were polygonal works boasting one casemate tier and one barbette tier of cannon. Fort Warren in

Boston Harbor, the largest of these, was designed for 300 cannon and a rambling area of 18 acres. Of somewhat lesser size were Fort Pulaski guarding Savannah Georgia and the Savannah River, with 146 cannon, and Fort Schuyler guarding the northern (Hell Gate) approach to New York City, with 250 cannon.

The decade closed with construction having at least begun on almost half of the forts built during the Third System. Bernard had returned to France midway through the decade, and Totten had firmly grasped the reins of the Fortifications Board. Nine completed forts then guarded our coastline, fully half of those begun. Most impressively, Fort Monroe stood as a completed work with her 63 acres of military might.

The Third Decade, 1838-1847

The third decade of construction opened slowly, with Congress reluctant to spend significant amounts of money on coastal defense. Building in Pensacola continued due to pressure from the Navy to protect the base being established, and a new Fort Barrancas was constructed as an adjunct to the Spanish water battery known as Fort San Carlos. This fort was primarily a land-defense work, with thirty guns bearing on the channel. These guns were nearly equally divided between the new fort and the modernized Spanish battery. Later in the decade, the Advanced Redoubt was constructed with a very similar design, but devoid of any seacoast-defense mission.

The only other new project in the final year of the 1830s was the construction of a new Fort Trumbull guarding the city of New London, Connecticut. This small-trace, three-tiered work was designed for water defense, with only minimal provisions to withstand a siege. The 62 guns were to be concentrated along the river faces, and a masonry ravelin in the rear of the fort would provide protection for the gorge.

In the mid-1840s, Congress loosened the purse strings and building began to flourish once again. In the next three years, nine forts were begun, making this the most active period of the Third System. Maine received its first Third System fort, the impressive Fort Knox on the Penobscot River. This unique fort had two external batteries providing the bulk of the seaward firepower, and a full counterscarp wall with galleries for land defense. The rock on which Knox sat was honeycombed with tunnels leading to external batteries and to detached caponiers protecting them.

The period also saw the commencement of the tall forts protecting the Florida Strait - Taylor and Jefferson. While both were designed primarily to defend against assault by ships, Fort Taylor was to have fairly elaborate protection for the gorge. These defenses had not been implemented, however, when war broke out, and the fort suffered the results of that lack of preparation.

Fort Jefferson, taking up virtually the entire island on which it stands, had no need for land defense and was built with six faces and no gorge. This impressive work was designed for 450 cannon, all housed within the perimeter of the fort, and a wartime garrison of 1,500 men.

The impressive tower forts of Delaware and Richmond were also begun, Fort Delaware replacing the boggled transitional work that mercifully burned prior to completion. Fort Delaware, guarding the Delaware River, and Fort Richmond, standing opposite the site of Fort Lafayette guarding the southern approach to New York Harbor, are both granite castles designed for four tiers of guns.[6]

Fort Tompkins, a unique land-defense fort guarding the rear of Fort Richmond, was begun

in this period, as was Fort Carroll, an island fort in Baltimore Harbor. Like Fort Jefferson in the Dry Tortugas, Fort Carroll had no outworks, but unlike Fort Jefferson, it had no bastions, either.

Also during that period, the two detached-scarp forts, Fort Clinch and the revised Fort Gaines, were begun. This innovative design had been implemented in Europe, and Totten decided to utilize the approach on these two southern forts.

Finally, Fort Winthrop, a defensive tower with adjacent batteries, was also constructed during the decade.

The Final Years, 1848-1867

Like the previous decade, the fourth decade of construction opened slowly. Four years passed until construction began on two new projects, and both of these projects were in the newly acquired California. Fort Alcatraz was begun in 1852 by sculpting the island into a rough scarp, supplemented by brickwork when necessary. Fort Point construction began a year later, and that impressive work still guards the entrance to San Francisco Bay.

During these final years Maine received two more forts, Fort Gorges and Fort Popham. Both forts were designed exclusively for sea defense, with Popham having a gorge with only minimal defensive capability and Gorges taking up its own entire island. Fort Gorges was to mount 95 cannon, while the much smaller Fort Popham was designed for only 42 guns.

Defenses were also built on Ship Island off the Mississippi coast, with a small work, Fort Massachusetts, mounting only 37 cannon. Also begun during this final period was Fort Taber (officially Fort at Clark's Point), an impressive tower fort designed to mount 150 cannon.

The defenses of New York City were finally realized with the beginning of construction on the

Figure 33: The construction of Endicott Period batteries in the fort at the tip of the Sandy Hook of New Jersey - defining New York's Outer Harbor - is shown in this period photograph. The amount of money spent on labor and materials to construct a Third System fort was an incredible boost to the local economy. *(Photo courtesy NARA)*

final two Third System forts, Hancock and Totten. Hancock was a sprawling work on the Sandy Hook on the north shore of New Jersey, designed to replace a series of forts projected by Bernard for that area. Fort Totten was designed to be a tower fort opposite Fort Schuyler, also guarding the approaches to the East River, from Throgg's Neck. Fort Totten had the honor of being the last fort started in the Third System - begun in 1863, it was never completed.

In all, 42 forts were begun during the period of the Third System. By 1867, 31 of them had been virtually completed.[7] During these final years, of course, the nation was embroiled in a civil war and many of these newly built forts were put to the test. Others served as training centers, and many as prisons. Some were damaged to varying degrees, while others were completed in great haste by either Union or Confederate engineers, some by both at different times.[8]

Notes

[1] Forts Morgan and Gaines were of identical design, but construction on Gaines was halted before the fort was completed. When resumed, a newer Totten design was used. Fort Jackson shared the same pentagonal shape as Morgan, but was smaller in size, had different interior features, and had fewer casemates.

[2] The casemated batteries of Fort Pike and Fort Wood consisted of 24-pounder seacoast cannon, while the barbette batteries mounted 32-pounders.

[3] Fort Adams also had sweeping arches for two cannon, but like McRee had a tier of cannon below. Fort Warren had very similar casemates to Fort Pickens.

[4] Fort Sumter had less than half of its design armament mounted, lacked in provisions, and had a "skeleton crew" for a garrison. This, coupled with its exposed gorge wall facing toward land, brought about the surrender of the fort.

[5] This fear indeed proved to be well based. Fort Sumter was destroyed by Union shore batteries but never surrendered to Union forces. The confederate troops

proved they could hold on to the fort indefinitely, and left only when Charleston held no further strategic value.

[6]Two external batteries were also located on this side of The Narrows, working in conjunction with Forts Richmond and Tompkins. These were Batteries Hudson and Morton.

[7]Many more forts underwent upgrades during the period, several Martello towers were constructed, and numerous batteries were built. The efforts mentioned here relate only to new-construction forts.

[8]Fort Massachusetts, on Ship Island, Mississippi, may be the most interesting in this regard. Begun by Federal engineers, construction continued by Confederate engineers after the Federal troops had been expelled, and construction was continued to near completion by Federal engineers after the Confederates abandoned the site.

Effectiveness of Third System Forts

As was mentioned previously, one of the great successes of the Third System was the fact that none of the forts was ever fired upon by a foreign invader. It is ironic that in most cases the same organization – and several times the same individuals – who built the forts, prosecuted the fighting against them. Such can be the nature of civil war, and in the case of the Third System, their sole test of effectiveness occurred during the American Civil War.

The fact that the forts were being attacked by their builders obviously gave the attackers a significant advantage. Federal forces besieging a fort were able to study the architectural drawings of the fort in advance of the attack. This allowed the exploitation of weak areas in the design, as well as the targeting of powder magazines by the siege guns. In some cases, an officer involved in the construction of the fort was brought forward to assist in planning the attack.[1]

Also working to the disadvantage of the forts was the very rapid development of weaponry taking place during this period. The time immediately prior to and during the Civil War saw the implementation of rifled cannon and the development of a casting method that allowed the production of much larger ordnance than had been feasible previously.

A common belief, put forth in park brochures and several books about individual forts, indicates that the development of rifled cannon caused the obsolescence of the Third System.

The serious student of fortification history often debates this conclusion. While the increase in the muzzle velocity of a rifled gun and the increase in the weight of a cylindrical projectile certainly played a role in the effectiveness of these cannon against masonry walls, the largest benefit of these weapons was their increased range. As discussed previously, earthen outworks protected masonry designed to defend against a siege, while masonry protecting only against ships was generally left unprotected. This unprotected masonry fell within the range of these modern guns.

Certain fronts of certain forts now became vulnerable to siege cannon. The remedy for this was not difficult – protective outworks needed to be constructed on these now-vulnerable fronts. Were the forts without these outworks now obsolete? Many believe they were not. What then, caused the obsolescence of the Third System? The answer to that is unclear.

J. R. Hinds states the belief that only the size of the ordnance brought about the obsolescence.[2] Others believe that the Third System ended due to the lessening of the need for the protection of coastal guns from land-based attack.

Whether or not rifled cannon caused the demise of the Third System, they certainly tested the robustness of the designs. The higher muzzle velocity, increased accuracy, and longer range of these guns pushed well beyond the design criteria of the forts. In spite of this, Third System forts gave a good accounting during the Civil War. With this principal caveat in mind, we will review how well these forts responded to a period of radical change in military engineering.

Another extenuating circumstance that the defenders of the Third System forts had to overcome relates to the equivalency of armament between the invader and the defender. While an advantage to the defender can be expected through the existence of a fort, it is not reasonable to assume that this advantage can fully compensate for major differences in armament between the attacker and defender. It would not be reasonable to expect someone with a musket to defend a position against someone with a sniper's rifle, even if the musketeer is in an excellent defensive position. In the same way, it is not reasonable to expect the conventional smoothbore Confederate ordnance in Third System forts to be able to respond to a siege conducted with longer-range Parrott rifles.[3]

Finally, in evaluating the effectiveness of the Third System, one must consider the mission of the forts. Third System forts were designed to repel a foreign invader for a short period, until reinforcements could arrive. In remembering the statements made in the 1821 report, it was the mission of the Third System forts to **delay** an enemy landing party for 7-21 days until the army could be moved to that location. During the Third System period, it was believed that **no** fort could stand up to a protracted siege. To force an enemy to both halt their naval advance and to lay siege to a fort was considered a victory to the fort designers.

In the Civil War, however, holding out until a reinforcing army arrived was not a realistic hope. In most cases, when a fort was attacked the surrounding countryside and major cities in the area had already fallen, and there was no army to relieve the garrison. Often, the inevitability of the success of the siege lessened the resolve of the garrison.[4]

Forts Monroe and Jefferson

Two southern Third System forts, occupied throughout the war by Union forces, were located in areas that made them highly desirable targets to the Confederacy but were never attacked. Fort Monroe, the largest of all Third System forts, was located well south along the Virginia coast, and controlled the entrance to Hampton Roads and the James River. It also provided indirect control of the Chesapeake Bay by providing a strong point at its entrance, a refuge for the navy, and covered the western channel directly. The fort stood amid Confederate-

held territory, and was truly a thorn in the side of the Confederacy. The famous Peninsula Campaign was launched from Fort Monroe, and possession of the fort and complimentary Fort Calhoun (by this time renamed Wool) across the channel controlled access to the Hampton Roads area.

Due to the occupation of Fort Monroe, all major water routes to the interior of Virginia were blocked. Communication between the capitol at Richmond and the ocean was eliminated, and the fort and the ships under its guns made access to the Rappahannock virtually impossible. In addition to local ships, the fort provided both succor and safe haven for the entire Union Atlantic blockade fleet.

Despite the desirability of its position, Fort Monroe never came under Confederate attack. Lee, in one of many ironies of the Third System, had been the engineer to finish the construction of Fort Monroe, and he knew well the strength of its defenses. His generals also felt that the development of a campaign to lay siege to the fort would be a waste of time, as its size, its considerable defenses, and the ease of reinforcement[5] made a successful siege highly unlikely.

Similarly, Fort Jefferson in the Dry Tortugas was a desirable site, controlling the major deep-water anchorage in the Gulf and serving as a supply center for the Gulf of Mexico blockading fleet. This massive fort, designed to mount as many as 450 cannon, also remained untouched by the Confederacy. Its size and formidable armament provided a strong deterrent to naval attack,[6] and its location precluded the mounting of a land-based siege. Even though it was never considered "complete," the massive scarp and the considerable armament mounted in the fort was enough of a deterrent to prevent a Confederate challenge.

These two forts actually provided the reverse of the function for which they were designed. They were built as defensive structures that would deprive an enemy of a strong point and prevent their entrance into the harbor, as well as protecting a harbor of rendezvous and refuge for the defending fleet. Instead, both forts served as strong points for the invading forces and protected harbors of rendezvous for the attacking and blockading fleets. Their role in depriving the Confederacy of materiel was very significant in the prosecution of the war.

Fort Sumter

Fort Sumter, in Charleston Harbor, underwent three major attacks during the Civil War, and performed admirably. The first and most famous attack was in the opening days of the conflict, when only a small garrison occupied the fort that was still under construction. Ringed by cannon in surrounding Confederate forts, short of both men and supplies and with little ability for defense, hours later the fort was surrendered after receiving only moderate damage and few casualties.

Having fallen in the "first" battle of the war, Fort Sumter had become a Confederate stronghold. Construction of the fort was completed, extensive armament was emplaced, and a substantial garrison manned the ordnance. Further fortification of the surrounding land points took place, and Charleston Harbor became a safe haven for both naval and blockade-running vessels.

The strategic importance of the fort was well known to Union officers, and a naval attack on the fort ensued. Fort Sumter was attacked by a flotilla consisting of eight newly built monitors and an ironclad frigate, but to no avail. The smoothbore and rifled cannon of the attacking ships pummeled the fort, but only moderate damage was sustained. The ships, however, faired

Figure 34: This historic photograph shows the parade of Fort Sumter after the initial bombardment at the beginning of the Civil War. Note the unfinished barracks, the construction materials scattered around the parade, and the Confederate flag flying over the fort. *(Photo courtesy NARA)*

less favorably. Serious damage to the attacking ships caused the Union Navy to break off the attack, demonstrating once again that ships, in this case even ironclads, were no match for masonry fortifications.

Failing in the naval encounter, Union troops began a bloody campaign to secure the shore areas in proximity to the massive stronghold. Rifled cannon and massive Rodman smoothbore cannon turned the tide. The extreme range of these guns allowed them to be mounted at distances up to two-and-one-half miles from the fort, far beyond the range of the smaller Confederate smoothbores.

It was at this point that Sumter became a "rubble fort." The garrison, however, continued to resist both land-based cannon and Union warships. While there were no heavy guns to return the fire of the ships in the harbor, the collapsed brickwork still protected the garrison. A demand for surrender was strongly rebuked by Beauregard, and the Union Navy had to resort to other means.

An alternative was to storm the now-reduced walls of the fort with marines. Late on the night of September 8, 1863, Union sailors and marines were put ashore along the walls of the fort under cover of darkness.[7] Again the massive fort held, with the entire Union contingent captured with no Confederate casualties.

For almost one and one-half years, the bombardment of Fort Sumter continued. While many times these cannonades were devastating, the garrison rebuilt with sand and timber. The musketry of the defenders and two rebuilt batteries provided defense, and the collapsing masonry made the bombproofs all the more protected. Although out-manned and out-gunned, the fort remained in Confederate hands.

The Confederate garrison finally abandoned the fort when Charleston held no further strategic value. Sherman had divided the coastal areas of the Carolinas from the remainder of the Confederacy, and the garrison quietly withdrew from the fort they had so gallantly defended. Under great ceremony the Stars and Stripes were raised again over Fort Sumter, but not because it had been captured. The only fall of Fort Sumter was in the "first" battle of the war when the small Union garrison surrendered.

Fort Jackson

Fort Jackson, guarding the Mississippi River, is often used as an example of the failure of the Third System in the Civil War. First, the fort failed to prevent some of the faster ships of Farragut's flotilla from passing the fort. Second, after a relatively short bombardment by Porter's mortar boats, the fort surrendered. A Third System fort had failed to secure the Mississippi.

The major failure was in the inability of the fort to prevent the passage of ships. Plaquemines Bend, where Fort Jackson is located, was an area of the Mississippi where sailing ships would slow as they maneuvered the sharp bend in the river. The steam-powered vessels of Farragut's squadron, however, were not at the mercy of the wind. They maneuvered the bend and steamed past the two tiers of cannon of Fort Jackson.

Being one of the earliest of the Third System forts, Fort Jackson did not carry the larger amount of armament that later Third System forts boasted. Its casemates lined only two fronts, and the barbette guns could control only the area immediately in front of the fort due to the large number of trees blocking the fields of fire to the south. The fort truly was inadequate for the task it was asked to perform.

Fort St. Philip, a colonial fort that was modernized during the Third System, cooperated with Fort Jackson in the defense of the river. It had only barbette guns, and was significantly less heavily armed than Fort Jackson. Its location across the river placed it further from Porter's

Figure 35: Fort Pulaski fell victim to the extended range of the more modern Union artillery, which could reach the unprotected masonry seacoast front. The breach, shown here, was relatively small, but jeopardized the powder magazine, and the fort was surrendered. *(Photo courtesy NARA)*

mortar boats, and its cannon did not have the range to reach these vessels.

The capture of Fort Jackson, however, was due to the experience of the Union officers who had been involved in Fort Jackson's construction. From the time the construction of the fort had begun, Jackson was plagued by the encroachment of the Mississippi River. Work constantly was required on the dike that held back the waters, and the swampy areas of the fort had caused the death of many of the workers attempting the construction. Knowing this, the Union gunners took full advantage of the situation. Rather than concentrating their fire on the fort, they aimed for the protective dike. Once breached, the dike allowed the water to flood both casemate areas and portions of the parade. The garrison mutinied and surrendered the fort.

Fort Pulaski

Fort Pulaski stood on the southeast end of Cockspur Island, a medium-size island near the mouth of the Savannah River. A large ravelin protected the gorge of the fort, facing the mass of the island, but the seacoast fronts were unprotected masonry.

Tybee Island was opposite one of these seacoast fronts, and it was not believed that siege batteries located there could do significant damage to the fort, being located more than 1,000 yards away. For this reason, no coverface was constructed on this front of the fort. Even the Union gunners were amazed at the power of their new ordnance, and it was put to good use.

Knowing the location of the main powder magazine, the salient of the bastion of the fort opposite the magazine was targeted. Bombardment by both smoothbore Rodman guns and Parrott rifles breached the bastion, opening a direct path to the magazine. With the entire garrison in peril, the fort was surrendered.

Fort Pulaski went down in history as the fort whose siege marked the beginning of the end of Third System fortification technology. The bombardment and early breach of the walls of the fort "proved" that masonry forts could not stand up to rifled cannon, signifying the Third System's death knell.

Figure 36: The interior of the breach in Fort Pulaski is shown here. The value of the separation of the scarp from the casemates is clear, as though the scarp is breached, the casemates of the fort remained intact. It is this same phenomenon that allowed Fort Sumter to remain as a "rubble fort" long after its scarp was destroyed. *(Photo courtesy NARA)*

Figure 37: The citadel at Fort Morgan fell victim to the Union bombardment. Although the exterior wall is standing, the entire interior of the citadel was destroyed, necessitating its demolition. *(Photo courtesy NARA)*

The author believes that while Pulaski did not live up to its expectations, extenuating circumstances were present. While it demonstrated once again the vulnerability of unmasked masonry walls, many of the arguments made regarding the fall of Pulaski as "ending the Third System" are overstatements.

Fort Pulaski was a victim, primarily, of the extended range of rifled cannon and very large Rodman smoothbore cannon. It was well known that masonry walls could not hold out to siege cannon indefinitely, and that was why outworks were built to protect the landside masonry. The extended range, however, of the newly developed Union cannon made the shore of Tybee Island a suitable site for siege batteries.

Exacerbating the situation, the Confederate artillerymen in Fort Pulaski were unable to return fire against these siege cannon, as the cannon in the fort had a much shorter range. This allowed the Union guns to fire with impunity at the Confederate fort.

The "obsolete" fort was immediately repaired and rearmed by the Union Army, and was a vital part of the coastal defense of Savannah harbor until the concrete emplacements of the Endicott Board took over in the later years of the nineteenth century.

Fort Morgan

Fort Morgan joined Fort Jackson in showing that while Third System forts alone could not close a harbor, they were not vulnerable to a naval bombardment.[8] In the famous Battle of Mobile Bay, Farragut steamed past Fort Morgan with little damage to his ships from the guns of the fort.[9] The fort was designed and armed to prevent hostile entry to the bay, but it failed to keep the ships out of the bay. Bombardment of the fort, however, also failed to do significant damage to the fort, and it remained a significant "thorn in the side" of the Union forces. At length, the fort fell to a protracted siege by the Union Army. Holding for more than a fortnight, Bernard's original goal, it was finally shelled into submission by Union artillery.

Forts Pickens, McRee, and Barrancas

Before the opening shots of the Civil War at Fort Sumter, the decision was made to abandon the mainland forts in Pensacola harbor and move all Union personnel into Fort Pickens on Santa Rosa Island. Fort Pickens was the biggest and strongest of the Pensacola forts, and its island location added another degree of isolation.

During the majority of the war, Pensacola remained divided with Fort Pickens in Union hands and the other forts occupied by Confederates. In November of 1861, an artillery duel between the various Confederate positions and Fort Pickens took place. In addition to the cannon firing from Fort Pickens, two Union warships participated in the battle and led the attack on Fort McRee. These ships positioned themselves approximately one and three-quarters miles from the fort, outside of the range of the forts guns but within the range of the shipborne rifled cannon.

While both Lieutenant William McKean, commander of the Union naval forces, and Colonel Harvey Brown, commander of Fort Pickens, claimed to have inflicted major damage on Fort McRee, Major Stephen Elliott, Fort McRee's commander, only credited the bombardment from Fort Pickens. This, along with previous accounts of the ineffectiveness of shipboard cannon against masonry fortifications, leads to the belief that the land-based guns of Fort Pickens were responsible for the most significant damage.

A second exchange of artillery occurred in January of 1862, with even more significant damage to Fort McRee. In addition, hot shot was used against land-based targets in the Navy Yard. This resulted in the burning of the town of Warrington and other nearby buildings. In all exchanges, Fort Pickens sustained no significant damage.

These incidents again underscored the effectiveness of land-based cannon on exposed masonry, but give no credit to ship-borne cannon. Of the two ships attacking Fort McRee, one received minor damage and one severe damage from a sand battery erected closer to the southern shore.

Fort Macon

Early in the war, October 1861, General Ambrose Burnside led an expedition along coastal North Carolina in an attempt to seize the major harbors. This would accomplish two objectives: first, it would provide a source of supply via the sea for the inland operations in the area; and second, it would deprive the Confederacy of their source of supply.

The first goal of the expedition was to control the Hatteras Inlet and to capture Fort Macon, near Morehead City, North Carolina. This fort guarded the entrance to Bogue Sound and Beaufort Harbor, both controlling the major supply point and providing a strong point in the Union rear. Fort Macon had been seized by the Confederacy on April 14, 1861, just two days after the capture of Fort Sumter, the first action of North Carolina in support of the Confederacy.

The first Union action against the fort was an infantry probe to determine if the fort was well defended. This was easily repulsed, and Burnside concluded that a protracted siege would be necessary to take the fort.

As preparations for the siege began, Burnside demanded the surrender of the fort "In order to safe the unnecessary effusion of blood…"[10] Colonel White, commanding the fort, declined the offer, determined to hold the fort.

These communications took place on March 23, 1861, and mark the beginning of the time that Fort Macon was to delay the Union advance and itself ask for reinforcement. April 12, 1861, is stated as the official date for the beginning of the siege.[11] It was on this date that the fort was completely cut off from outside communication and the work on the siege batteries was begun.

On April 25, more than a month after the demand for surrender, bombardment of the fort began. The Union forces had more effective cannon and an ample supply of mortars to use against the fort, while the fort was under armed and the quality of the powder was very inconsistent, making ranging very difficult.[12] Still, however, the fort held out.

The Union blockading squadron sent four ships against Fort Macon to support the siege and to bring a quicker end to the fort. Both the attacking ships and the aim of the fort's guns were hampered by bad weather, but in a ship-vs.-shore battle, Fort Macon was providing the defense for which she was built. Driving off the ships and damaging two of them, the fort received no damage in the exchange. The ships did not return.

The land siege, however, was a different situation. The mortars were the most effective weapons, driving the unprotected gunners away from their guns with the shells exploding overhead and on the terreplein. The Parrott rifles did significant damage to the walls of the fort, concentrating their fire on the areas where the magazines were located.

The Union gunners had a significant advantage in this regard. Using the construction plans of the fort and information from one of Burnside's brigade commanders, a former engineer officer who had visited the fort in that capacity, they were able to target the key areas of the fort where the most damage could be done.

After 10½ hours, the guns of the fort were silenced. The accuracy of the mortars had driven the Confederate gunners off the ramparts, and Fort Macon had no casemated guns. Cracks in the outer walls near the magazines threatened the loss of the entire garrison should a shell find the magazine, and Colonel White raised the flag of truce in preparation for establishing the terms of surrender.

The fort had delayed and occupied the Union forces for 34 days, and had been under siege for 14 of those days. This was accomplished with a fraction of the ordnance it was designed for, and with a supply of munitions that were badly substandard.[13]

Fort Gaines

Fort Gaines did not fair well in the struggle for possession of Mobile Bay, and was the least successful Third System fort in withstanding a siege. The fort was constructed with the detached scarp design, which required that all guns be mounted *en barbette*. Coupled with the fact that a sand dune to the west of the fort had been allowed to grow beyond the height of the fort walls, Fort Gaines was left woefully unprepared for the Union attack.

Even still, the fort gave a good accounting of itself in the initial days of the siege. When it surrendered, it was still had a strong defensive capability, and Confederate General Page of Fort Morgan personally met with Fort Gaines' commander in an attempted to stop the surrender. His efforts were unsuccessful, and he referred to the surrender of his sister fort as a "deed of dishonor and disgrace."[14]

Conclusions

The effectiveness of the forts of the Third System can best be judged by the intent of the designers of these forts. As derived from the 1821 Report of the Board of Engineers,[15] these intentions can be divided into three basic elements:

1. To close a harbor or waterway to enemy shipping, and to withstand a naval attack;

2. To prevent the taking of a fort by a rapidly executed coup de main (storming by infantry);

3. To withstand a land-based siege **until reinforcements could arrive** to lift the siege. This time period varied by area of the country, but was typically 7-21 days. A fourteen-day period (one fortnight) could be considered typical.

The following table lists each of these goals, and how well several Third System forts met these expectations. From the table it is clear that most of the goals of the forts were achieved, even though some of the forts were reduced by siege. No forts were lost to a coup de main; both armies were well aware of the strength of these forts and did not wish to unnecessarily lose troops to such a futile effort.[16]

The time from the initiation of the siege until the fall of the fort was sufficient, in all except one case, to allow for a potential reinforcement of the garrison. The fact that none of the garrisons was reinforced is related to the course of the Civil War, and had no bearing on the strength of the forts.

Fort	Closed Harbor	Repelled Ships	Repelled Coup de Main	Length of Siege
Monroe	Yes	N/A	N/A	Not besieged
Jefferson	Yes	N/A	N/A	Not besieged
Sumter	Yes	Yes	Yes	31 days
Jackson	No	No	N/A	12 days
Pulaski	Yes	N/A	N/A	17 days
Morgan	Partially	Yes	N/A	15 days
Macon	No	Yes	N/A	14 days
Gaines	No	Yes	N/A	5 days

Notes

[1] Branch, Paul, *The Siege of Fort Macon*, Herald Printing Company, Morehead City, North Carolina (1988).

[2] From Hinds, James R., Stone Walls and Iron Guns: Forts and their Effectiveness in the Civil War, in *Bulwark and Bastion*, by Hinds and Fitzgerald, as well as a personal interview with Hinds.

[3] Fort Sumter was able to respond to such a siege with some success. This does not weaken the caveat, however, but rather speaks for the determination of the garrison and the robustness of the design.

[4] For example, refer to the siege of Fort Gaines in Dave Page's *Ship versus Shore*, Rutledge Hill Press (Nashville, TN, 1994), p219.

[5] The control of the seas by the Union Navy made a Confederate blockade of the fort impractical.

[6] Had the Confederate Navy had the offensive strength to mount an attack.

[7] See the Report of Lieutenant-Commander Williams, U. S. Navy, Roxbury, Mass., September 27, 1864, to Gideon Welles, Secretary of Navy. Available in *Official Records of the Union and Confederate Navies in the War of the Rebellion.*

[8] While Fort Jackson fell victim to naval fire, it was from platform - albeit floating - based mortars, not from direct cannon fire from warships. The attacks by warships were repulsed with significant damage to the ships and little damage to the fort.

[9] The first ship attempting to pass Morgan was sunk by a mine (torpedo), not by the guns of the fort.

[10] War of Rebellion, A Compilation of the Official Records of Union and Confederate Armies (Washington, U.S. Government Printing Office, 1880-1901), Series I, Vol. IX, p. 277.

[11] Branch, Paul, Jr., ., The Siege of Fort Macon (Morehead City, NC, 1982), p. 45.

[12] Ibid.

[13] For a detailed account of the actions against Fort Macon, see Branch, Paul, Jr., The Siege of Fort Macon, Morehead City, NC, 1982.

[14] Bergeron, Arthur W., Jr., Confederate Mobile, University Press of Mississippi (London and Jackson, 1991), p.146.

[15] ASP-MA, Vol II, p.304-312.

[16] A coup de main was attempted at Fort Sumter, but only after the massive Union bombardment had left the scarp in ruins. Even in this state, the coup de main was repulsed with the loss of the entire Union force.

Part II:

Forts of the Third System

The Northern Frontier

Figure 38: Fort Mackinac, located on Mackinac Island, Michigan, has a masonry scarp to seaward and a wooden scarp to landward. It also has no defense against the high ground seen behind the fort, a flaw that necessitated the fort's surrender to the British. *(Photo by author)*

Several forts period to the Third System protected the northern frontier of the country, primarily concerned with invasion from Canada. Most, but not all, of this frontier consisted of bodies of water dividing the two countries. Some of these bodies were vast – the Great Lakes – while some were rivers of varying width. The length of the frontier, the multitude of locations

Figure 40: The sally port of Fort Wayne is located in the only casemated portion of the fort, the bastion flanks. No Third System fort shares this characteristic. *(Photo by author)*

where troops and supplies could be landed, and the relatively short distance across the water at many points provided a unique problem for its defense.

While similar in architectural form to the seacoast forts of the Third System, the forts of the northern frontier were significantly different in function. Henry Wager Halleck, in his

review of the coast for his course at West Point in 1862,[1] states of these forts, "They are entirely different in their character from those on the coast, the latter being intended principally for the use of our citizen-soldiery, in the defence of our seaport towns, while the former are intended merely as auxiliaries to the operations of more disciplined troops."

Like the Third System, this group of forts consisted of a combination of newly constructed forts and the modernization and repair of existing forts. Three forts, newly constructed for the defense of the northern frontier, bear great similarity in design to the seacoast forts of the Third System.

Fort Wayne, located on the Detroit River between Lake St. Clair and Lake Erie, was a square, bastioned fort with barbette cannon and casemated

Figure 39: Fort Wayne, in Detroit, Michigan, was a Northern Frontier fort period to the Third System. The design of the fort was simple - a square with casemated bastions and barbette cannon around the entire perimeter. Additional cannon were provided by a ravelin that faced the Detroit River.

DETROIT RIVER

Ravelin

Casemated bastion flanks

Figure 41: The gorge front of Fort Niagara, at the mouth of the Niagara River, was designed and built during the Third System. Shown in this photograph is the flank of one demibastion, as seen from the opposing demibastion. *(Photo by author)*

bastions. The firepower of the fort was supplemented by a large ravelin facing the river, also containing barbette cannon.

Fort Ontario, in Oswego, New York, was a pentagonal bastioned fort, reminiscent in design to Fort Jackson on the Mississippi River below New Orleans. This masonry fort boasted very large,

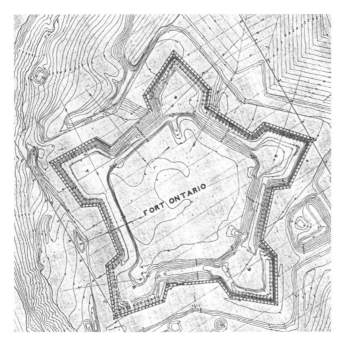

Figure 42: Fort Ontario, on the shore of Lake Ontario, has the familiar bastioned pentagonal shape of a Third System fort. *(Drawing courtesy of NARA)*

casemated bastions – far larger than those at Fort Jackson – with barbette guns on the bastions and the curtains. The fort is a New York State Historic Site, and is open to the public from May through October.

Fort Montgomery, guarding the northern ap-

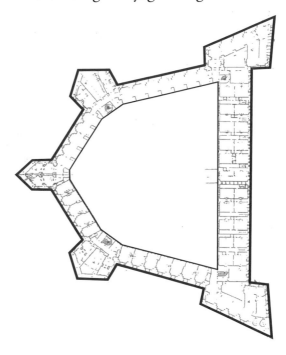

Figure 43: Similar in deisgn to Third System forts, the fully casemated Fort Montgomery is on the plan of an irregular pentagon. Only a small portion of this once-magnificent fort now remains near Rouse's Point, New York. *(Drawing courtesy NARA)*

proaches to Lake Champlain, bore the greatest similarity in design to Third System forts. This bastioned work contained two casemated tiers of guns, capped with a barbette tier. Its all-granite scarp and substantial height were reminiscent of Fort Delaware near Delaware City, Delaware. In his 1836 report, Totten refered to Fort Montgomery as "the only permanent military work now recommended for the northern frontier."[2] For this reason, some historians include Fort Montgomery in the Third System.

Fort Porter, near Buffalo, New York, was a defensive tower reminiscent of the tower at Fort Winthrop in Boston Harbor.

Supplementing these forts were older forts that were repaired and modernized during the Third System period. Fort Niagara and Fort Erie, located on either side of the Niagara River joining Lake Ontario with Lake Erie, were masonry forts that received these repairs and modifications. Both were irregular works with non-classical designs. The relatively small Fort Erie had a modified tenaille trace, while Fort Niagara had an irregular trace that conformed to the point of land on which it was located.

Fort Mackinac, located on Mackinac Island where Lake Michigan and Lake Huron join, was an infantry fort with a masonry front toward Mackinac Harbor and a wooden stockade on the landward sides.

While not considered part of the Third System, these forts are wonderful examples of military architecture of the 19th century and are very enjoyable to visit. Fort Montgomery and Fort Wayne are currently closed to the public except for special tours, but Forts Erie, Niagara, and Mackinac have been restored and have excellent interpretive programs.

Notes

[1] Halleck, Henry Wager, Elements of Military Art and Science, Appleton (New York, London, 1862)

[2] ASP, MA

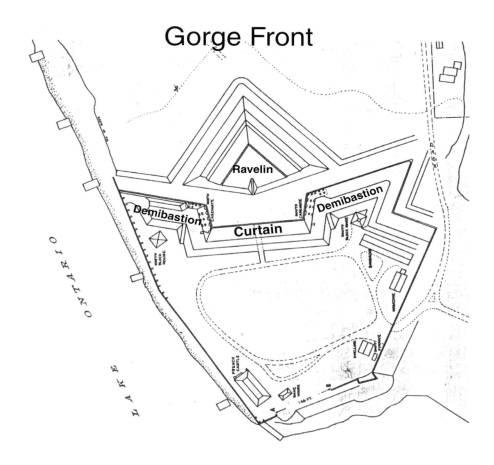

Gorge Front

Figure 44: Fort Niagara is a compilation of several generations of fortifications, blended together in the overall plan shown in the above drawing. The landward front with two demibastions flanking a curtain and a ravelin in advance was built during the Third System period. *(Drawing courtesy NARA)*

The Defenses of the
Maine - New Hampshire Coast

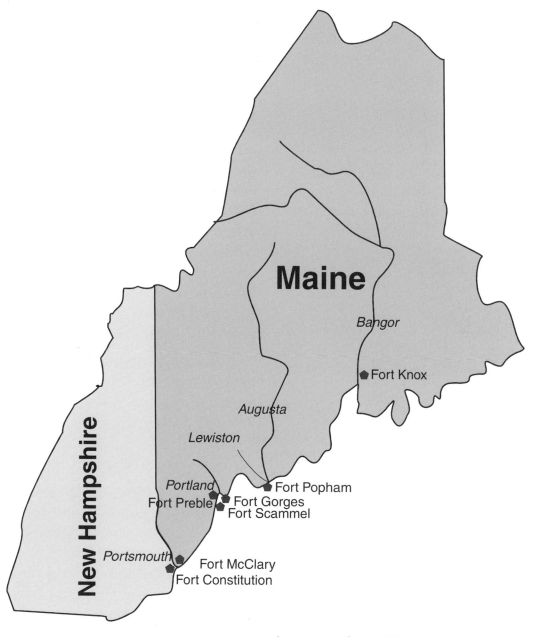

History

The defenses of the Maine and New Hampshire coastlines came long after the conception of most of the Third System. Maine was not considered an area of primary importance because of its small population and limited amount of industry. As with most things, however, when there is a fear of losing something, its value quickly becomes apparent. The Aroostook War (1839) and the threat that Canada was going to consume Maine provided the impetus for development of defenses along the coastline of Maine.

The wealth of Maine was in the natural resources in its interior and its fishing industry on the coast. The interior communications were quite primitive, and the only method of moving

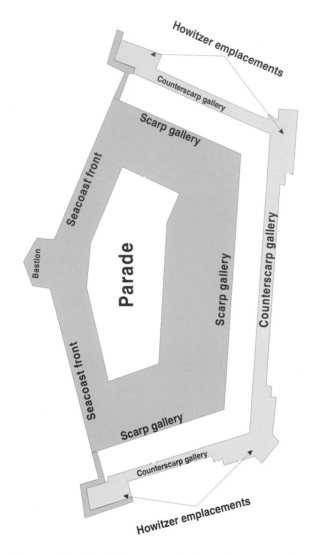

Howitzer emplacements

Counterscarp gallery

Scarp gallery

Seacoast front

Bastion

Parade

Scarp gallery

Counterscarp gallery

Seacoast front

Scarp gallery

Counterscarp gallery

Howitzer emplacements

Figure 45: Fort Knox was designed as a pentagon with two very short sides. This elongated shape fit well on the hilltop location and provided long fronts bearing on the river.

the inland resources, especially timber and granite, to their points of use was by water. The two principal rivers in Maine, the Penobscot and the Kennebec, provided the basis for most of the interior communication. The Penobscot River led to Bangor, and the Kennebec led to Bath and on to Augusta. As supplies for any action in the interior of the state would by necessity be transported on these rivers, control of the river mouths would provide great hardship to any attempt to control the interior.

In addition to the river mouths, Maine boasted Portland as its finest harbor and largest population center. This city and Portsmouth, New Hampshire, the next major harbor and population center south of Portland, were valuable assets to the Maine economy. The fishing industry established itself in the hundreds of small bays and inlets that cover the coastline, and in the principal harbors of Portland, Brunswick, and Bangor.

Third System Strategy

In planning the defenses of Maine, it was clear that a system of fortifications could not be provided to protect the diverse fishing villages, but the main harbors and communication channels could be defended. Two Second System blockhouses guarded the northern areas of the coast, Fort Sullivan at Eastport and Fort Edgecomb at Wiscasset. As these areas were of secondary importance, an updating of the armament was considered sufficient.

The area where Penobscot Bay narrowed at the mouth of the Penobscot River was chosen for the first Third System fort in Maine, Fort Knox. Eighteen years later, the mouth of the Kennebec River was defended by a significantly smaller work, Fort Popham.

In Portland Harbor Fort Gorges, the largest of Maine's Third System forts, was constructed at the junction of the two channels leading to the port. In advance of Fort Gorges on the main channel sat two works from the Second System, Forts Preble and Scammel. A unique detached-bastion fort replaced Fort Scammel, and Fort Preble was surrounded by a new fort of the same name, with the old fort remaining in use as a battery.

Two Second System forts, Fort McClary and Fort Constitution, guarded Portsmouth. A Martello tower, Walbach Tower, built in 1812 immediately west of the old Fort Constitution, supplemented these defenses. Fort McClary, a blockhouse with external batteries, was built in

1809 on the site of a 1715 work.

Toward the end of the Third System, plans were drawn for the construction of a new Fort Constitution, but the fort was never completed. The scarp wall on the seaward fronts was complete enough, however, to allow the mounting of guns at the first-tier embrasures. This provided a significant coastal battery to protect the

Figure 46: Fort Knox, one of the few hilltop forts of the Third System, stands above the Penobscot River near the Maine coast. Note the seacoast embrasure above the sally port - it is the only single-tier fort with a seacoast casemate above the sally port in the Third System. *(Photo by author)*

harbor, with the ancillary functions being supplied by the older fort.

A replacement for Fort McClary was begun shortly after Fort Constitution, but was further from completion when the construction program was terminated.

Fort Knox

As one sails through the fog of the Penobscot River approaching Bucksport, Maine, a massive stone structure covers the entire left bank, with the gaping barrel of a massive Rodman cannon pointed up the river. This scene today replicates an almost identical scene during the middle of the previous century. The only difference is that today's Rodman gun in the lower water battery would have been one of dozens of upriver guns mounted in two exterior batteries, within casemates, and atop the walls of the formidable Fort Knox. In the unlikely event that an enemy passed the fort,

more cannon mounted in the two upstream batteries would have provided further harassment.

Fort Knox constructed from 1844 through 1864, is strategically located at a sharp bend in the channel of the Penobscot River, a point where a sailing ship would be moving relatively slowly. A total of 137 cannon could bear on the channel.

The fort and its outworks made up a unique work, blending the skill of the local craftsmen with the basic principles of a mixed-defense fortification. The fort itself was an irregular five-sided work, with a small bastion at the shallow angle joining the two seacoast fronts. The outworks consisted of a counterscarp gallery that surrounded the fort on three sides, and four external batteries. The fort and its outworks followed the contour of the land, which sloped gently down a rocky hillside parallel to the water.

Two casemated batteries of heavy guns anchored the river defenses of the fort. A barbette tier above these casemates provided further gun positions, and the four external batteries provided the remainder of the seacoast cannon. Interestingly, the channel side of the fort contained the main sally port. This feature was shared with Fort Hamilton and Fort Tompkins, defenses of New York City, where the sally ports also faced the channel.

Figure 47: Relatively large external batteries supplimented the armament of the main fort. This 14-gun battery was just below the fort on the slope of the hill. *(Photo by author)*

An interesting architectural feature of the fort involved the design of the sally port such that it did not eliminate a gun position. As the ground sloped upward, the walls of the fort and the levels of the embrasures followed that slope. Taking advantage of this grade, the sally port was located low in the wall, and a casemated gun position was mounted immediately over it.

Communication with the external batteries was from the road that passed the main sally port. The two upper batteries were on the same level as the road; tunnels led from the upper batteries to the lower batteries. The upriver tunnel also had a branch that led to the wharf.

The batteries were each controlled by a protected structure with rifle loopholes and howitzer embrasures. For the upper batteries, this structure was a branch from the counterscarp galleries, entered through the galleries. For each lower battery the structure was a "casemated traverse" at the termination of the tunnel from the upper battery. These structures controlled the area behind the parapet of the battery, thus preventing the use of the guns or the spiking of the guns should the battery be overrun.

The fort was located at the top of a steep slope that led to the river, with only a narrow roadway separating the slope from the two casemated curtains. A projection of the curtain extended beyond the body of the fort, closing the ditch at each end. Projecting beyond the curtain from the counterscarp galleries were two bastion-like structures that provided flanking fire down the scarp. These structures supplemented the bastion at the intersection of the fronts, for a total of four howitzer embrasures opening onto each curtain. Six additional embrasures faced the river.

The three sides of the fort to landward had more extensive defenses. A casemated rifle gallery extended around these three curtains, with loopholes opening into the ditch. Across the ditch was a similar gallery behind the counterscarp wall, entered from the ditch. The reentering angles of the counterscarp contained embrasures for six howitzers, completing the formidable defenses of the ditch.

These rifle galleries, scarp and counterscarp, were similar to the stone galleries in Fort Tompkins, defenses of New York City. Fort Warren in Boston Harbor had a similar stone scarp gallery in one curtain, but it was much smaller than these impressive structures. Fort Barrancas and the Advanced Redoubt in Pensacola and Fort Livingston south of New Orleans had brick galleries of similar size and nearly identical design. Fort Caswell, North Carolina, had brick scarp galleries but no counterscarp galleries.

Four small powder magazines were located in the counterscarp works, one at each reentering angle and at each end, near the intersection of the curtain. The fort itself had two magazines, a two-level magazine on the downstream end of the river front, and a single-level magazine at the upstream front. Each of these main magazines was located adjacent to the parade, but protected by the circular stair towers. Additional magazines were located outside the fort, near the external batteries.

A unique feature of the fort was the presence of food storage areas beneath one end of the parade. These shallow, arched rooms provided underground storage accessible from a trench along the edge of the parade. Thus, the casemated areas away from the channel were available for living quarters and other storage, an efficient design.

The most striking feature of Fort Knox was the outstanding craftsmanship displayed in the granite work. The exterior walls, the casemates and counterscarp works, and the interior facades all display the marks of skill and caring that demonstrate that this fort was built by true artisans.

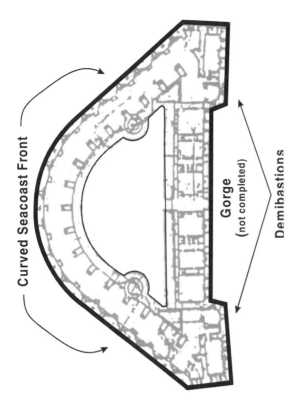

Figure 48: Fort Popham used a parabolic trace for the seacoast front of the fort, closing the gorge with a straight wall. Note that the gorge was designed with casemates, but only the scarp wall was constructed on this front.

Few structures in the world boast stonework of this quality.

Today, Fort Knox is a state historic site, well cared for by the Maine Bureau of Parks and Lands and a volunteer organization, The Friends of Fort Knox. The fort is in such good condition that it appears a garrison could move in at any time. Good interpretive signs and unlimited access to virtually all parts of the fort make this one of the more enjoyable Third System forts to visit.

Fort Knox is located just off US 1 just across the Penobscot River from Bucksport, Maine, about 20 miles south of Bangor.

Fort Popham

At Popham Beach, at the mouth of the Kennebec River, stand the remains of the uncompleted Fort Popham. Though very small in

trace, this tower fort was to mount an impressive 42 heavy guns to guard the entrance to the critical Kennebec River. Construction began in 1862, but the fort was never completed.

The location of the fort was well chosen. Standing at the tip of a peninsula that divided the river from Atkins Bay, a land-based attack would have been very difficult. This was also at a narrows in the river where the current was very strong, slowing a ship approaching from the ocean. This would leave the ship under the guns of the fort for a longer period of time.

Fort Popham was of the "closed lunette" design, essentially a half-moon shape with a straight wall closing the gorge. Demibastions protruded beyond this wall to provide flanking fire through howitzer embrasures. The curved front provided casemates for the primary seacoast cannon, designated to be a combination of 10-inch and 15-inch guns.

While the fort was designed for three tiers of cannon, it was never completed. The two tiers of casemates were constructed, but the

Figure 49: A portion of the unfinished Fort Popham can be seen in this photograph, including the unfinished gorge wall. Loopholes were opened in the gorge, but were left open to the parade. *(Photo by author)*

barbette remained unfinished. While many of the arches were turned above the second tier of cannon, the earthen fill of the terreplein was not put in place and the parapet was not constructed. While this left the cannon of the second tier somewhat more vulnerable and the fort with one-third less firepower, the entrance to the Kennebec was quite well defended.

Figure 50: This aerial view of Fort Popham shows that while unfinished, the fort was in a very defensible condition. *(Photo courtesy MHI)*

The land defenses were much less developed. The gorge was designed for two tiers of casemates, with loopholes, and a barbette tier of cannon. Neither tier of gorge casemates were constructed, but the scarp wall closed the gorge. This wall was penetrated by loopholes, and contained the main sally port. Additional land defense was provided by a moat across the gorge, effectively isolating the fort from the land. This was considered to be an adequate defense against a coup de main, but would not provide significant resistance to a siege.

Two circular stair towers provided access between the tiers of the fort, but the magazines were not located behind these towers as in most Third System forts. Instead, the magazines were located in the interior portion of each demibastion. The demibastions also provided loopholes defending the land approach along the gorge and the narrow strip of land leading to the curved seacoast front.

While of quite small trace, the massive granite walls and beautiful brick arches make Fort Popham an interesting site. The uncompleted work allows the visitor to observe casemates, stair towers, etc. in various stages of completion, assisting in an understanding of the construction techniques employed.

The fort is managed by the Maine State Park Commission, and is open to the public in the summer months. Signs explain the history and function of the fort in the half of the fort that is open. The remainder of the fort can be viewed from these public areas. The exterior of the fort can be visited all year.

Fort Popham is located on State Route 209 about 20 miles south of Bath. To reach the fort, located in Popham Beach State Park, follow Route 209 to the end of the road. You will have reached the Fort Popham parking area.

Fort Gorges

The key to the defenses of Portland Harbor was Fort Gorges, occupying a man-made island at the junction of the two main channels leading from the Atlantic. The fort still dominates the view from the city, and stands as a silent sentinel watching the approach of all types of ship-

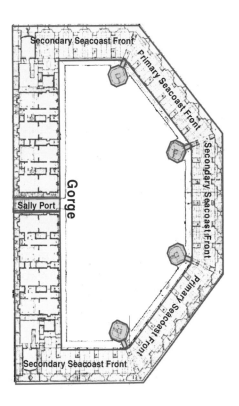

Figure 51: Fort Gorges was built on the plan of a truncated octagon, with deep barracks along the gorge wall. Built on an artificial island, it had no land defenses other than the very tall scarp. *(Drawing courtesy of NARA)*

74

Figure 52: The unprotected masonry scarp of Fort Gorges allowed a maximum number of cannon and unobstructed views of the channels coming into Portland Harbor. This fort would have been a formidable sight for a warship attempting to run past the guns. *(Photo by author)*

ping toward Portland's docks and marinas.

Begun in 1848, Fort Gorges was a six-sided truncated octagon, with no bastions or demibastions. Occupying its own island, land attack was not considered a problem so the land defenses were minimal. They consisted only of a wet moat along the gorge wall, complete with drawbridge, and loopholes in both casemated tiers of the gorge. The barbette of the gorge was designed for seacoast cannon.

Fort Gorges was a masterpiece of granite work. While the arches of the casemates were brick, they rested on granite piers and both the scarp and the interior facade of the fort were granite. While all of the granite work was magnificent, particular attention is directed to the hexagonal stair tower. Unlike the stair towers in most Third System forts, this one was not attached to the ramparts. It stood about four feet from the nearest casemates, with a bridge[1] connecting the tower to each tier.

The stonework in this stair tower demonstrates impressive craftsmanship, but the size of the granite blocks that were used is even more impressive. Of particular note is the single piece of granite that forms the uppermost step of the tower and continues as the

platform supporting the bridge to the terreplein. Also interesting are the mitered joints in the granite, strengthened by iron splines through the joint.

A notable fact regarding the fort is the use of iron in the construction process. Suspended iron bars supported many of the shallow arches in the ancillary structures, and iron beams were used extensively in the construction of the barracks building. The casemates did not utilize iron supports, however. They were constructed completely of brick and stone. Such extensive

Figure 53: This photograph of the parade of Fort Gorges shows the gorge wall on the right, with the sally port extending slightly beyond the barracks area. On the far end of the parade are the open-backed casemates, with a stair tower to the left edge of the picture. *(Photo by author)*

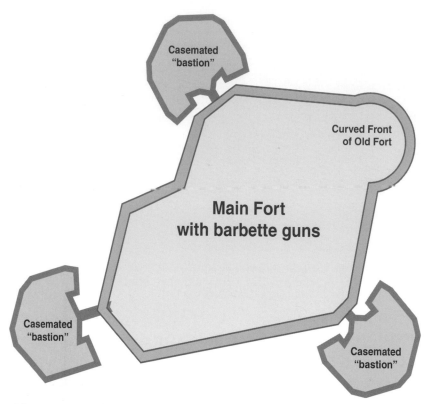

Figure 54: Fort Scammel is the only fort in the Third System to use the concept of "detached bastions." Each of these structures were free-standing, casemated forts whose primary mission was seacoast defense. The central earthwork fort communicated to each bastion through tunnels from the parade.

pearance of the seacoast fronts gave way to the beautiful granite facade of the barracks building. Plastered quarters with ornate woodwork were the hallmarks of the interior of this area, with loopholes opening from the rear rooms of the barracks.

Toward the end of the Third System an addition to the fort was designed. This addition was to be a three-tiered, v-shaped structure that would sit immediately opposite the gorge. While not attached to the existing fort, it would be separated only by a narrow passageway, which would provide access. The loopholes of the gorge would have controlled this open-backed structure.

The purpose of this structure was to increase the armament of the fort, principally to the rear. In that time period, it had become clear that iron-clad, steam-powered vessels could successfully run past the guns of a fort, and Fort Gorges was relatively vulnerable to rear attack. Because this was designed late in the Third System and the fort was located in the North, funds were not forthcoming and the addition was never constructed.

Today there are numerous pieces of precut granite strewn around the area behind the fort. It is not known whether these pieces were destined for the never-constructed addition or whether they were from proposed or actual construction within the existing fort. Several of the pieces are obviously shaped for a stair tower.

At present, Fort Gorges is only accessible by private boat. Extensive work has been completed, however, to make such a visit very worthwhile. The parade and the casemates have been

use of iron in the structure of the fort was seen in only the latter Third System forts.

The fort had five seacoast fronts, with one front parallel to the gorge. The orientation of this front was such that its cannon could be brought to bear on ships in either channel. Off this front were the two main fronts, each pointing toward a channel. Finally, two more secondary fronts each provided fire on their respective channel.

Each of these fronts was utilitarian in design, containing only casemates. They boasted six seacoast cannon on each of two tiers of casemates, with provision for a further six cannon mounted *en barbette*. This allowed 90 cannon to bear on the two main channels, with a further five cannon on the barbette of the gorge.

The design of the gorge contrasted with the design of the seacoast fronts. The utilitarian ap-

Figure 55: Fort Scammel is somewhat overgrown, as shown in the above photograph, but the parade and the masonry bastions have been very well preserved by the fort's owners. This unique fort is an extremely interesting structure to visit. *(Photo by author)*

cleaned and interpretive signs have been placed around the area. A bridge has been constructed across the ditch, and another connects the stair tower to the terreplein.

The terreplein itself has been cleared, and it provides great views of Portland Harbor and the city. Also in this area is the tube of a well-preserved Parrott Rifle.

Also present is the granite wharf that provided access to the fort. This relatively large area contains large granite blocks and massive iron mooring rings. It is still the preferred location for the landing of today's visitors, regardless of the size of craft.

Significant efforts by volunteer organizations have begun to return Fort Gorges to its original splendor, and these efforts are applauded. This beautiful granite fort is well worth the efforts of arranging transportation across Casco Bay.

Fort Scammel

A unique fort in the Third System was Fort Scammel, located on House Island in Portland Harbor. This fort was the only Third System fort and, to the author's knowledge, the only fort in the United States to use the concept of detached bastions. It was located opposite Fort Preble, with both forts guarding the main (south)

shipping channel entering the harbor.

Fort Scammel was a relatively large stone-revetted earthen fort with mountings for 51 heavy guns, *en barbette*. There was also provision for the mounting of several additional guns on the coverface in advance of the sally port. The fort was a seven-sided structure, one curved, with each side being constructed as a seacoast face. Since its island location allowed all sides to bear on various portions of the entrance to Portland Harbor, each face was designed for heavy cannon. The semicircular barbette battery facing the main channel was adapted from the previous Fort Scammel that controlled the island during the Second System.

What was unique about Fort Scammel was the design of three detached bastions, actually small forts in themselves. Although called bastions in the plans of the fort, in function their primary design was not to provide flanking fire along the curtain, but to mount three tiers of seacoast-defense cannon that could be brought to bear on the main shipping channels into the harbor.

Each bastion was designed to mount 15 guns per tier, which would have added another 135 guns to the armament of the fort. This was more than twice the 51 guns in the main structure, underscoring the seacoast defense mission of these "bastions."

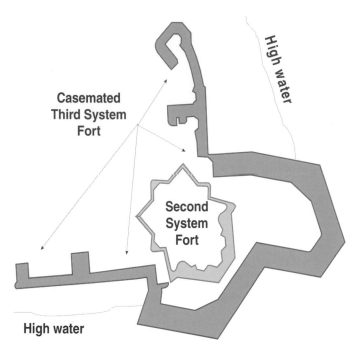

Casemated Third System Fort

Second System Fort

High water

High water

Figure 56: Fort Preble, occupying Preble Point on the main channel leading to Portland Harbor, was to be a blending of a closed Second System fort and an open-backed, casemated Third System fort.

The bastions were constructed of granite, with a high level of craftsmanship going into the structures.

Communication within each bastion was provided by straight stairways at the rear, near the powder magazines, and a circular stairway immediately behind the center casemate. The straight stairways connected the two casemated tiers, while the circular stairway provided access to the barbette.

Each bastion was entirely self-sufficient and individually defensible, such that it could serve as an independent fort. Howitzers in the embrasures at the extremes of the bastions provided flanking fire along the walls of the main structure in a manner similar to conventional bastions.

Only two of the three detached bastions were constructed. They connected to the parade through long, downward-sloping tunnels that opened onto the casemates of the multi-tiered structures. Further tunnels led to the barbette tier of each bastion.

Fort Scammel is privately owned, and is being maintained in very good condition by its owners. They provide tours of the fort and lobster bakes for various groups, and have done an outstanding job of keeping this historic fort available. A boat ride around House Island provides the visitor with a good view of the bastions, but a visit to its interior is the only way to appreciate the magnificence of this unique fort.

Figure 57: The Third System portion of Fort Preble had a stone scarp with Totten embrasures. Behind and above this casemated structure stands the Second System fort of the same name, also with a stone scarp. The barbette guns of the old fort were a suppliment to the casemated guns of the new structure. *(Photo by author)*

Fort Preble

There is some question whether Fort Preble, on Preble Point on the south shore of the channel into Portland Harbor, was a new-construction fort of the Third System or whether it was a modernization of the former Second System fort. While a portion of the Second System fort was planned as a battery for the new fort, an entirely new scarp was planned, and the portion of the old fort incorporated in the design was minimal in comparison with the new structure. This, coupled with Totten referring to it as the "new Fort Preble" in his documentation,[2] leads the author to treat it as a new-construction fort.

The design of the "new Fort Preble" is very interesting. The fort itself was designed to sit in advance of the old fort, with a single tier of casemates and no barbette guns. Barbette guns mounted on the terreplein of the old fort were to fire over the casemated structure. No barracks or quarters were provided within the fort.

Flanking this structure, two large barbette batteries provided positions for an additional 16 heavy guns to bear on the channel. These batteries were protected by howitzer positions on the barbette of the old fort. The rear of the complex was likewise protected by a howitzer position. This strange structure, had it been completed, would have provided 62 heavy guns to control the channel, with three howitzers for the minimal land defenses.

The seacoast defenses were constructed in what was then the latest technology. Iron-throated Totten embrasures, with Totten shutters to protect the gunners while not firing, penetrated the thick scarp.

In fact, the land defenses of the fort were so minimal that no rear scarp of the fort was designed. This made Fort Preble the only open-backed fort in the Third System. The three howitzers were placed *en barbette* on the old fort, facing away from the channel.

Unfortunately, very little of the fort was actually constructed. Only a small portion of the scarp wall stands today as a monument to the impressive plan developed for the defense of the south shore of the main channel. The area containing the remains is part of the Southern Maine Technical College. It is open to the public, and a series of informative signs trace the history of Forts Preble and Scammel.

Fort Constitution

Fort Constitution is the name given to two forts which both exist on the same point of land guarding the entrance to Portsmouth, New Hampshire. As would be expected, this causes considerable confusion when it comes to establishing the history of Portsmouth's coastal forts.

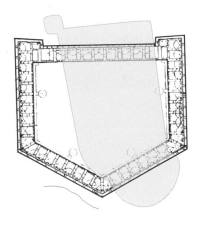

Figure 58: The Third System Fort Constitution was designed to completely replace its Second System namesake, shown here in gray. Construction of the new fort, however, was never completed and the circular water battery of the old fort was used in conjunction with the completed embrasures of the new fort. *(Sketch based on NARA drawing)*

79

Figure 59: The masonry scarp of Fort Constitution is shown in the photograph above. Although the casemates were not completed, the scarp wall was finished to the top of the first tierand the Totten embrasures were installed. This allowed cannon to be emplaced in the new fort. *(Photo by author)*

Adding to the confusion is the fact that cannon were mounted in both the old fort as well as in the unfinished portions of the new fort during the Civil War. Historic photographs describe "cannon mounted at Fort Constitution," sometimes showing the Second System fort and sometimes showing the Third System fort.

The Second System Fort Constitution had an irregular trace, forming three sides of a quadrilateral with the fourth side consisting of a semicircular water battery. A single bastion protected the gorge wall and the wider side of the peninsula. All cannon were to be mounted on the terreplein – there were no casemates.

The newer Fort Constitution is a classic Third System design. Designed in 1863, it was being constructed around the earlier fort when Third System construction was discontinued in 1867. It was designed as a five-sided truncated hexagon, very similar in design to Fort Pulaski in Savannah, Georgia. The fort was designed to have no bastions, but two demibastions flanking the gorge. While the older Fort Constitution was quite small in trace, the new fort was designed to cover the entire end of the peninsula.

The primary purpose of the fort was seacoast defense, and this was to be accomplished through the mounting of 36 guns en casemate and another 37 guns *en barbette*. Landward defenses were to be provided through loopholes in the casemates of the gorge wall and 10 barbette guns. These were to be supplemented by a flank howitzer in each demibastion. Four circular stair towers were to provide communication between the tiers.

Only a small portion of the new fort was constructed. The scarp of one primary seacoast fronts was built, and a small portion of the second primary front was constructed. The remainder of this front was where the semicircular water battery of the Second System fort projected through the location for this front. The old fort was temporarily left intact while work began on the two secondary fronts.

When construction was halted, none of the casemates had been built. The portion of he scarp wall that had been constructed had functional Totten embrasures, the pintles and traverse rails had been set, and guns had been emplaced.

It is in this condition that the fort stands today, unfortunately without the cannon. A good cross-section of the granite construction can be observed in the unfinished portions of the scarp, and the Totten embrasures and shutters give the viewer a sense of how this invention functioned. The massive granite blocks are impressive both in size and in the craftsmanship of the artisans that sculpted the shapes into arched recesses in the scarp wall.

The remains of the old fort and the incomplete "new" fort are open to the public, and provide an interesting contrast in construction methods of two generations of coastal fortifications.

To reach Fort Constitution, follow US 1B from Portsmouth, New Hampshire, crossing the bridge to New Castle Island. Fort Constitution is on a short peninsula on the northeast corner of the island.

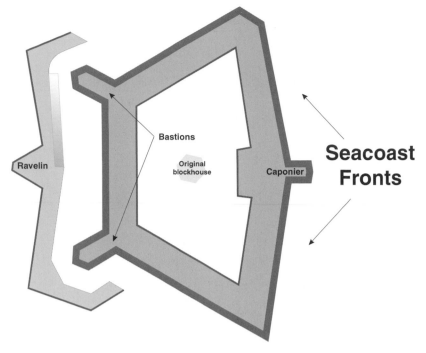

Figure 60: Fort McClary was an irregular pentagon, maximizing the length of the seacoast fronts while providing land defenses to the rear. Only portions of the fort were completed when construction halted.

Fort McClary

Fort McClary was a blockhouse with external batteries, built during the Second System. When Totten put together a plan to strengthen the defenses of the Maine-New Hampshire coast during the latter portion of the Third System, a new Fort McClary was proposed.

The Third System Fort McClary was to cooperate with Fort Constitution in defending the entrance to Portsmouth, New Hampshire. Located across the Piscataway River from the island on which Fort Constitution stood, the fort was located at a point where sailing ships were dealing with a bend in the river.

The new fort was to be an irregular five-sided work, with two seacoast fronts forming a shallow angle along the shore. Joining these fronts was a caponier with loopholes sweeping the curtains. Entered through a stairway and tunnel from the parade, it provided small-arms defense of the seacoast fronts. Only limited defenses were needed to protect these faces of the fort, as the rocky shore sloped very steeply downward to the water.

The three remaining fronts provided land defense only. Two small bastions, each designed for four howitzers, joined these landward curtains.

Begun in 1863, very little of the new Fort McClary was completed. The partially completed walls, however, provide a clean vision of the shape of the fort. The scarp of the north bastion was raised several feet, and the embrasures were completed. Other portions of the walls of the fort give the visitor a good feel for the design of the work.

To reach Fort McClary, take Maine Route 103 (Kittery Point Road) eastward from Route 1 and Interstate 95, past the old Portsmouth Naval Station and prison – now a Coast Guard Station. The park and the fort are on the right.

Notes

[1] Two secondary sources refer to these bridges as *drawbridges*, but this seems unlikely. Examination of the granite near the bridges leads one to believe that the bridges were wooden, but there is no evidence of a lift mechanism and no reason to believe there would be a need to isolate the stair tower from the casemates.

[2] ASP-MA, various reports on the status of the Third System.

The Defenses of Boston Harbor

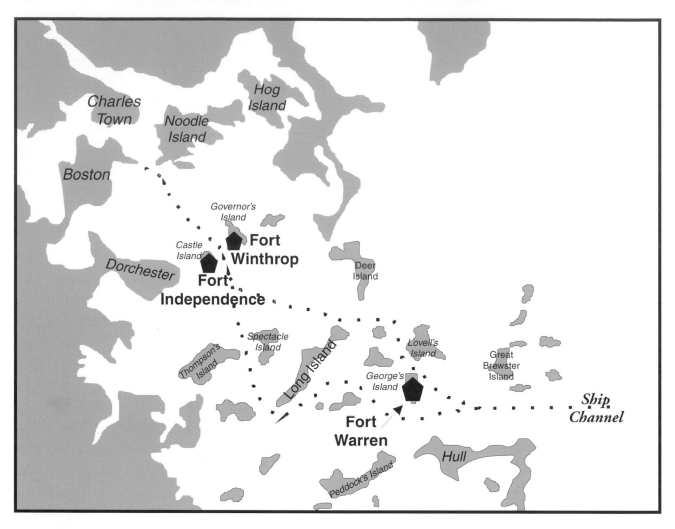

History

Boston was a premier seaport in North America before the United States became a nation. Indeed it was the sea borne commerce of Boston that led to the dissent that caused the Revolutionary War. Second only to New York City in size and second to none in political influence, it both required significant defenses and could afford to finance the construction of these defenses during the first two "systems." Therefore, it possessed some of the best harbor defenses in the nation when the Coastal Fortifications Board did its initial survey of the coast. Because it was quite well protected, Boston was not near the top of the priority list for the construction of new fortifications.

Like New York City, Boston harbor actually consisted of two parts, the inner harbor and the outer harbor. The large outer harbor, containing numerous islands, was entered by two main channels passing between Nantasket Head and Deer Island. Between these two peninsulas were several islands that protected the outer harbor from Massachusetts Bay and the Atlantic Ocean.

The inner harbor looks much different today than it did in the early nineteenth century. Islands have been joined together and to the mainland, and areas of the harbor were filled in to provide more waterfront property. In the early 1800s, several islands dotted the inner harbor in proximity to the mainland port of Boston.

Third System Strategy

When the Fortifications Board surveyed Boston Harbor, it found several forts protecting the Inner Harbor, but the Outer Harbor was defenseless. The entrance to the Outer Harbor was to receive the initial treatment in the Third System, with the defenses of the inner harbor following.

Two major channels provided access to the Outer Harbor; located between these channels was George's Island. Fort Warren was designed to occupy a large portion of the island, with the majority of the remaining island consumed by its outworks.

The two channels entering the Outer Harbor converged to a single channel entering the Inner Harbor. This channel passed between Governor's Island and Castle Island. The First System fort on Castle Island, Fort Independence, was replaced by a Third System fort with the same name and nearly the same trace. Fort Winthrop, a large defensive tower with external batteries, was constructed on Governor's Island, guarding the north side of the Inner Harbor entrance. Both these forts were considered secondary defenses of the city, as they were located very close to the seaport.

Fort Warren

Fort Warren, on George's Island in Boston's Outer Harbor, ranked fifth in size of the 42 Third System forts. Occupying a strategic position that was recognized prior to the American Revolution, the fort overlooked the two major channels leading into the port of Boston. Begun in 1837, the fort was not completed until the beginning of the Civil War.

The fort was what may be termed a "squashed pentagon" in shape. While the plan of a regular pentagon was chosen for the design of the fort, this shape was modified to make

maximum use of the existing island. This elongated the pentagon slightly along one axis while narrowing it along the other.

The design of Fort Warren required special features. Although situated on an island well out in the harbor, the fort was vulnerable to siege guns placed on nearby islands. For this reason, some of the seacoast fronts required significant earthworks protecting the scarp and the place d'armes mentioned later.

The bastions of Fort Warren were the largest on a fort of the latter Third System, though somewhat smaller than those of Fort Adams and Fort Monroe. The interior area of each bastion was open to the sky, with the rampart of the fort following the trace of the scarp wall.[1]

The ramparts were formed by the construction of casemates that were divided into two parts. The section of the casemates adjacent to the scarp wall was fitted with loopholes and/or embrasures for defense. Toward the parade from these rooms there was a dividing wall, and very

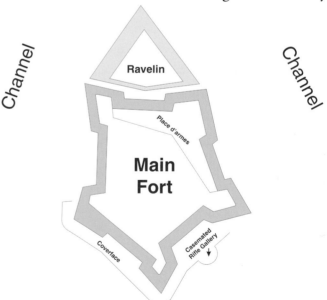

Figure 61: Fort Warren was an irregular pentagon, with a large water battery housed in a ravelin that "pointed" at the point of divergence of the two main channels. Additional seacoast cannon were also emplaced on a coverface on a secondary seacoast front facing the main channel.

Figure 62: This historic photograph of a seacoast front of Fort Warren shows a line of 10-inch Rodman cannon emplaced on the ramparts. The beautiful stonework that is a characteristic of this magnificent fort can also be seen. *(Photo courtesy NARA)*

ornate quarters opened onto the parade. Joining these two portions of the casemate were rectangular archways of granite, identical in design to those of Fort Adams.

Also like Fort Adams, Fort Warren had an interior ditch. This ditch was, however, very small in comparison to the ditch at Adams. About six feet wide, the ditch allowed access to the casemates on the lower level of the gorge wall. It was accessed from the parade by four stairways spread across the length of the gorge.

The most dramatic feature of Fort Warren was the granite work, said by some to be the finest in the United States. Compound arches, spiral staircases, even door lintels bespeak the craftsmanship that was applied during the construction of this massive fort. As one stood in the parade, three sides of the fort were faced with beautiful granite facades. Inside the casemates, the quarters had fireplaces, false ceilings, and extensive trim work. They were very elegant compared to the quarters at most Third System forts.

Like most Third System forts, however, the quarters were not very functional. In later years, loopholes were broken out to form windows that would let more air circulate, and extensive work was done to attempt to eliminate the dampness. Most remarkable was the construction of double walls of brick in many of the rooms, with heat

from the fireplaces circulating between the two walls.

Two sides of the parade terminated in the place d'armes. This angle of the fort consisted of an earthen slope rising from the parade to the ramparts, fronted with more gently sloping ramps. This extensive use of earth provided further strength to the seacoast front. There was no need for casemates on these walls, as the ravelin and coverface precluded the use of casemated cannon on these fronts.

The design of the defenses of the fort was unique, and each front was customized for its particular mission. The gorge wall, containing the sally port, was the primary land-defense front of the fort. The curtain and flanks of the bastions contained two levels of casemates, pierced with loopholes for small-arms fire. The face of the bastions had two tiers of loopholes about halfway to the salient, and then only the upper tier continued. Embrasures for four flank howitzers, two per tier, were located in the flank of each bastion.

In front of this formidable wall was a dry ditch, crossed by a drawbridge. The sally port had two chambers, with the first of these closed by the drawbridge. Four loopholes in each wall opened into this chamber from guardrooms on either side of the sally port. The second chamber was divided from the first by a portcullis,

Figure 63: The demilune guarding the sally port of Fort Warren is a beautiful structure and is still accessible. The ditch and counterscarp that stood in front of this demilune are no longer visible. *(Photo by author)*

and had no openings in the granite walls. Doors opened from this chamber onto the parade.

Beyond the ditch was a covert way, then a counterscarp wall that tapered from full height at the seacoast front to a very low wall at the dock end. This was curious, as the earthen mound and glacis maintained a constant elevation; only the granite counterscarp wall tapered downward. A ramp led from the covert way to the parapet of the outworks.

Immediately in front of the sally port, midway along the outworks, was a very elaborate demilune. This demilune was reached by a spiral stairway from the covert way, and was located at the base of the glacis. The crescent-shaped, granite structure was protected by a ditch with a granite counterscarp, the ditch now filled with sand. The demilune itself contained loopholes opening across the ditch to the shore of the island.

The land front facing the dock area was of a different design. The face of the bastion adjacent to the gorge was casemated and was penetrated by one tier of loopholes. The curtain, however, was not casemated and had neither loopholes nor embrasures. The opposite bastion was not casemated, but contained a rifle gallery along the face of the bastion. This narrow, rather primitive structure was accessed from the ramparts by a stairway. It consisted of granite-walled rooms joined by rectangular arches, with each room containing two loopholes. Off the end of the gallery, at the flank of the bastion, were casemates for two flank howitzers. They opened across from another pair of embrasures in the opposite, casemated bastion.

A very large ravelin that formed a triangle pointing toward the sea covered the front of the fort facing the ocean. While the grade of the land indicates the ravelin's shape, all traces have been obscured by construction during subsequent periods.

The channel front of the fort had a coverface with a substantial water battery. This battery extended from the salient of the bastion near the ravelin, along the entire channel front, and around the salient of the gorge bastion. At that point it became a classic covert way for small-arms fire. This battery, along with the barbette guns of the fort, provided two tiers of cannon guarding the main channel into Boston harbor.

The use of a coverface on this front yielded two advantages over a traditional casemated curtain. First, the earthen coverface provided protection for the masonry scarp from siege guns that could be located on nearby islands. More significantly, however, was the increase in armament using this approach. The coverface, located across the ditch, provided a significantly longer trace, which allowed an increase in the number of gun positions.

At the end of the counterscarp, just beyond the right gorge bastion, stood the "guardhouse." The structure was of granite, with arched brickwork in the same style as the fort. It had a solid back and side walls and a front wall with a large entrance door and two very large windows. Photographs[2] show the structure was a shelter for

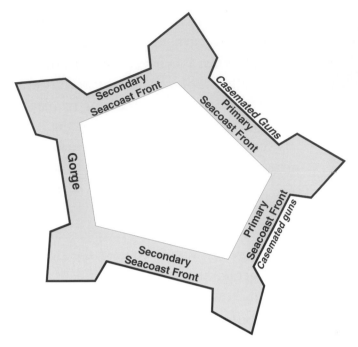

Figure 64: The Third System Fort Independence was built on the same foundation as its predecessor. The trace, therefore, remained as a bastioned pentagon. The ramparts were not quite as thick on the new fort, causing the parade to grow slightly.

the sentries guarding the approach to the sally port from the dock.

Today, Fort Warren is in very good condition. The channel front has been obscured by the construction of a concrete emplacement during the Endicott period, as has been the ravelin, but the remainder of the fort appears as it did during the Third System, minus its armament. Modifications to quarters and one bastion during the late nineteenth century make it necessary to do some "detective work" to determine the age of some of the structures, but the park rangers provide valuable insight into the clues.

Fort Warren can be reached by private boat or by two tour boats that leave from Long Warf in downtown Boston, and provides a very pleasant excursion through Boston Harbor en route to the fort. The fort is well-managed by the Metropolitan District Commission, and the site includes an excellent historical program with costumed reenactors. Signs with photographs and historical information do a very nice job of interpreting the history of the fort.

Fort Independence

Standing on Castle Island along the main ship channel into Boston Harbor is Fort Independence. The current Fort Independence replaced a late-Second System fort of the same name. Interestingly, the new Fort Independence followed the trace of the earlier fort, and was therefore able to use the same foundation. The newer fort, however, was casemated with cannon embrasures in the seacoast fronts. This more modern design made the fort far stronger than its predecessor.

There is significant confusion among historians regarding Fort Independence as a Second System or Third System fort. This confusion is for good reason. Sylvanus Thayer, who was the superintending engineer at the site, used money designated for "repair" of Fort Independence to construct a new fort on the old foundation. Effectively covering his tracks with Congress, he has also outwitted a number of historians!

Begun in 1834, Fort Independence was located on Castle Island, a small island at the junction of the two main channels leading to Boston's Inner Harbor. The island was located in a key strategic position, occupying the shore immediately south of the only deepwater channel to the port.

Figure 65: The primary seacoast front of Fort Independence is still best viewed from the main channel into the port, as shown in this photograph. *(Photo by author)*

86

Figure 66: The parade of Fort Indepence, while significantly smaller, bears a strong resemblence to the parade of Fort Warren. *(Photo by author)*

Fort Independence was a five-sided regular pentagon with bastions at each corner. All of the bastions were casemated with howitzer embrasures in the flanks. All of the salients of the bastions were earth-filled in the traditional manner.

All of the curtain walls were casemated, but only the two seacoast fronts had embrasures. The gorge front, with the sally port in its center, had loopholes for small-arms fire while the remaining two fronts had no openings.

The casemates were used for quarters, support functions, magazines, and storage, as well as for gun positions on the two seacoast fronts.

Figure 67: The seacoast fronts of Fort Independence open with embrasures, while the landard front opens with loopholes for small arms. *(Photo by author)*

Wooden walls separated the gun positions from the adjacent living quarters. The beautiful granite facades facing the parade bespoke the high level of workmanship demonstrated by the masons.

The barbette tier of the fort was designed to hold the majority of the armament, atop the bastions as well as the curtains. Gun emplacements were located on all fronts of the fort, with the largest concentration of cannon on the seacoast fronts.

Fort Independence is in very good condition, managed by the Metropolitan District Commission. Costumed guides from the Castle Island Association provide knowledgeable tours of the fort, and a few signs assist the visitor in appreciating this beautiful fort. The interior of the fort is open on weekends during the season.

Castle Island is now connected to the mainland, and is easily accessible. Take the Columbia Road/UMass/JFK Library exit from Interstate 93/Southeast Expressway to the rotary adjacent to the Bayside Expo. Follow signs for Day Boulevard. Follow the roadway east along the shore all the way to the end.

Fort Winthrop

Immediately opposite Castle Island and Fort Independence was Governor's Island, now joined with other islands to form Boston's Logan International Airport. Occupying the north side of the main shipping channel into Boston, this island held a very high strategic value.

The original fort on Governor's Island was named Fort Warren, but that name was transferred to the new Third System structure being built on George's Island. The old Fort Warren was given the name Fort Winthrop, which was applied to the defensive tower that replaced it.

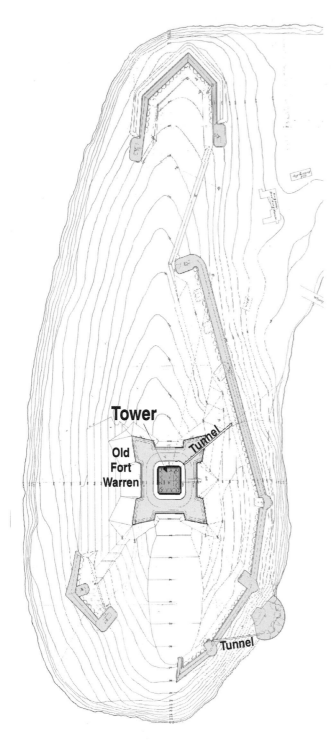

Tower

Old Fort Warren

Tunnel

Tunnel

Figure 68: Fort Winthrop is a group of four batteries that surround a defensive tower atop the center of the island. The tower uses old Fort Warren as a coverface. *(Sketch from NARA drawing)*

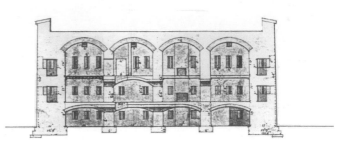

Figure 69: This drawing shows a section view of the Fort Winthrop tower. The interior levels open with loopholes - all cannon are mounted en barbette. *(Drawing courtesy of NARA)*

perimeter of the island with one battery on the shoreline. It was designed as an auxiliary to Fort Independence immediately opposite the main shipping channel.

The defensive tower was a square with rounded corners, each face being 138 feet in length. Casemates opened to loopholes on all fronts. The lower tier had 40 loopholes, while the upper two tiers each had 52 loopholes. The three casemated tiers were surmounted with an

Figure 70: This rare photograph of the Fort Winthrop tower shows a roof that was apparently added during a later period. *(Photo courtesy of NARA)*

The Third System Fort Winthrop consisted of a square defensive tower atop the crest of the island, with external batteries located along the

open barbette tier surrounded by a breast-high parapet. It was on this tier that artillery could be mounted, and emplacements for 16 guns were designed.

Encircling the tower was a massive coverface – actually the mass of the old fort – that concealed the lower two stories of the tower. The square coverface had a masonry counterscarp wall that had rounded corners, while the parapet of the coverface sported the bastions of the original work.

The only entrance to the tower was a sally port located on the third story, reached by a drawbridge over the ditch. The drawbridge opened onto the glacis, and onto two stairways leading down into the ditch. From the ditch a tunnel led under the coverface and glacis to the southwest battery.

Inside the tower, a spiral staircase near the sally port provided communication between the three stories and the barbette tier.

The external batteries consisted of a very long battery extending along about half of the length of the island, a battery on each end of the island, and a masonry battery near the water line below the long battery. In addition to the tunnel mentioned that connected the long battery to the ditch surrounding the tower, a second tunnel connected the long battery with the battery at the shoreline. Communication between the long battery and the battery on the north end of the island was provided by an earthwork trench extending along the crest of the hill.

Unfortunately, no trace of Fort Winthrop remains. Governor's Island was joined with other islands to expand Logan International Airport, and Fort Winthrop fell victim to that expansion.

Notes

[1]One bastion was subsequently covered, and used as an interior training and recreation area during later periods of occupation of the fort. Two of the remaining bastions reflect the original design.

[2]Still Pictures Branch, National Archives.

Figure 71: The guardhouse that controls the entrance to the ditch leading to the sally port of Fort Warren is shown in this Civil War photograph. The photograph is taken from the area of the warf, under the guns of the gorge of the fort. *(Photo courtesy MHI)*

The Defenses of the
Southern New England Coast

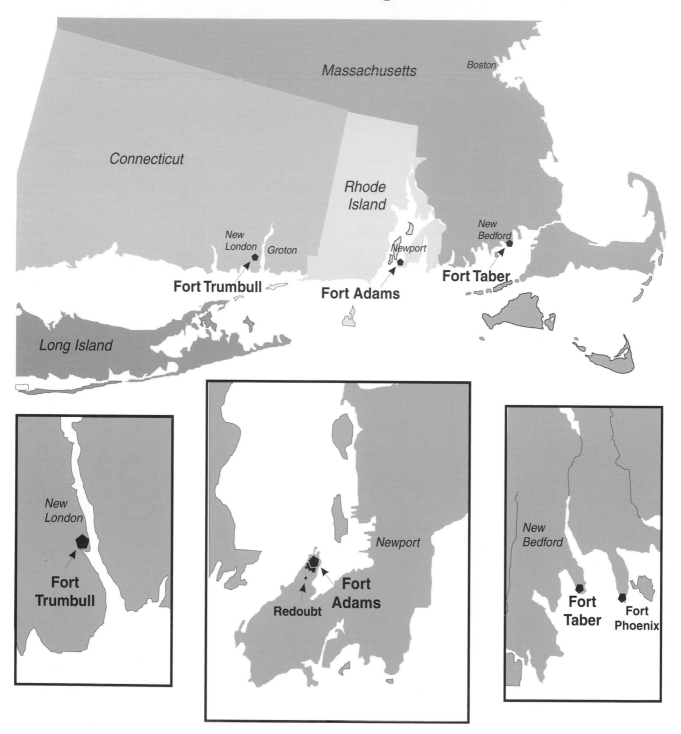

History

The southern coast of New England, from Cape Cod to New York, was a populous area sustained by the fishing and manufacturing industries. Several major cities dotted the coastline, located at the harbors and river mouths. The major rivers of New England tend to run north to south; therefore this southern coast con-

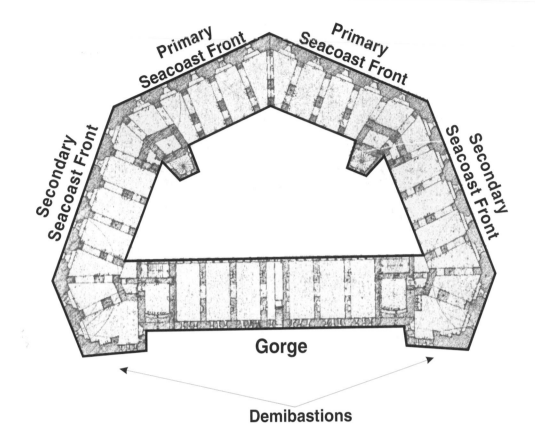

Figure 72: The plan of the Fort at Clark's Point, known as Fort Taber, was a truncated octagon. Two arms of the octagon were substantially shortened and the gorge was closed with a straight wall. *(Sketch based on NARA drawing)*

trolled waterborne access to most of the inland areas.

The most important area on this coast was Narragansett Bay, considered the finest bay in the United States. The location and shape of the bay was such that it could be entered during unfavorable wind conditions that would close many of the harbors.[1]

Other major cities in the region were considered critical to national security. First, New London and Groton, Connecticut, stood on opposite shores of the Thames River, a principal waterway leading to Norwich and beyond. New Bedford, Massachusetts, was a center of the fishing industry, and controlled access to

the Acushnet River. It also had a sheltered harbor that would provide a stronghold for an attacker who wished to control southern Massachusetts.

The defenses of the region were in poor repair. Fort Adams, a Second System fort on Brenton's Point, guarded the principal entrance to Narragansett Bay. This fort, however, had fallen into disrepair and was not considered an adequate defense of so critical a harbor.

Two other forts guarded the Thames, Forts Trumbull and Griswold. While the first Fort Trumbull was destroyed during the War of 1812, Fort Griswold did provide some defense for the area.

Third System Strategy

The major priority of the Fortifications Board was the protection of Narragansett Bay. The focus of activity in this area became Newport, Rhode Island, the key to the deep-water channel into the bay. Brenton's Point, opposite Newport, was chosen for the site of a major new fort – the same location as the Second System Fort Adams. A Third System fort of the same name was to be built on the site and obstructions were to ensure that only one channel was available to ships-of-the-line. Of lower priority were forts on adjacent islands and several smaller batteries. None of the latter were constructed during the Third System.

As the Third System progressed, two more areas were slated for construction. The first was the replacement of the Second System Fort Trumbull, which was destroyed during the War of 1812. This new Fort Trumbull was to cooperate with Fort Griswold across the river to guard the Thames River and the harbors of Groton and New London, Connecticut.

The last of the Third System forts designated for this region was at Clark's Point near New Bedford, Massachusetts. The "Fort on Clark's Point" was constructed late in the Third System. Construction was not completed until near the end of the Civil War.

Figure 73: This aerial photograph of Fort Taber shows two structures built on the ramparts during later periods of use. *(Photo courtesy NARA)*

Figure 74: The gorge of Fort Taber opened with loopholes, with howitzer embrasures in the flanks and faces of the demibastions. *(Photo by author)*

While Fort Trumbull and the Clark's Point fort were relatively small works, Fort Adams was one of the truly magnificent works of the system.

Fort Griswold, destroyed during the War of 1812, received some repairs, and was replaced by an angular 16-gun battery to cooperate with Fort Trumbull in the defense of the Thames River.

Fort Taber

The fort on Clark's Point, just south of New Bedford, Massachusetts, was not officially named – it remained the "Fort on Clark's Point" throughout the Third System. Local citizens, however, called it Fort Taber after the small Civil War earthwork that guarded the point until the granite fort was completed. Even the garrison referred to it as Fort Taber in letters home,[2] but that was never its official name. The entire reservation, including the Third System fort, was later named Fort Rodman, the only official name that the fort had. The local citizenry has continued with the name of Fort Taber, however, and there has even been a Fort Taber Society dedicated to preserving the granite fort. To differentiate the Third System fort from the remainder of the Fort Rodman reservation, and to maintain the name used by the original garrison, it will be referred to here as Fort Taber.

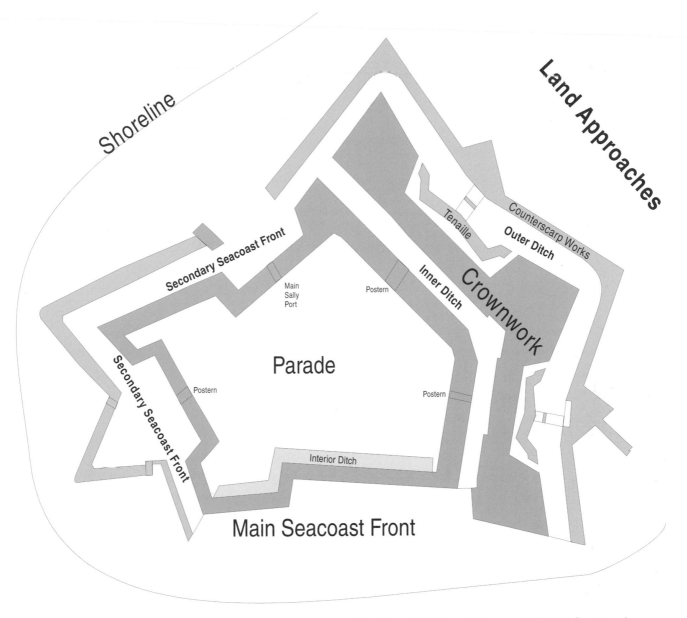

Figure 75: The magnificent Fort Adams embodied all of the thinking of the early Third System in one fort. An innovative approach to increasing the seaward firepower, remarkable land defenses, and a scarp protected from all shore areas combined to make this fort nearly invulnerable.

The fort was an imposing tower fort – begun in 1857 – with two casemated levels and a barbette tier of guns. The truncated octagon can be said to have had either five or seven sides, depending on the way they were counted. The four seacoast fronts were equal in length, each being 108 feet long and mounting five cannon per tier. The next two sides, which would continue the regular octagon, were truncated to 47 feet and mounted only two cannon per tier. If these two short sides were counted, Fort Taber was a seven-sided fort. These terminated in demibastions that protected the gorge wall with one howitzer embrasure and one loophole per tier.

The gorge wall was casemated with 20 loopholes on the upper tier and 18 loopholes on the lower tier. It is interesting to note that the scarp wall extended much higher above the second-tier embrasures than would be justified by the casemate height. This increase in vertical scale gave the fort both a more impressive demeanor and a greater resistance to an attacker attempting to scale the walls.

Also interesting is the nature of the stonework. While some of the granite blocks had a relatively flat exterior face, others projected well out from the wall. It is not known whether this was for artistic expression on the part of the masons or if it related to the variable quality of the granite that was available during the span of construction.

An internal design feature unique to the fort was the presence of iron railings protruding from the portals of the circular stairways. These railings added a very pleasing, finished touch to the interior of the fort that was missing on many of the other forts of this period.

Today, only the exterior of Fort Taber is accessible. While it is clear that some relatively thin, intrepid souls have broken out a portion of one of the lower-tier loopholes and gained entry by squeezing through, that is certainly not recommended. The loopholes do provide a view into the former barracks areas of the gorge and across the parade to the stair towers and casemates of the fort. A stroll around the perimeter of the fort reinforces the height of the walls and the obstacle that they would have provided to an attacker.

Plans are underway to open the fort to the public, and to create a park to interpret the military history of the area. These efforts are applauded, and the author looks forward to the ability of the public to view this interesting fort.

Fort Adams

One of the grandest of all the Third System works was Fort Adams, on Brenton's Point outside Newport, Rhode Island. The second largest of the mainland works behind Fort Monroe, it had both heavier armament and more impressive land defenses. This fort, more than any other in the Third System, was representative of the various elements of fortification integrated into one formidable unit.

This irregularly shaped fort used the available land on the peninsula as efficiently as practical, consuming all but a short distance between the outer walls and the shore. Very large, irregular bastions provided enfilading fire down the curtains, from as many as eight guns on the channel front. While the channel front provided a tremendous amount of firepower, it was the land defenses, not as much from the massive bastions as from the intricate system of outworks, that made Fort Adams truly impressive.

Built from 1825 through 1857, this massive work was located on a narrow point overlooking the harbor, giving only one direction

Figure 76: Dividing Newport Bay from the main channel of Narragansett Bay, Fort Adams still provides a dominating presence. *(Photo by author)*

Figure 77: The ideal location and the extensive landward structures of Fort Adams are visible in this aerial photograph. The covert way to the Redoubt followed the ridge along the near shore. *(Photo courtesy Terrance McGovern)*

from which a significant land-based attack could be launched. A detached redoubt defended this approach up the peninsula, in itself a small but impressive fort, and by multiple levels of land defenses for the fort itself. It was a classical application of Vauban's principle of siege defense in designing positions that could be successively abandoned as the siege continued.

The first level of defense for Fort Adams was a redoubt located approximately 650 yards from the landward wall of the fort. This redoubt bore a remarkable similarity in design to a defensive tower, but was designed wholly for land defense. The main structure was a six-sided, truncated octagon, with demibastions on the gorge wall. The main level was casemated for

five guns on elevated platforms and the demibastions had embrasures for two howitzers guarding the drawbridge.

A unique feature of this redoubt was the beautifully designed double spiral staircases that wound to the ramparts. This is the only place that the author has seen two spiral staircases winding over each other and providing access to the same place. While a portion of one staircase has been broken out, the remains of this magnificent piece of construction give a clear indication of the original design.

The ramparts included breast-high walls and a banquette around the perimeter. The vantage point atop the redoubt gives a clear view of the impressive outer defenses encircling this structure.

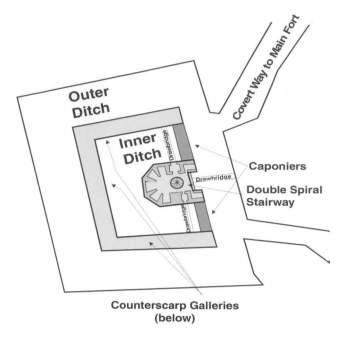

Figure 78: The redoubt of Fort Adams is an impressive small fort in itself. Like the main work, the redoubt uses innovative designs and defense in depth.

Two deep ditches encircled the redoubt, with the inner ditch extending around the three main fronts. The outer ditch extended around all four sides of the work.

Between the two ditches was an impressive counterscarp gallery with loopholes opening to the inner ditch. This ditch was closed at each end by caponiers connecting to the counterscarp galleries. Loopholes in the caponiers also opened into the inner ditch. A further tunnel, now underwater, extended from the counterscarp gallery toward the bay. Evidence of arched brickwork along the shore indicates that a tunnel may have extended to the water, but this has not been confirmed.

Tall masonry walls with no openings defined the outer ditch. This made the outer

Figure 79: The interior of the redoubt had a passageway connecting the casemates, the sally port, and the two posterns. The casemates were elevated from the floor of the passageway, as evidenced by the steps in the photograph. *(Photo by author)*

ditch a passive, but formidable, obstacle.

Two drawbridges provided communication to the covert way and banquette above the counterscarp galleries, each opening into a postern in the redoubt.

A long wooden bridge provided passage across the outer ditch, with a drawbridge at the sally port. Demibastions on the gorge flanked the bridge and drawbridge, with loopholes and howitzer embrasures providing both enfilading fire and forward fire on the bridge.

Beyond the ditch was a large, masonry-revetted outwork facing the distant Fort Adams. This group of three structures consisted of a V-shaped redan and two wedge-shaped structures. From the westernmost of these structures an extremely long parapet and covert way extended to the outworks of the fort. Over a good por-

Figure 80: The gorge of Fort Adam's redoubt sports two demibastions with flanking howitzer embrasures and loopholes for forward fire. Also of note are the two caponiers that close the inner ditch and provide communications with the counterscarp galleries. A long narrow bridge ended with a drawbridge at the sally port. *(Photo by author)*

tion of this distance, the covert way ran parallel to the channel and provision was made for mounting seacoast guns behind the parapet.

All evidence regarding the terrain between the redoubt and Fort Adams has been obscured by subsequent construction, and a Navy housing project now stands on that ground. The plans of the fort called for a long glacis connecting the parapet of the ravelin with the parapet of the outworks of the main fort. Little is left of this covert way, but in a few areas the outline of the breast-high wall can be seen.

A beautifully curved passageway led to an opening in the parapet of the outworks of the main fort, allowing access from the covert way. This led to a very long parapet at the termination of the glacis of the main work.

It is interesting to note that the covert way between the fort and the redoubt was located near the water, and designed such that it would not provide a protected area for an attacker down the narrow peninsula. It was designed, however, to provide completely protected communication between the redoubt and the main fort from ships in the channel. This complex design was a masterpiece of military engineering and planning.

As the covert way met the outworks of the main fort, a parapet, banquette, and covert way provided the next line of defense from a land-based attack. Immediately toward the fort from these works was a stone counterscarp wall fronting a deep, wide ditch – the widest in the Third System. This counterscarp wall contained

Figure 81: The unique double spiral staircase of the Fort Adams redoubt is shown in the above photograph. *(Photo by author)*

galleries in each curved face with loopholes opening into the ditch. The only access to these galleries was through the incredible tunnel system that will be described later.

Within the ditch were a series of land defenses that were unique to Fort Adams. Communication between the covert way and the ditch was gained from a stairway leading to a small chamber that has sometimes been mislabeled a caponier. This chamber ended in a stone rifle gallery that controlled entry to an arched passageway through the tenaille. The rifle gallery was roofed, with the roof supported by stone columns in the rear and the loopholed wall in the front.

The tenaille was bastioned, and two howitzer casemates were located in the flank of each bastion. Access to these casemates was via a tunnel, which is now filled with dirt and debris. The casemates were open-backed, opening to embrasures in the very large crownwork to the rear. This allowed the tenaille to be fully controlled by the crownwork, making it of no strategic value to the attacker.

This defensive system, including the tenaille and rifle gallery, was repeated between each demibastion and the full bastion.

The crownwork was of classic design, with a demibastion at each end and a full bastion in the center. The demibastions of the crownwork were casemated and embrasures opened to the ditch. The rear of the crownwork contained counterfire galleries, as well as ramps leading to the rampart. The rampart of the crownwork contained a breast-high wall and banquette for small-arms fire. The height of the crownwork was such that it commanded the entire glacis.

Immediately behind the crownwork was the ditch and the scarp of the fort. This wall was not bastioned as the counterfire galleries in the crownwork defended this portion of the ditch. Embrasures as well as loopholes provided forward fire from the scarp of the fort.

Two posterns provided communication with the ditch, immediately opposite the archways through the crownwork. Along the scarp on each side of the posterns there were embrasures and loopholes on two levels, one even with the parade and one near the bottom of the ditch. Communication with the parade was through two arched passageways under the ramparts. These passageways sloped rather steeply from the ditch up to the parade.

The scarp wall along the seacoast front extended from the main work to the parapet of the outworks. This wall joined the end of the crownwork and the covert way, closing the inner and outer portions of the ditch. An archway closed with an iron gate[3] led from the inner ditch to the shore.

In each postern, a stone stairway descended to a (now water-filled) tunnel that appeared to lead in the direction of the crownwork. A complementary set of steps in the crownwork also led to a water-filled tunnel. If these tunnels led to other passageways, which indeed they may have, the intrepid explorer would need a SCUBA to solve the mystery. Construction progress drawings in both 1831 and 1833 give a good indication of the tunnels completed at that time, but a physical inspection of the tunnel system has revealed tunnels that are not indicated on those drawings.

Also in the crownwork was a spiral stairway leading to an impressive array of tunnels that terminated at the counterscarp gallery at the extreme of the ditch. These tunnels formed a diamond shape with two cross-connecting tunnels. From the counterscarp gallery, further countermining tunnels extended under the glacis. All these tunnels were arched, brick-lined

Figure 82: Each massive casemate of Fort Adams was designed to hold four cannon on two levels The lower level of casemates was accessed by a unique interior ditch, the upper tier by bridges over that ditch. *(Photo by author)*

passageways that had periodic openings in the brickwork. These openings, closed with loose granite blocks, allowed further countermining should the sounds of mining tunnels be detected.

The outworks along the Newport side of the fort extended beyond the sally port, but only scattered remains indicate their shape. Immediately outside the sally port, within the perimeter of the now-destroyed outworks, stood a small granite structure. While called a "redoubt" on the original drawings of the fort,[4] this structure functioned as a caponier to provide further defense of the sally port. The outwork contained both howitzer embrasures and loopholes for the defense of the ditch at the main entrance to the fort. It was modified in a later period for use as a storage shed, but the original design is obvious, especially when viewed from inside the structure.

The channel side of the fort mounted an impressive number of guns on two tiers of casemates, as well as a tier of guns mounted en barbette. A unique aspect to Fort Adams is that the parade was on the level of the *upper* tier of casemates. An interior ditch, open to the parade but with a very steep slope, allowed access to the lower casemates. Access between the parade and the upper casemates was via bridges over this ditch.

Also interesting was the use of the faces of all the bastions for seacoast cannon. With the extremely large size of Fort Adams' bastions, this added significantly to the amount of armament that the fort could mount. This practice applied to the Newport side of the fort as well as the main seacoast front.

The casemates were very large arches, with provision for mounting two cannon per tier in each casemate. The intervening flooring was of timber, similar to the design of Fort McRee in Pensacola, Florida. This timber flooring was supported by a row of transverse

Howitzer Embrasures

Figure 83: The gorge of Fort Adams has embrasures for seacoast cannon interspersed with embrasures for howitzers for land defense. A platform in the sally port held a howitzer directly above the main gate of the fort. *(Photo by author)*

"arches," which are rectangular rather than curved. These large pieces of granite formed a long colonnade supporting the interior of the rampart.

An impressive feature of the fort was the granite work forming the perimeter of the parade. The inner portion of the casemates was designed as quarters, and the granite entrances and windows opening on the parade were a beautiful piece of architecture. The interiors of these quarters were equally impressive, with very attractive architectural features. Of particular note are the rosettes in the ceilings, below which chandeliers once hung. Toward the scarp wall from these quarters were gunrooms that ringed the entire perimeter of the fort.

Above the quarters, accessible from stairways in each bastion and demibastion, were the ramparts with the barbette tier of guns. An interesting note is that the demibastion on the landward side of the fort had a crenellated parapet on its flank, while the remainder of the parapet was smooth. This crenellated section allowed a further depression of the guns mounted *en barbette*, implying that the cannon at that location were howitzers guarding the sally port rather than heavy guns. This use of a crenellated embrasure was also used at the Advanced Redoubt in Pensacola, Florida.

Another interesting feature of the fort was that the walls of the fort sloped downward from the land front to the end of the peninsula, following the contour of the land. This meant that there were periodic steps downward in the casemates and on the rampart of the fort as one proceeded along the seacoast front. Intervening walls on the land front made this descent less obvious than when viewed from the exterior of the fort.

While Simon Bernard designed Fort Adams, Joseph Totten superintended construction there for several years and used the fort to carry out research on embrasure design. Possessively considering the fort his own, he played a very major role in the design as it was finally implemented.

Today, the impressive fort is once again open to the public, as a Rhode Island State Park. Many areas of the fort are open, and work continues on the restoration and stabilization of this magnificent structure. Plans have been made for an even more complete interpretation of the fort, and the addition of a museum and bookstore is planned. The redoubt to the south of the fort is fenced, and the interior is weed-infested. Little of the structure can be seen from outside the fence.

Fort Adams can be reached by traveling south from downtown Newport, Rhode Island, and following the shoreline to the west. Turn north into the entrance of Fort Adams State Park and continue to the end of the road.

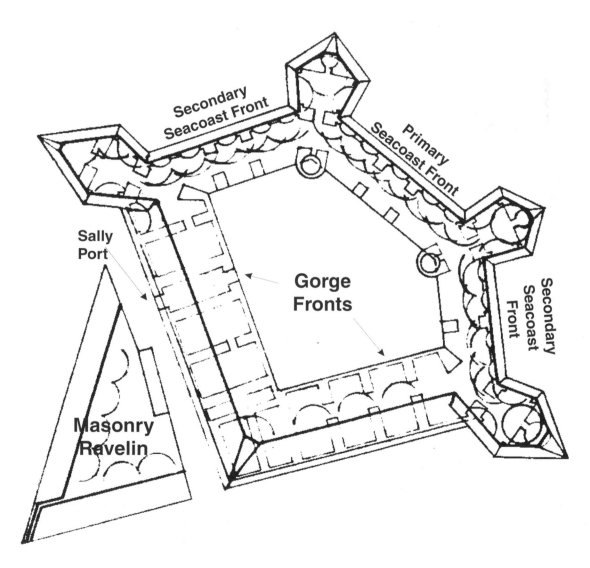

Figure 84: The irregular Fort Trumbull was designed to provide maximum firepower on the main channel of the Thames River with a relatively modest trace. The massive ravelin guarding the main sally port is unique to this fort. *(Drawing courtesy NARA, labels by author)*

Fort Trumbull

Overlooking the Thames River just below Groton and New London, Connecticut, stood the granite Fort Trumbull, built from 1839 through 1850. Replacing a Second System fort of the same name, this granite fort of modest trace was designed to cooperate with the older Fort Griswold across the Thames.

Fort Trumbull was a five-sided irregular work overlooking New London Harbor, about one-half mile south of the old city and approximately two miles upstream of the Long Island Sound. Three seacoast fronts faced the Thames River, with two landward fronts forming the gorge.

A short seacoast front faced directly downstream, and would have contained the first cannon to fire on an approaching enemy. To the left of this front were two equal-length fronts that would come to bear on an enemy as he moved toward the city. The second front was angled to the channel at roughly 45 degrees, and the third front ran roughly parallel to the channel. The gorge was closed by two nearly perpendicular fronts.

Bastions were located at the ends of each of the seacoast fronts, but there was no bastion at the gorge angle. Each of the seacoast fronts was casemated for one tier of cannon with a second tier mounted en barbette. Center-pintled cannon were mounted atop each bastion, except the one furthest upstream. This bastion was designed for three fore-pintled cannon.

The three fronts were designed for 14 seacoast cannon, and the barbette could mount another 28 guns. In addition to this armament, two flanking batteries outside the fort were designed for 10 heavy cannon.

The gorge walls were casemated to contain barracks areas, and were loopholed to provide forward small-arms fire on an attacker. Forward fire was also to be provided from a howitzer embrasure at the eastern end of the north gorge. Flanking fire was to be provided by howitzers mounted in the flanks of each bastion.

Two spiral stair towers, one behind each of the two seacoast bastions, provided access to the ramparts.

Immediately north of the gorge angle was a sharply angled granite cover face, with a place d'armes and accommodation for six barbette guns. This coverface protected the rear of the fort and also controlled the northeast external battery. The southwest external battery was controlled from the southwest bastion of the main work.

Today, Fort Trumbull is open to the public as a Connecticut State Park. Work is continu-

Figure 85: This landward front of Fort Trumbull was closed by loopholes, with howitzer embrasures in the face of the bastion. The water-facing fronts contained embrasures for seacoast cannon. Note the masonry ravelin to the left of the fort. *(Photo by author)*

ing to restore and interpret more areas of this interesting fort. Its massive granite walls and dominating Egyptian Revival styling lend to its forbidding appearance dominating the Thames River.

Fort Trumbull can be reached by traveling south from downtown New London, Connecticut, on Jay Street to Shaw Street. Turn left on Shaw Street and follow it to Trumbull Street. Turn left and follow Trumbull Street to the end. Fort Trumbull is at the end of the street.

Notes

[1]Report of the Secretary of War, November 1, 1851.

[2]Letters folder, New Bedford Public Library, New Bedford, Massachusetts.

[3]It is not known whether the iron gate is period to the Third System fort, but it is strongly suspected that this was a later addition. It is expected that the door would have been the two-layer oak door with iron studs that was commonly used in sally ports.

[4]National Archives, Cartographic Branch, RG77.

Figure 86: While the use of Totten Shutters was common on seacoast embrasures in the late Third System, their use on howitzer embrasures was rare. The photograph above shows such a shutter on the demibastion of Fort Taber. *(Photo by author)*

The Defenses of New York City

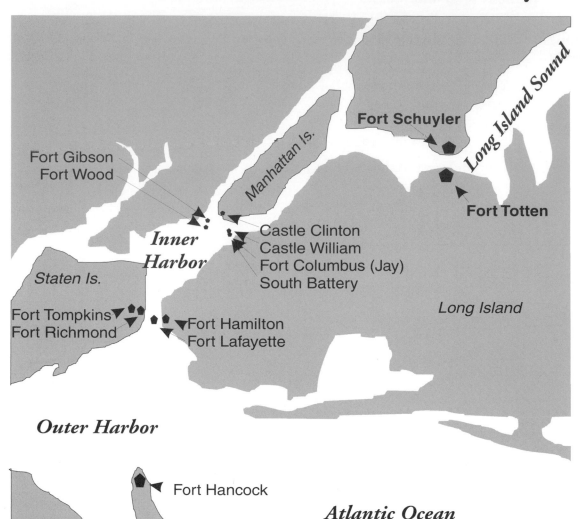

History

The largest population center of the United States, and the most heavily defended city at the beginning of the Third System, was New York City. Not only was New York a crucial prize in itself, it also controlled the Hudson River, one of the nations most important waterways. Being of great strategic importance and a wealthy metropolis, it was well defended during the First and Second Systems. For this reason, Bernard relegated further work on the defenses of New York until after several more vulnerable locations had been adequately protected.

There were two major water routes leading to the city from the Atlantic Ocean. The first, and most direct, route was south of Long Island, past the Sandy Hook, and into the Outer Harbor. From there, the channel led through The Narrows between Staten Island and Long Island into the Inner Harbor. The channel continued to the tip of Manhattan where the East River and the Hudson River met.

The second water route passed north of Long Island through the Long Island Sound and into the East River. Passing through the dangerous "Hell Gate," this channel then led down the East River to the Inner Harbor at the mouth of the Hudson River.

Believing that the rocks and shallows of Hell Gate provided ample protection against deep-draft men-of-war, all the early defenses of the city were located around the northern end of the Inner Harbor and at The Narrows dividing the Outer Harbor from the Inner Harbor. The later development of shallower draft, steam-powered vessels, however, would be able to navigate the upper reaches of the East River, leaving the city vulnerable from the north.

To the south of the city, the forts constructed on the shore of The Narrows were aging. Fort Lafayette, a transitional work on a shoal in The Narrows was an impressive casemated work, but it had little support from the land forts. The early forts on both the Staten Island and the Brooklyn side of the Narrows needed to be replaced.

Third System Strategy

Although the most important entrance into New York was through The Narrows, the modern Fort Lafayette and the aging forts Richmond and Tompkins protected this route. The Hell Gate approach, however, had no defenses.

It was to close off this approach that Bernard chose to locate the first Third System fort for the defense of New York, Fort Schuyler. The location was well chosen. A spit of land, known as Throgg's Neck, projected into the East River at the point where the channel turned from south to west. The channel then proceeded northwest around the point, then due west toward Manhattan Island. The tip of this point was chosen as Fort Schuyler's location.

Immediately across the channel from Fort Schuyler was another projection of land that lay bow-on to a ship progressing up the East River. The last fort built for the defense of New York, Fort Totten, was built on that point. These two forts effectively sealed off the approach to the city through the East River.

Following the construction of Fort Schuyler, attention was turned to The Narrows and the old forts there. The replacements for these forts, guarding what was considered to be the most important channel in the nation, comprised the most impressive defensive scheme of the Third System.

Utilizing the power of Fort Lafayette for a defense of the east side of the channel, a tower fort, Fort Richmond, was built immediately opposite on the west bank of The Narrows. On the ridges immediately above these two forts, two additional forts were built, Fort Hamilton on the east and Fort Tompkins on the west. Together, these four forts sealed off the shipping channel to the Inner Harbor and provided protection from a land attack from either shore of the Outer Harbor.

The final defenses of the city were built at the entrance to the Outer Harbor. The channel at this point was far too wide to be defended by forts, but an anchorage on the south side of this channel could allow an invader to safely anchor out of the weather of the Atlantic Ocean. This anchorage was protected by the Sandy Hook, a projection of land angling northwest from the New Jersey shore at the mouth of the bay. At the end of this projection, construction began on an extremely large fort. While this Fort on Sandy Hook was constructed to the extent that it was defensible, it was not completed. Also, the final structure was slightly smaller than the original plan.

The inner harbor was dotted with forts from earlier periods. While these forts were considered too close to the city to provide an adequate defense, they were in an excellent position to back up the new harbor forts, providing a secondary defense to the city. Fort Wood, on Bedloe's Island, is now the structure for the Statue of Liberty. This Second System "star fort" cooperated with Fort Gibson, another Second System fort on nearby Ellis Island. Governor's Island boasted

105

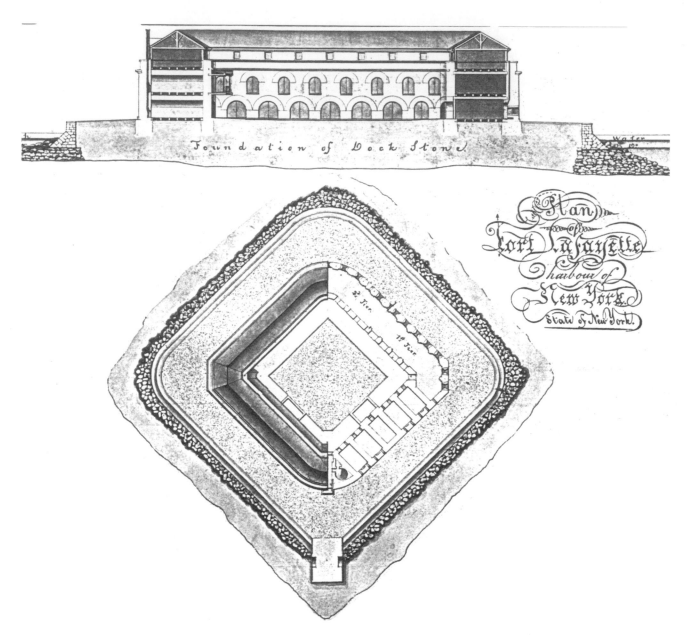

Figure 87: Fort Lafayette, also known as Fort Diamond, was designed and built prior to the Third System. For its day, this fort was a beautiful example of vertical fortification, mounting three tiers of cannon in casemates. The orientation of the square fort gave gunners a maximum length of time to be able to fire on ships entering the harbor, thus maximizing the effectiveness of the fort. *(Drawings courtesy NARA)*

three forts, First System South Battery, Second System Fort Columbus (later named Fort Jay), and Second System Castle Williams. Castle Williams cooperated with similar Castle Clinton on the southern tip of Manhattan Island.

By the close of the Third System, New York was defended by twelve forts, six of which were newly constructed and the seventh dated from the post-War of 1812 period. The combined firepower of these forts was unequaled at any harbor in the United States.

Fort Lafayette

Prior to the implementation of the Third System, but after the end of the War of 1812, it was decided that New York City was far too vulnterable to a naval attack. Forts Hamiton, Tompkins, and Richmond were badly aging and utilized outdated technology in their designs. A new fort to guard The Narrows was needed.

The concept of vertical fortification had been used successfully during the Second System in the design of Castle Williams and Castle Clinton. These two multiered structures mounted very significant firepower on a circular trace. These castles were located near the water so that their cannon would have maximum impact on ships passing near the forts, and would be able to engage ships further from shore.

Begun in 1815 under the name Fort Diamond, Fort Lafayette built on these principles. A three-tierd structure was constructed on a shoal that sat in The Narrows. This placement required ships to come near the fort when passing from the inner to the outer harbor, and the multiple tiers of cannon provided significant firepower on a small trace.

The shape of the fort was square, oriented such that one salient faces the oncoming ships. This allowed the fort's guns to be traversed at a maximum angle to fire on ships approaching the fort bow-on, with the ships receiving bombardment from two fronts. As the ships passed the fort, the cannon would be traversed to the other extreme, again allowing two fronts to fire on the ship. Finally, if the ship made it past the fort, it would receive stern-on fire from two fronts.

The principal vulnerability of the fort was to land-based cannon. The fronts of the fort

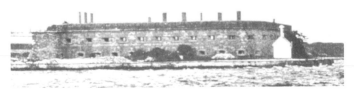

Figure 88: The magnificent Fort Lafayette once stood where now stands a pillar for the Verrazano Narrows Bridge. *(Photo courtesy NARA)*

were of unprotected masonry, and would therefore have difficulty standing up to a siege. This situation was mitigated by the forts along both shores of The Narrows that would provide the necessary land defense.

Unfortunately, Fort Lafayette no longer exists. In its place stands the eastern upright of the Verrazano Narrows Bridge, using the foundation of the fort in the support of the bridge.

Fort Schuyler

As the Long Island Sound narrowed to become the East River, it turned from south to west around a point of land originally known as Frogg's Neck. Crowning the tip of this peninsula, now known as Throgg's Neck, was Fort Schuyler, begun in 1833 and completed in 1856.

Fort Schuyler (pronounced SKY lur) was an irregular, five-sided fort, shaped like a truncated hexagon whose parallel sides had been "flared" as they proceeded to the gorge wall. There were bastions at the junction of each of the fronts, but only demibastions protecting the gorge. Behind the gorge stood a classic hornwork.

The fort had significant land-defense capability as well as providing significant firepower on the channel. The four seacoast fronts were designed to follow a ship with cannon fire as it proceeded southward down the East river, made the turn to the west, then angled northwest to continue along the channel. This created a situation where the ship was under the guns of the fort for an incredible length of time.

Controlling the traffic though the channel were 312 guns mounted on three tiers. The casemates were extremely large, arched chambers, with a wooden deck dividing the two tiers of guns. This design, mounting four guns per casemate, was shared only with Fort McRee in Pensacola, Florida and nearby Fort Adams in Newport, Rhode Island. The guns of the

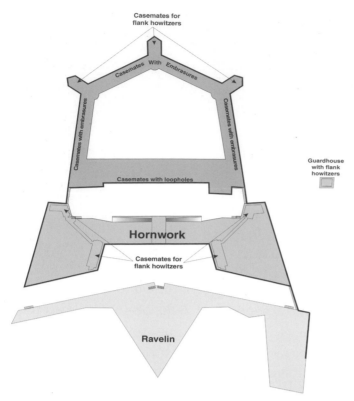

Casemates for
flank howitzers

Casemates With Embrasures

Casemates with embrasures

Casemates with embrasures

Casemates with loopholes

Guardhouse
with flank
howitzers

Hornwork

Casemates for
flank howitzers

Ravelin

Figure 89: Fort Schuyler's location on a narrow neck of land - Throgg's Neck - allowed only one land approach to the fort. This approach was well defended by an earth-and-masonry ravelin, a massive masonry hornwork, and the gorge main fort. It is interesting to note that the hornwork had flanking casemates not only on the front, defending the outer ditch, but also on the rear to assist in the defense of the inner ditch.

third tier were mounted en barbette. The bastions on the seacoast fronts were long and narrow, mounting two howitzers per tier in the flanks and one heavy gun per tier at the salient.

The landward side of the fort was considered the most vulnerable. There were many locations that a land force could be put ashore before the fort was reached, and this force would stand more of a chance against the fort than ships would. For this reason, the landward defenses of the fort were considerable.

The passageway to the fort was well defined, as the land narrowed to a small spit before widening at the tip where the fort stood. The gorge of the fort, facing this spit, was protected by the two demibastions, with flank howitzers, and a dry ditch. In addition to the howitzer embrasures, loopholes for riflemen penetrated the gorge wall and the faces of the demibastions.

Beyond this ditch stood a massive hornwork, with two bastions protecting its curtain. The rear of these bastions protruded behind the rear wall of the hornwork and the flanks were equipped with loopholes. The faces of these protrusions, actually the flank of the bastion, contained howitzer embrasures sweeping the side of the fort. Tunnels within the hornwork connected the various gun positions. These tunnels were accessed through a postern to the ditch in the rear of the hornwork.

Toward the fort from the howitzer embrasures in the hornwork were walls closing the interior ditch between the fort and the hornwork. These walls had embrasures where howitzers or field guns within the ditch could provide further defense. An arched opening, closed by massive two-layer oak doors with iron studs, provided access to the ditch and the main sally port.

The flanks on the landward side of the bastions of the hornwork were casemated for four howitzers per bastion, opening into an

Figure 90: Three tiers of cannon were emplaced on each of the seacoast fronts of Fort Schyler. The unique location of the fort caused ships to traverse three sides of the fort on their way through Hell Gate. *(Photo by author)*

Figure 91: Fort Schuyler's location out into the passageway known as Hell Gate allows forward fire on approaching ships, broadside fire as the ships turn to go around the peninsula, then rear fire on any ship fortunate enough to pass the fort. *(Photo courtesy NARA)*

outer ditch, also closed at each end. The entire top of this hornwork was built with a parapet where both artillery and riflemen could discourage the approach of an enemy. Stairways and a ramp provided communication between the ditch and the hornwork.

Beyond the hornwork was the outer ditch with a masonry counterscarp and outworks, including a covert way and a large ravelin. A stairway behind the ravelin provided access to these outworks. From the parapet of the outworks, a long glacis sloped toward the narrow isthmus. To the west of the fort, along the sea wall, a small redoubt mounted howitzers to prevent an approach outside the sea wall, flanking the outworks.

Today Fort Schuyler has been adapted for use by the State University of New York Maritime College, and it also houses a maritime museum. It is a very pleasant location to visit, and the flavor of the fort definitely shows through the interior modifications. The fort's exterior is in very good condition, and one can imagine the cannon projecting from the now-closed em-

brasures. All of the hornwork and most of the other outworks remain, which is rare among Third System forts.

Fort Schuyler is located at the Bronx terminus of the Throgg's Neck Bridge. From the exit just north of the bridge, proceed south to the entrance of the SUNY Maritime College. Continue south to the fort. The entrance to the museum is from the parade of the fort.

Fort Totten

The Third System Fort on Willett's Point, immediately opposite Fort Schuyler on Throgg's Neck, was not completed and was never officially named. During a later period, the entire reservation was named Fort Totten, in honor of General Joseph G. Totten, and the name has been applied to the Third System work as well. For clarity, the name Fort Totten will be used to refer to the Third System fort. It must be noted, however, that the Third System fort – begun in 1863 and never completed – was simply the Fort on Willett's Point.

Figure 92: Fort Totten as seen from Fort Schyler, across Hell Gate. Only the primary seacoast fronts of what was to be a massive fort were constructed, and even those were not completed. *(Photo by author)*

Fort Totten was designed as an irregular pentagon, with two seacoast fronts and three gorge walls. The two seacoast fronts had a relatively shallow angle, and were divided by an abbreviated bastion. Moderate-sized bastions were to be located at the other four corners. While all five walls were to be casemated, only the seacoast fronts were to have embrasures.

The seacoast front was to have four tiers of casemates, while the landward sides of the fort, sloping up a hill from the shore, were to have two tiers. This would keep the top of the ramparts level, but the height of the wall would vary with the level of the surrounding terrain.

The land defenses of the fort were to be secondary to the seacoast fronts. The scarp wall would be half the height of the seacoast scarp, but even this 22-foot granite wall would provide a substantial barrier to an invader. Medium-sized bastions on each corner were to provide howitzer embrasures to wash the walls, and barbette guns would provide counterfire against attacking siege guns. Additionally, a ditch with a substantial covert way and three ravelins would supplement the defenses provided by the main work.

The casemates of the landward side of the fort were to be used as quarters and storage areas. These areas were to be the primary support for the massive water battery, and would house the considerable munitions and stores required by a fort of this size.

The primary mission of the fort was to be seacoast defense. Four tiers of heavy guns were designed to line the two seacoast fronts, with a total of 68 cannon. The latest technology was to be used, with the entire fort constructed of granite. Totten embrasures with iron throats would have provided a wide angle of fire, and Totten shutters closed the embrasures between firings. Iron reinforcement on the outside of the embrasure protected the corners of the granite.

The four tiers were to be joined by a central spiral staircase. On each level, a magazine was

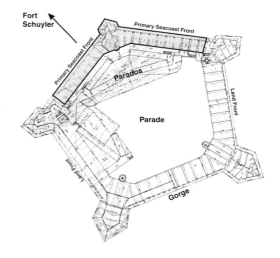

Figure 93: The plan of Fort Totten is shown in the above drawing. Note that the indicated areas at the top of the drawing are the only portions of the fort that were constructed. *(Drawing courtesy NARA)*

110

Figure 94: The construction of the massive stone arches of the first tier of casemates for Fort Totten is shown in this period photograph. *(Photo courtesy NARA)*

to be sheltered by the staircase on the rear and the small bastion on the front. Square stair towers, again sheltering a magazine, were to be provided at the medium-sized bastions abutting the seacoast fronts. A large parados was located behind the seacoast fronts, sheltering the casemates from the rear. This unique arrangement would have provided rearward protection to the casemates while allowing good ventilation for the gun crews and easy communication through the road dividing the place d'armes from the casemates. The retaining wall and two stairways of this place-of-arms still remain.

Construction of the fort was never completed. Only the seacoast portion of the fort was built: two curtains joined by a central bastion. The first tier of casemates was completed and made ready to receive its armament, and the second tier, partially constructed, was modified to receive guns which would fire through embrasures but would not have the overhead protection of a casemate. Construction had begun in 1863, and ceased only 18 months later.

Today the fort is inaccessible to the public, but the exterior can be viewed from Fort Schuyler across the channel and from the nearby Throgg's Neck Bridge. Special tours of the fort are given periodically.

Fort Hamilton

Guarding The Narrows at the entrance to the Inner Harbor on the Brooklyn side stands the remains of Fort Hamilton. This fort was a dual-purpose fort, supplying barbette-mounted cannon for defense of the channel and the primary land defenses for Fort Lafayette below. Construction began in 1825 and the fort was completed in 1831.

The principal mission for the fort was to prevent a siege of the seacoast forts Lafayette and Richmond from the high ground on the Long Island side of the channel. There was a concern that an invading force could land somewhere on Long Island and move overland to assault the forts guarding the Narrows. The relatively small Fort Hamilton was charged with preventing such an assault.

The trapezoidal Fort Hamilton was a small, unbastioned work surrounded on three sides by a dry ditch. The fourth side of the fort – the seacoast front – opened on the steep embankment that led down to the water.

Figure 95: This view of the partially completed seacoast casemates of Fort Totten is taken from the now-tree-covered parados. Note that little progress was made between the construction photograph on the previous page and this current-day photograph. *(Photo by author)*

111

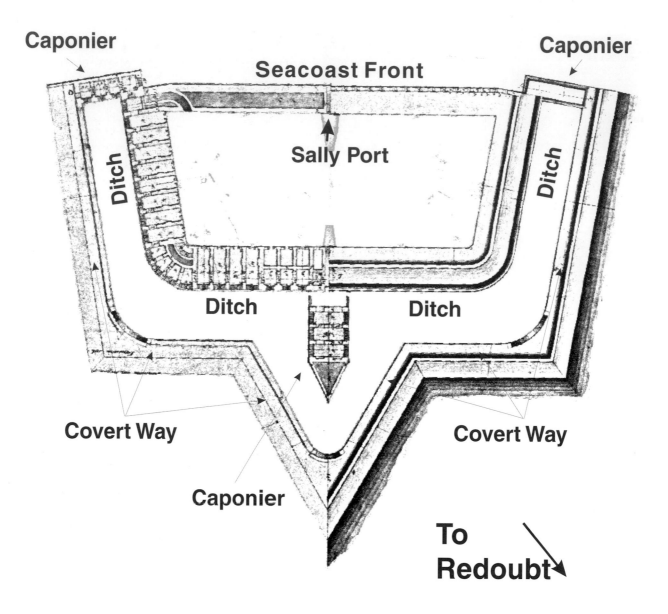

Figure 96: Support of Fort Lafayette was the primary mission of Fort Hamilton, which controlled the high ground on the Brooklyn side of The Narrows. Extensive land defenses on three fronts and two tiers of seacoast cannon on the side facing the older fort combine to that end. *(Drawing courtesy NARA)*

To the landward, casemate embrasures were each flanked by two loopholes, providing both cannon and small-arms defense. Above was a tier of barbette guns providing additional support against a land attack.

In the ditch, at the midpoint of the landward face, stood a relatively large caponier. This structure, with loopholes and howitzer embrasures, provided the principle defense of the ditch. Beyond the caponier were the covered way and parapet of the outworks, angled to appear similar to a ravelin.

Beyond the glacis stood a square redoubt as the first defense against an attacking enemy. This redoubt had counterscarp galleries in each corner, with howitzer embrasures designed to protect its ditch.

The seacoast defenses of the fort consisted of a tier of barbette guns and one tier of casemated guns. It is interesting to note that the main sally port of the fort opened from the sea-

Figure 97: The entire seacoast front and portions of two land fronts have been removed from Fort Hamilton, as shown in the above photograph. The remaining portions of the main work have been extensively modified during later periods of use. Only the caponier, shown to the right of the photograph, and portions of the outworks remain in their original condition. *(Photo courtesy Terrance McGovern)*

coast front rather than the gorge. This certainly shows that the principal mission of the fort was land defense.

Today, the caponier stands as the only unmodified portion of the fort. It houses a very nice museum, and gives the viewer a sense of the harbor defenses of New York through the ages. This caponier and the caponier at Fort Washington, Maryland, are the only preserved caponiers of the Third System remaining.[1]

Figure 99: Both the interior and exterior of the Fort Hamilton caponier are well preserved, the former holding the fort museum. Shown here is a flank howitzer in position to defend the ditch. *(Photo by author)*

Unfortunately, the entire seacoast front of the fort was removed during later periods of construction. Also gone are significant portions of the two secondary fronts. The remaining portions of the fort show many of the original features, but one must look beneath the modifications to the structure that were performed for its more modern uses. A stroll through the dining room, however, requires little imagination to picture the windows as embrasures and cannon defending this vital point on the approaches to New York. In front of the fort is a 20-inch Rodman cannon, one of two still in existence.[2]

Figure 98: Although a roof has been added over the parapet and barbette tier of Fort Hamiton, the masonry scarp and embrasures remain. *(Photo by author)*

Fort Hamilton can be reached by taking the 92nd Street exit on the Brooklyn side of the Verrazano Narrows Bridge. Turn right on Battery Avenue and follow it to the entrance of the Fort Hamilton reservation. Proceed back toward the bridge to reach the old fort.

Fort Richmond

The small but mighty Fort Richmond guarded the Staten Island shore of The Narrows, now dwarfed by the Verrazano Narrows Bridge overhead. Before the bridge was constructed, however, the 67-foot-tall granite walls dominated

113

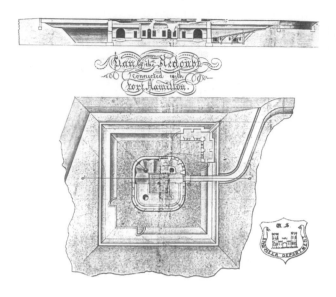

older work also named Fort Richmond, leads to a significant amount of confusion in identifying the structure. Construction of the fort began in 1847, and ended in 1864 with the fort esssentially complete.

The four-sided, truncated hexagon sported three tiers of casemates with a fourth barbette tier of cannon above. Each of the channel fronts were 286 feet, with the gorge wall being 450 feet. At each of the corners stood a small bastion, and behind that a circular stair tower joined the tiers. This design provided for 116 cannon to bear on the channel, with a further 24 howitzers for land defense.

The principal mission of the fort was seacoast defense, and it was well equipped to accomplish that mission. Standing on a point adjacent to the channel, all 116 heavy guns could fire on a ship directly opposite the fort. Before and after that time, guns from the two secondary fronts could provide additional fire.

The landward defenses of the fort were minimal. A ditch with drawbridge provided protection from a coup de main, along with the loopholed gorge wall and the flanking bastions with their howitzer embrasures. The high ground behind the fort, however, would make

this passageway. The fort was named Battery Weed during later periods, and is part of the Fort Wadsworth military reservation. This variety of names, coupled with the fact that it replaced an

Figure 101: The formidable Fort Richmond stands at water level with its four tiers of cannon on three fronts. Immediately above this work is the seacoast front of Fort Tompkins, supplimenting Fort Richmond's firepower and, more importantly, guarding the land approach and high ground above the massive shoreline fort. *(Photo by author)*

withstanding a siege virtually impossible, and the fort had to depend on Fort Tompkins to protect its rear.

The gorge wall of the fort was not casemated, but it did provide loopholes. The main sally port, the only entrance into the fort, was guarded by a two-story, pitched-roof guardhouse. This guardhouse provided flanking fire on the sally port and a protected area for the sentries.

While a number of soldiers could camp on the parade or arrange temporary quarters in the casemates, the fort was not intended to house its garrison. Quarters would be provided by nearby Fort Tompkins, or by out buildings on the site.

The two most remarkable features of the fort were its vertical scale and its magnificent granite work. It exists essentially intact today, as if the garrison had just moved out. It is an excellent example of the late-Third-System tower forts that emphasized seacoast defense over land defense. The National Park Service has taken over management of this property, and the fort is open to the public. It can also be viewed from the Brooklyn side of The Narrows, particularly from Fort Hamilton and from the Verrazano Bridge, passing above the fort.

Fort Richmond is reached by taking the first exit on the Staten Island side of the Verrazano Narrows Bridge, Tompkins Avenue. Proceed south on Lilly Pond Avenue to Richmond Avenue. Turn left and enter the Golden Gate National Recreation Area. Park in the lot, and proceed down the hill to reach Fort Richmond at the water's edge.

Fort Tompkins

On the ridge overlooking Fort Richmond stood Fort Tompkins, the land-defense fort on the Staten Island side of The Narrows. Replacing a Second System fort with the same name and modified for other uses during later periods, Fort Tompkins now stands as an empty sentinel alongside the Verrazano Narrows Bridge. Construction on the existing fort began in 1847.

Fort Tompkins was an irregular, five-sided work with two levels of casemates but with no embrasures. The only seacoast cannon were to be mounted en barbette on the third tier of the fort.

Figure 102: Looking down at Fort Richmond from Fort Tompkins both points out the massive character of the former work and the importance of the defensive mission of the latter. The gorge wall of Fort Richmond merely encloses the work, with only token defensive capablity provided by flanking howitzers in the demibastions. *(Photo by author)*

Figure 103: This view of the interior of Fort Tompkins shows the large amount of area dedicated to barracks. These accomodations were designed to hold both the garrison of Fort Tompkins and the garrison of Fort Richmond, the latter having no barracks. *(Photo by author)*

The seacoast front was the longest face of the fort, originally designed with a caponier at its midpoint. This front, facing a steep slope to the flats along the shore, was the least likely to experience a land attack and accordingly had minimal defenses. Forward fire from this front was provided through loopholes opening from the first tier of casemates. The masonry wall extended only a short distance above these casemates, then an earthen slope angled all the way to the parapet of the barbette tier. Behind this earthen slope were the casemates of the second tier, used only for quarters and storage.

The design of this front was modified prior to the construction of the fort. The caponier was eliminated, and the counterscarp galleries were extended beyond the front to act as demibastions sweeping this curtain.

The main armament of this front was to be a battery of seacoast guns mounted en barbette. Protected by the long earthen slope, these barbette guns were separated by brick-faced traverses that also contained day-use magazines. They faced the portion of The Narrows where the Verrazano Bridge now stands.

The remaining four sides of the fort were much more vulnerable to land attack, and there-fore were better equipped for defense. The counterscarp walls, almost as tall as the walls of the fort, provided a significant barrier for attacking troops. Two levels of casemates opened into the ditch with loopholes, and a full counterscarp gallery provided a cross fire with the fort. Two corners of the gallery were equipped with howitzer embrasures, with each corner washing two walls.

Access to the counterscarp galleries was through a passageway at each end of the seacoast front. This passageway also closed the ditch on the seacoast side of the fort. Posterns at each end provided communication to the ditch. Two circular stair towers provided communication between tiers, as did iron stairways from the parade.

A principal function of Fort Tompkins was the quartering of the garrison of Fort Richmond as well as its own garrison. For this reason, both tiers of casemates along all five sides of the fort contained quarters. Iron balconies circled the parade on both upper tiers, and the impressive granite interior facade must have made the piazza a very pleasant place. The beautiful views of the entrance to New York's Inner Harbor would have added to the splendor of the fort.

Figure 104: This aerial photograph, taken prior to the construction of the Verrazano Narrows Bridge, shows the relative positioning of Fort Tompkins and Fort Richmond, as well as the general shape of the two forts. *(Photo courtesy NARA)*

Today, the fort is open to the public. While the areas that can be visited are limited due to safety concerns, the National Park Service is stabilizing the structure and hopes that soon more areas will be available to the public. It is a part of the Gateway National Recreation Area, and has a nice museum and bookstore.

Fort Tompkins is reached by taking the first exit on the Staten Island side of the Verrazano Narrows Bridge, Tompkins Avenue. Proceed south on Lilly Pond Avenue to Richmond Avenue. Turn left and enter the Gateway National Recreation Area. Park in the lot, and walk along the crest of the ridge to reach Fort Tompkins.

Fort Hancock

The "Fort on Sandy Hook" was not named during the Third System, but later works at that location were last named Fort Hancock. For reasons of convenience, the name Fort Hancock will be used to describe the Third System work; please be indulgent.

One might question the wisdom of the construction of a fort on the lonely peninsula referred to as the Sandy Hook. The guns of that day could certainly not control the miles of water comprising the entrance to the Outer Harbor, and one would have to dig deeply to think of a reason why an invader would wish to occupy the barren regions on the north shore of New Jersey.

Construction of this fort was, however, very logical. First, a very real fear was that an enemy fleet could blockade the entrance to New York Harbor, cutting off the largest commercial center in the country. The presence of a fort on the Sandy Hook inhibited an enemy from closing that channel, and gave a strong point where ships could find respite under the fort's guns.

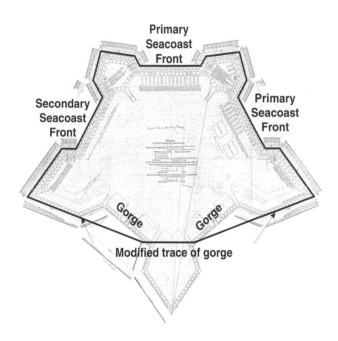

Primary
Seacoast
Front

Secondary
Seacoast
Front

Primary
Seacoast
Front

Gorge   Gorge

Modified trace of gorge

Figure 105: The very large fort at the tip of the Sandy Hook was modified during construction to lessen time-to-completion and cost. The gorge wall was closed with a simple trace, eliminating the flanks of two bastions and eliminating a third bastion altogether. *(Drawing courtesy of NARA)*

The fort also closed the harbor to a fleet wishing to find shelter from the temperamental Atlantic Ocean by hiding behind this spit of sand. Finally, the guns of the fort did control the deepest and most favorable entrance to the channel, and this passage would be denied to an enemy.[3]

The original plans for the defense of the Sandy Hook called for the construction of two tower forts, but eventually a single, much larger fort was constructed. This massive structure, designed by then-Captain Robert E. Lee, was to have a perimeter of more than three-quarters of

a mile. In addition to the massive fort itself, two masonry ravelins were to sit across the ditch, connected to the main work by bridges. Construction began in 1859, and was halted in 1867 with the fort in a defensible condition.

The fort was a five-sided irregular pentagon, with large, open bastions on each corner. The longest curtain wall was the primary seacoast front, facing the channel. This 320-ft curtain was designed to mount 16 guns en casemate and another 16 guns en barbette. The bastions on either side of the curtain were designed to mount a further 39 guns each. The adjacent curtains were designed for 26 guns each, with the seacoast face of the two large bastions mounting 25 guns each. This gave 173 guns to bear on the channel.

The non-seacoast faces of the two large bastions and both faces of the large gorge bastion were not casemated, but were to mount a further 35 guns. The four remaining guns were to be mounted to cover the bridges from the ravelins.

The ravelins were to be located on the landward side of the fort, up the narrow land passage. They were not to be casemated, but were to mount five guns each, en barbette. The bulk of the ravelin was to be made up of a banquette for small-arms fire. Between the ravelin and the fort, in the ditch, was to be a structure assumed to be a tenaille. It was not casemated, however, but a structure with a parapet guarding the bridge to the ravelin.

Beyond the ravelins was to be a ditch, with substantial outworks beyond. These outworks

Figure 106: This panoramic photograph shows Fort Hancock during its construction. Unfortunately, photographs and a small section of scarp wall are all that are left to envision this impressive fort. *(Photo courtesy USNPS)*

Figure 107: Only a small section of scarp with four embrasures remain of the once-mighty Fort Hancock. *(Photo by author)*

were to consist of a covert way with traverses, a banquette, parapet, and glacis. The outworks ended at the seacoast fronts that were protected by only a ditch.

Construction on this massive fort was never completed. The scarp of the seacoast bastion, the two primary curtains, and the seacoast portions of the two secondary bastions were raised well above the embrasures, and pintles and traverses were set for the mounting of the fort's cannon. Only the foundations and a few tiers of stone were completed on the two gorge walls and the gorge bastion.

At this point, a significant modification in design was made. Not only were the masonry ravelins scrapped, but the gorge bastion was also eliminated from the design. The rear of the fort was designed to follow a line that extended the curtain wall to intersect the face of the secondary bastions, and to the flanks of the gorge bastion. Another short curtain joined this curtain across the throat of the gorge bastion. These three curtains contained neither loopholes nor embrasures, but were simply earth-backed stone walls with a banquette providing the only rear defense.

In this way, the gorge of the fort was closed at minimum expense. While these modifications caused some of the foundation work and a little of the masonry to be wasted, most of the structure at the rear of the fort was used in the modified design, and the cost and time of construction were greatly reduced.

Today little is left of the uncompleted fort. A small portion of a scarp wall remains, complete with Totten embrasures and shutters. Beyond this portion of wall are two brick-arched structures below the level of the casemate floors. Also remaining is the salient of the gorge bastion, now the base for a water tower. Portions of the scarp wall can also be found in the structure of the nine-gun battery that was constructed during the Endicott period.

The fort is part of the Sandy Hook Unit of the Gateway National Recreation Area. Information on the old fort can be obtained from certain rangers, but the Third System period is not formally interpreted. An excellent photograph of the fort during its construction hangs on the wall of the museum.

Fort Hancock can be reached by taking exit 117 off the Garden State Parkway, State Route 36. Follow State Route 36 East until you reach Ocean Avenue, and take the exit to the Sandy Hook Unit of the Gateway National Recreation Area. Follow the road north until it ends. The remains of the fort are north of the parking lot, west of the concrete gun battery.

Notes

[1]Some caponiers of Fort Caswell on the Cape Fear River in North Carolina still exist, but are buried in sand. The caponier of Fort Washington on the Potomac River in Maryland is also in good condition. While Fort Washington is a transitional fort, the caponier was designed and built during the Third System.

[2]The other massive 20-inch Rodman cannon stands on the site of the Fort at Sandy Hook in the Sandy Hook Unit of Gateway National Recreational Area. These massive guns were among the largest muzzle-loading cannon ever built. Some records show that four were built.

[3]This main channel was the only channel available to deep-draft ships in the early nineteenth century.

119

The Defenses of the Mid-Atlantic Coast

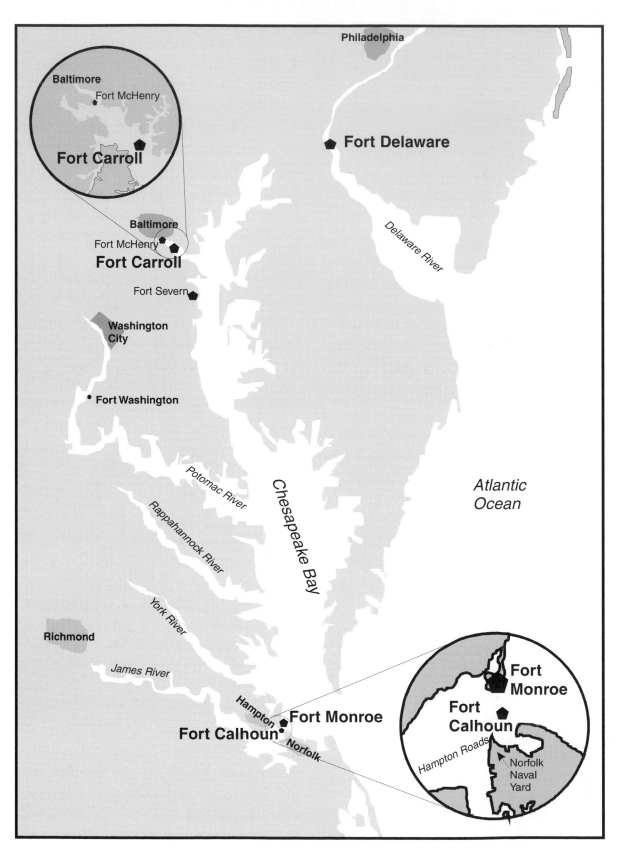

History

The defense of the middle portion of the Atlantic Coast, from New York City to Hampton Roads, was critical to the safety of the nation. The principal cities of Philadelphia, Baltimore, Richmond, and Norfolk, as well as the nations capital, were in this region. It was also the largest population center of the nation outside of New England. For these reasons, the Coastal Fortifications Board examined its defensive needs closely.

Two major bays joined these critical areas to the Atlantic: Delaware Bay and Chesapeake Bay. While the control of these bays would provide adequate defense to all of the principal cities, the bays themselves were too wide to be adequately defended by the short-range coastal guns of the day. Therefore, forts would need to be constructed closer to the cities.

Three of the most important cities already had defenses. Fort Mifflin, a First System masonry fort, guarded Philadelphia from very near the city. This fort was quite old and had minimal defenses, but a more modern fort, Fort Delaware, was under construction downstream in the Delaware River. This Transitional[1] fort was to provide Philadelphia's primary defense.

Annapolis was a principal city on the upper Chesapeake, and was defended by two older forts, Fort Severn and Fort Madison. Fort Severn had a circular scarp with an octagonal citadel, while Fort Madison was a of a trace common in the Second System – semicircular water battery with bastions and demibastions to landward.

Baltimore was defended by the famous Fort McHenry, which had just resisted a determined British invasion. Not only was Baltimore *considered* secure; its security had been *proven* in the recent war. Our National Anthem was written in tribute to the successful defense of the city provided by Fort McHenry.

Washington City was defended by Fort Washington, which was being replaced with a Transitional fort, following the destruction of the older fort by its garrison. This new fort was ideally located to provide an adequate defense of the capital.

The only defenses in the Hampton Roads area were provided by Fort Norfolk, a Second System fort located in the city of Norfolk. Its location was specific to the defense of Norfolk, leaving most of the roadstead virtually defenseless.

Hampton Roads provided access to the largest natural harbor in the country, and the area had become the most important seaport on the portion of the East Coast south of New York City. In addition to its own value, the roadstead controlled the entrance to the James River and the principal city of Richmond, the Elizabeth River and its tributaries, and the Nansemond River. It even had significant influence on the Chesapeake Bay. While it was well understood that no fort could control the wide entrance to the Chesapeake, a powerful fort could shelter a fleet that could easily control this vital bay.

Third System Strategy

Hampton Roads was the area where the Coastal Fortifications Board concentrated its efforts. At the beginning of the Third System, two powerful forts were designed to protect this crucial area, and construction began a short time later. Fort Monroe, the largest fort in the Western Hemisphere, guarded the northern shore of the roadstead and provided some control over the mouth of the Chesapeake. Fort Calhoun[2] sat on the southern side of the channel on an artificial island created solely to hold the fort. Together they were designed to mount some 600 guns to control this critical area.

Fort Washington, on the Potomac just south of Washington City, was being constructed when Bernard came to America. While pleased with

121

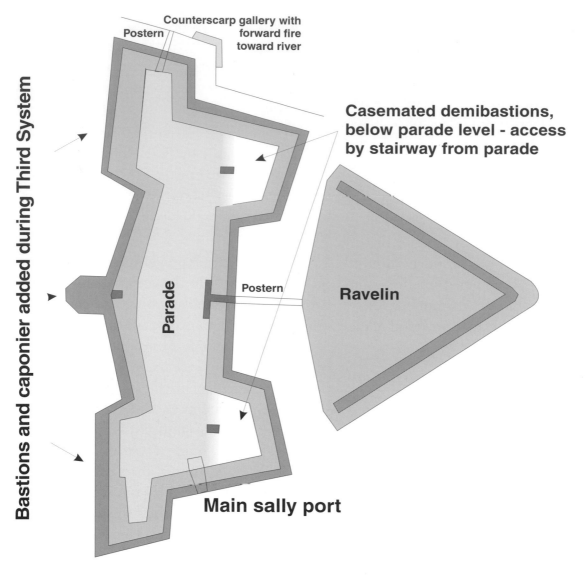

Figure 108: Fort Washington, Maryland, was designed and construction began prior to the Third System. The basic design was by L'Enfant, but Bernard was unhappy with the lack of land defenses to the rear of the fort (left in the above sketch). He added the two bastions and caponier during the Third System, and made some overall modifications to the scarp of the fort.

portions of the L'Enfant design, he made some rather dramatic changes to the design of the gorge. Thus, the transitional fort had very significant Third System characteristics.

The construction of Fort Delaware, protecting the approach to Philadelphia, did not go well. The problems were blamed on the incompetence of the superintending engineer, who was replaced and subsequently court-martialed. His replacements, therefore, were left with a poorly constructed foundation and scarp. It appeared that nothing could be done to rectify the problems,

and work was suspended indefinitely.

Mercifully, a fire broke out in the fort, destroying most of the unfinished structure. This provided the impetus to tear down the useless hulk and construct a modern Third System fort. Retaining the same name, but with a completely different design, construction of the new Fort Delaware began in 1847.

That same year, work began on a new fort to protect Baltimore. Advances in artillery had made Fort McHenry too close to the city to provide an adequate defense. Fort Carroll was begun on an artificial island at the entrance to the lower harbor, and was to mount many more cannon than Fort McHenry.

Fort Severn received minor updates, while Fort Madison was replaced with a closed barbette battery mounting 21 guns.

Thus designed, the mid-Atlantic coast was defended by four newly constructed Third System forts and one transitional fort. These forts controlled the water approach to each of the major cities in the area, as well as the mouths of the principal rivers that provided interior communication. While modest in number, these four forts were some of the most powerful of the Third System.

Fort Washington

The fall of Fort Washington and the burning of the nation's capital during the War of 1812 was a significant embarrassment for the American military. Congress, meeting in temporary quarters and many living in temporary housing, developed a "never again" mindset, immediately appropriating money to rebuild the fort to ensure the defense of the city. A new Fort Washington was designed by Pierre L'Enfant, and construction began shortly after the end of the war. Since this was prior to Bernard's coming to America and the formation of the Coastal Fortifications Board, this fort was not considered a Third System fort. Bernard and Totten both put Fort Washington into the category of "older works to be included" on either a temporary or long-term basis. Falling between the Second and Third System, it is labeled a Transitional fort.

Bernard, however, significantly influenced the final design of the fort. Unhappy with the lack of defenses to the rear of the fort, he added bastions to the rear curtain and designed an impressive multi-level caponier located midway between the bastions. Additionally, Bernard increased the height of the scarp, and modified the gun positions to accommodate the larger cannon that had then been developed.

Fort Washington was a rectangle, with its long sides roughly parallel to the Potomac River. Large bastions to the rear of the fort and even larger demibastions toward the river dominated

Figure 109: The seacoast front of Fort Washington consists of two very large demibastions with a curtain between. All three faces were casemated for seacoast cannon, as shown in the above photograph. A postern in the center of the curtain leads to the ravelin, modified in later periods, that was in advance of the fort, toward the Potomac River. *(Photo by author)*

Figure 110: The sally port and landward front of Fort Washington is shown in the above photograph. In addition to forward fire from the ramparts, the bastion to the left provided enfilading fire to this curtain. Deterioration of the scarp wall can be seen to the right of the sally port - stabilization funds are desparately needed or this historic landmark will be lost. *(Photo by author)*

the trace – the faces of the demibastions were longer than the curtain between them.

Control of the Potomac River was provided by casemates that covered the entire river front, including the faces of the demibastions. This design resulted in two tiers of cannon down the entire length of this front.

Complementing this firepower was a large ravelin, located in advance of the fort and down the hillside. The location of the ravelin allowed cannon to fire on ships well before they were within view of the fort. The ravelin, designed as a closed-back inverted V, had a sally port midway down the upstream leg of the V.

The land defenses of the fort were unique to Fort Washington. While the bastions were of the classic trace, they were not casemated – only top of the ramparts would provide for rifle and cannon fire. The downstream bastion face and the curtain had an earthen scarp, albeit steeply sloped, while the upstream bastion face and both bastion flanks had a masonry scarp.

The caponier was also of a unique design. Entered from the parade of the fort by descending either of two facing stairways and proceeding down a tunnel under the ramparts, the caponier extended slightly beyond the faces of the bastions. In the classic style, it provided how-

itzer positions to defend the curtain and bastions, but also provided rifle positions at its extreme that could provide either enfilading or forward fire.

From the ramparts of the fort, defenders could enter the barbette tier of the caponier that provided a banquette for the defense of the curtain as well as forward fire into and across the valley behind the fort.

The two short fronts were defended by the flanks of the bastions, again not casemated, with the downstream front also defended by a counterscarp gallery. Entered from the ditch across from a postern, this gallery provided reverse and enfilading fire along the fort, as well as forward fire toward the river.

Fort Washington is open to the public, and well managed by the National Park Service. A small museum and bookstore is supplemented by knowledgeable park rangers and costumed interpreters who give tours and provide detailed information on the fort.

Fort Washington is located south of Washington, D.C. Take the Indian Head Highway exit off 495, just east of the Potomac River bridge. Continue south to Fort Washington Road. Turn west, and follow the road to its end. Enter the park and continue to the end of the park road. The fort and visitor center are just beyond the parking area.

Fort Delaware

With the devastation of the original (1815) Fort Delaware by a fire, the damage compounding construction flaws, a new fort was needed to defend Philadelphia. The new (1833) Fort Delaware, located at approximately the same site on Pea Patch Island, was a well-designed, powerful replacement for the former fort bearing this name.

Fort Delaware was an irregular five-sided work, and could be described as a regular penta-

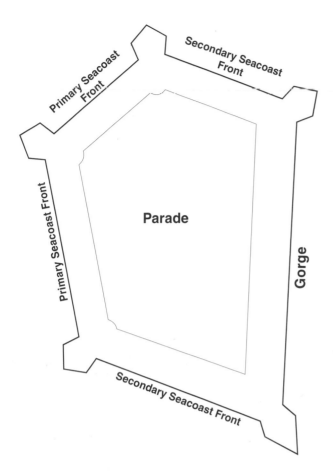

Figure 111: Fort Delaware was an irregular work designed to make the best use of the tip of Pea Patch Island. The relatively short curtains were offset by the three tiers of cannon.

gon that had been skewed to one side. The angles of the walls were defined to bring the maximum number of cannon to bear on the two channels leading up the Delaware River. A granite scarp wall surrounded the all-brick ramparts and interior.

The fort had four seacoast fronts and one gorge wall. The two longest seacoast fronts bore on the primary channel and the two shorter seacoast fronts bore on the shallower west channel. Together, these fronts were capable of mounting 123 heavy guns. Another fifteen heavy guns were to be located in the bastions - including positions at the salients — and the typical barbette mounts above. Eleven more cannon were to be located on the gorge

wall barbette, and twenty howitzer positions were located in casemates in the flanks of the bastions, sweeping the walls of the fort.

The gorge wall, the longest wall of the fort, boasted 68 loopholes for small-arms fire as well as the eleven gun positions on the barbette. The center of the gorge contained the sally port, opening to a drawbridge over the moat. The moat surrounded the perimeter of the fort, and had a tide gate to control its water level. This tide gate opened into a granite-faced canal that connected to the Delaware River.

The original design called for a large, two-story barracks building along the length of the gorge wall, but two separate, three-story buildings were actually constructed. While the rooflines of these buildings extended higher than the perimeter walls, they were designed such that they would not interfere with the barbette-tier gun positions.

These barracks buildings were beautifully constructed, with numerous large windows. The original designs called for ornate iron balconies and open stairways joining the floors, but it is not known if these were ever constructed. Whether or not the balconies were in place, these barracks must have been some of the most pleasant in the Third System.

Figure 112: The gorge of Fort Delaware traded embrasures for loopholes on the two casemated tiers, with the barbette mounting cannon to combat a siege. Note that the salients of the bastions had embrasures on the second tier. *(Photo by author)*

Figure 113: The seacoast fronts of Fort Delaware had three tiers of guns - two casemated tiers and the barbette tier. The indentations in the top of the wall made attacking ships beileve that there was an additional tier of embrasures. *(Photo by author)*

Today, Fort Delaware is well managed by the Delaware Park Commission. There is a ferry from Delaware City that provides access to Pea Patch Island, and it is also accessible by private boat. A well-informed staff and summertime re-enactors complement the views of the fort. A very nice gift shop stocks a variety of historical books and souvenirs. The very large number of people who visit the fort annually is a tribute to the quality of the programs provided.

Fort Carroll

The channel into Baltimore Harbor passed between two points of land as the Patapsco River became Baltimore Harbor. These points, about two miles apart, are now spanned by the Francis Scott Key Bridge. When constrcution began in 1847, however, this was simply a narrows well below the city.

It is in this narrows, on Soller's Point Flat, that the Coastal Fortifications Board decided to put the fort that would continue the function that Fort McHenry had performed so well. By this time artillery had progressed to such a level that Fort McHenry could no longer prevent ships from shelling Baltimore, as that city had grown southward to meet the area of the fort. A more modern and more heavily armed fort was needed, and it needed to be located well southeast of the city. Fort McHenry would then provide a secondary defense should ships be able to run past the guns of the new fort.

Fort Carroll, constructed on an artificial island on the shoal, was as close to a regular hexa-

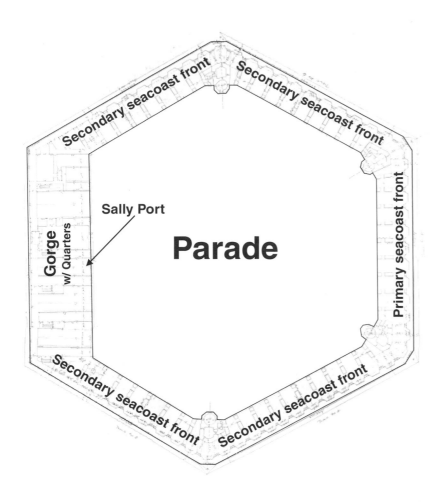

Figure 114: Fort Carroll was built on an artificial island in the shape of a regular hexagon. The gorge of the fort, containing quarters, was significantly thicker than the casemated fronts that did not contain quarters. *(Sketch based on NARA drawing)*

bility of mounting 225 guns on four tiers. This tower fort, similar in section (but not in plan) to Fort Delaware, was to be one of the more powerful of Third System forts. The choice of its location, however, is ironic. Built farther from the city than Fort McHenry to provide better protection against "modern" artillery, it was rendered obsolete before it was built by still-longer-range artillery. For this reason, construction was halted before the fort was completed.

Being a fort located on an island precisely the size of the fort, there was no need for land defenses. The only defenses against a land-based attack were those facing the granite wharf opposite the gorge. The entire gorge wall was designed with tall, narrow windows to provide ventilation to the barracks area. Their shape allowed them to be closed as loopholes should this become necessary. Two of these windows were modified to receive cannon. These windows, on either side of the sally port, were fitted with granite-and-iron Totten embrasures, complete with Totten shutters. The windows were allowed to continue intact above the embrasure, thus minimizing the impact on the ventilation of the room.

The only other concession to defense against a coup de main was the drawbridge between the wharf and the sally port. The sally port itself contained no loopholed guardrooms, and as previously mentioned, no bastions or demibastions provided flanking fire. Even though the windows of the gorge were large enough for a per-

gon as practical, with only hundredths of a foot variation in the length of the sides.[3] It was not bastioned, and contained no citadel. It was a very simple yet effective design, embodying the concepts used in the late Third System. Very similar in design to Fort Sumter (but with one more tier of guns), it was a classic design for an island fort, where Totten used virtually no land defenses and utilized unprotected masonry walls on all sides.

The fort was designed with five seacoast fronts and one gorge, and was to have the capa-

Figure 115: Only the first tier of Fort Carroll, and less than that on some fronts, was constructed. These embrasures, however, were readied for seacoast cannon and the fort received a portion of its armament. *(Photo by author)*

blocks. These iron keys locked into rectangular slots in the edges of adjacent blocks, preventing lateral movement. While these keys would have been hidden were the construction completed, its incomplete condition allows one to see this interesting construction technique.

son to pass through, iron beams connected the wharf to the fort. These beams would preclude even a small boat from sailing near the gorge and discharging marines through the windows.

The entire design of Fort Carroll was directed toward its ability to defend the harbor from attacking ships. The powerful seacoast fronts were to be casemated on three tiers, with a tier of barbette guns above. Totten embrasures with iron shutters opened onto the two shipping channels from five fronts. Located at the middle of the narrows, ships would be required to pass very close to the formidable armament of the fort.

The casemates of the fort were brick, with concrete fill between the brick faces. Like several forts from the latter part of the Third System, concrete was used inside the brickwork for mass, but was not considered structural support. Since *reinforced* concrete had not been introduced, concrete was not used for anything other than masonry-faced fill.

The scarp consisted of a layer of granite backed by a layer of brick, making it the only scarp in the Third System that used both brick and granite layers in its construction. The embrasures did not use brick, but were framed in granite. The iron throats developed by Totten were also used.

Of particular interest to the visitor are the hexagonal keys used in the joining of the granite

Figure 116: Some of the casemates of Fort Carrol were completed, while others were left open to the sky. The photograph above shows a front where all of the first-tier casemates were completed. *(Photo by author)*

An interesting anomaly of the casemates is the lack of smoke vents in either the embrasure area or the center of the casemate. Most forts of this period had vents in either place, with some forts, such as Fort Pickens in Pensacola, Florida, having vents in both locations. It can only be assumed that the strong breezes in the area and the relatively shallow casemates would be considered adequate to clear the smoke.

At the junction of each front was a stair tower providing communication between tiers and protecting a powder magazine behind it. The entrance to these service magazines was aligned with the row of arches for communication behind the gun positions. Larger main magazines were located at either end of the gorge. One of these magazines was open to the sky, but there is no evidence of damage

Figure 117: The exterior of the completed casemates is shown in the above photograph. Good views of the fort requre the use of a boat. *(Photo by author)*

from an explosion. The likely explanation is that the roof had not been constructed when work on the fort was halted.

While the casemated fronts of the fort were relatively shallow, the gorge was very deep. Flanking the sally port were rooms containing barracks, kitchens, and support areas of the fort. These rooms had elaborate iron columns, and opened to the parade with large windows. While some of the rooms were quite narrow, others were very wide.

The ceiling of this area consisted of shallow arches supported by iron beams. These flat beams were tapered in thickness, having been approximately one inch thick at the piers and a full two inches thick at the center. Rods connected the beams, with large turnbuckles midway between the beams. Periodically, there were small arches, approximately four feet by twelve feet, running perpendicular to the remaining arches. The brickwork of these arches is inferior to the nearby brickwork, leading one to suspect that stairways to the unbuilt second tier were to be located in these areas. The existing brickwork would have been a later addition, probably during the Endicott Period.

During construction of the fort, there were problems with the stability of the foundation. While not the serious problem that Fort Calhoun fought, there was some settling of the grillage forming the foundation of the fort. Two fronts of the fort had considerable settling, and granite was piled on these fronts to accelerate that settling. When the settling stopped, construction resumed but was short-lived. By this time the decision to abandon work on the fort had been made and the first tier of casemates was not completed on this front.[4]

Construction of the fort halted before it obtained much of its planned grandeur. The first tier of casemates was completed, and the scarp of the second tier was raised to breast height. On this tier, the pintles were set to allow the mounting of cannon en barbette, but the scarp was raised only to the bottom of the embrasures. One of the secondary fronts was not completed – only a low wall with barbette mounts provided any defense.

Today, Fort Carroll is a lonely sentinel near the Key Bridge. Abandoned to an overgrowth of vegetation, the parade resembles a rain forest. From pear trees to poison ivy, access to the various portions of the fort must be gained by the use of machetes and pruning shears. Even portions of the terreplein are overgrown, but quite a bit of this area can be easily reached. The views from the ramparts are very enjoyable.

A portion of the parade and two seacoast fronts have been modified for the construction of a concrete gun battery, but the original facade of the sally port still admits those who wish to enter the fort. Its single level of casemates is in good condition, as are the barracks areas of the gorge. Fort Carroll is privately owned, and can be visited only by special arrangement.

Boat tours of Baltimore harbor travel past the fort and provide the tourists with good views of the embrasures and granite facade. Travelers over the Key Bridge may look down into the fort, but it is advised that only *passengers* in the cars do the sightseeing on that windy, high-traffic bridge.

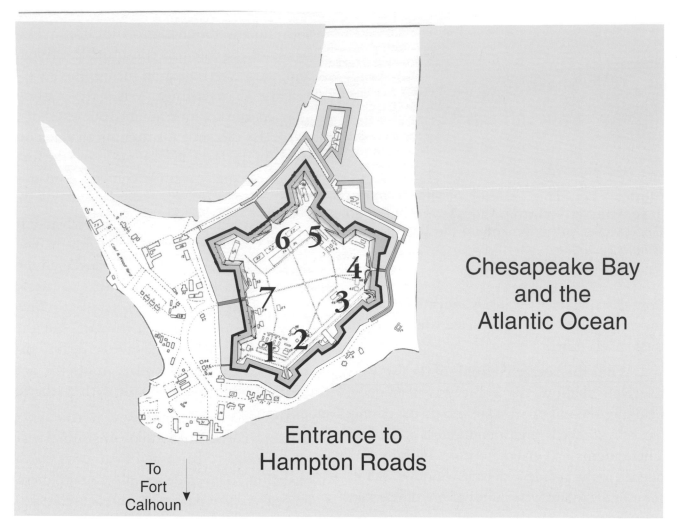

Figure 118: Fort Monroe occupied almost the entire area of Old Point Comfort. The largest fort in the system, this incredible work amazes even the most casual visitor. *(Sketch based on NARA drawing)*

Fort Monroe

The fort that is considered Bernard's masterpiece is Fort Monroe along Hampton Roads, Virginia. The largest of all Third System forts, this 63-acre marvel guarded the entrance to the Chesapeake Bay, the James River, the York River, and the harbor at Norfolk. Its strategic location caused Bernard to choose this site for his "headquarters" fort for the entire system of fortifications.

The site of Fort Monroe was chosen for two principal reasons. First, Old Point Comfort had a full command of the entrance to Hampton Roads, and was located in the easternmost area on the north side of the channel. This allowed additional control over shipping entering Chesapeake Bay as well as the shipping entering the Roadstead. Second, Old Point Comfort was well situated for easy defense. Connected to the mainland by an isthmus, the land approaches were minimal and the strength of the fort could be concentrated on seacoast defense.

Begun in 1819, Fort Monroe was one of the first forts of the Third system. Due to its massive size, construction spanned an 18-year period, with construction being completed in 1837.

Fort Monroe was a six-sided, irregular work with very large, open bastions. In addition to a bastion at each corner, a bastion at its midpoint broke the longest side of the fort. This side of the fort was the main channel front, with casemates on

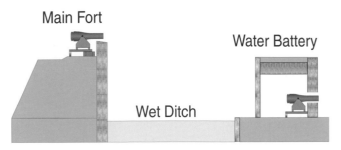

Figure 119: The famous Fort Monroe Water Battery was called by Bernard, its designer, a casemated coverface. As shown in the above sketch, it cooperated with the main fort in providing two tiers of seacoast cannon to bear on the channel.

the curtains and on the flanks and faces of the bastions. The guns of these casemates joined with the guns of the barbette tier to provide direct fire on the channel. Additional fire on the channel was provided by the two secondary fronts that came off of the main front at 45° angles.

To simplify references to areas of a fort of this size and irregular shape, the curtains were each numbered. The numbers begin with the first face of the fort, the southwest secondary front. From this front, which is fully casemated, they proceeded counterclockwise around the fort. The two curtains of the main front were numbered 2 and 3.

The southeast secondary front, curtain number 4, was a curiosity of Fort Monroe. This front, bearing on the entrance to the channel, was *not* casemated. Instead, a magnificent casemated water battery across the moat covered it. This 40-gun battery was reached by a postern and bridge, and contained magazines to service the guns. The firepower of this battery was supplemented by the barbette guns of the fort, and by two emplacements in the salient place d'armes flanking the battery in front of curtain number 5.

By using a "casemated coverface" rather than casemates in the main work, Bernard was able to greatly increase the number of guns bearing on the channel. Being outside the wide moat, the length of the water battery was much greater than the length of the walls of the main work. Unfortunately, this no longer remains.

Curtain number 5 faced the isthmus that provided the only land route to the fort. For this reason, this face had the most extensive set of land defenses. The flank of the northeast bastion was casemated, with embrasures for five howitzers to cover the ditch. In advance of the

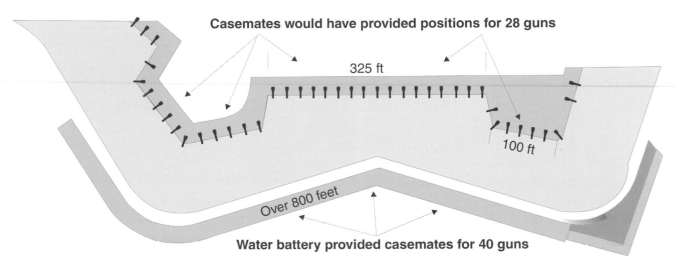

Casemates would have provided positions for 28 guns

325 ft

100 ft

Over 800 feet

Water battery provided casemates for 40 guns

Figure 120: By using a water battery placed outside the very wide ditch, Bernard took advantage of the significant increase in length to increase the number of casemates from 28 to 40. The earthen coverface in front of a non-casemated front at Fort Warren, Boston Harbor, was the only other example of this concept, and it was nowhere near this elaborate.

131

Figure 121: The longest side of Fort Monroe was broken into two fronts, with a full bastion at the midpoint. This is the only instance in the Third System that a bastion was placed in a straight wall. *(Photo by author)*

moat was an extensive outwork with a ravelin at its midpoint and a salient place d'armes in front of the southeast bastion.

In advance of the northeast bastion was a small masonry redoubt, the most significant of the land defenses of the fort. The redoubt, ravelin, and remaining outworks were fronted by a wide, deep-water moat fed from the main moat encircling the fort. Only the tide gate controlling the water flow to this secondary moat remains today.

Curtains number 6 and number 7 were approximately equal in length, and formed the two gorges of the fort. Each curtain was penetrated by a sally port at its midpoint, each sally port having a drawbridge over the moat. The defenses of these sally ports, however, varied. In addition to the barbette defenses common to both entrances, the North Gate in curtain number 6 was defended by a series of loopholes high in the northwest bastion. These loopholes opened into a small, independently defensible structure in the flank of the bastion. On the other hand, two howitzer embrasures on either side of the gate defended the Main Gate in curtain number 7. These embrasures opened

into conventional guardrooms flanking the sally port. The flanks of the bastions on this front, however, were earth filled. In all cases, the long flanks of the bastions provided both cannon and rifle positions atop the ramparts. These positions controlled the bridges, the moat, and the area in advance of the moat.

In addition to providing defensive fire in the event of a siege, the barbette cannon of curtains number 6 and number 7 each provided a secondary function. Curtain number 6 defended the large creek, Mill Creek, which ran behind the fort and curtain number 7 guarded an anchorage in the roadstead beyond the channel.

An interesting element in Bernard's design of Fort Monroe was the lack of flank embrasures in the bastions. Flank embrasures protected the seacoast fronts, but only two other bastion flanks provided any defense. The remaining six bastion flanks were solid, a design not duplicated

Figure 122: The magazines of Fort Monroe are also unique. Built into the flanks of the bastions, these structures have an independent brick room built inside the outer building shown here. An air gap between the inner and outer building lessened the vulnerability of the structure to cannon fire, and the vents shown provided circulation to keep the powder dry. *(Photo by author)*

in any other Third System work. It must be surmised that Bernard relied on the extensive outworks covering all but the seacoast faces, the large areas atop the bastions, and on the fully encircling moat to provide the required protection for the scarp.

Today, Fort Monroe remains in remarkable condition. While the only remaining outworks consist of one salient place d'armes and one magazine, the entire fort is intact. Modernization of most of the interior rooms for use in later missions has hidden many of the original details, but a portion of the Casemate Museum has been restored to its original condition. While abandoned and in only fair condition, other portions of the casemates are accessible with special permission.

The museum does a very nice job of bringing to life the history of coastal defense in general and Fort Monroe in particular. A bookstore/gift shop provides a wide variety of publications as well as souvenirs and memorabilia.

In addition to this excellent museum, a walk around the ramparts provides a true flavor of the incredible fort. Additionally, the Moat Walk provides the visitor with the vantage of a potential attacker and the defenses he would face. A visit to Fort Monroe is an experience that will not be soon forgotten, and will entice the visitor back for repeated tours.

To reach Fort Monroe, take exit 268 off I-64 just north of the Hampton Roads Bridge-Tunnel, and proceed eastward on Mallory Street. Turn south (right) on East Mellen Street. Continue south (the road changes names twice) across the bridge onto the Fort Monroe reservation, and continue to Ruckman Road. The old fort is on the left.

Fort Calhoun

The most troublesome fort in the Third System was Fort Calhoun, later known as Fort Wool.[5]

This fort, built on the "rip-raps" opposite Fort Monroe at Hampton Roads, Virginia, was begun in 1820 and had not been completed by 1867. In fact, only one level of casemates was completed around two-thirds of the perimeter of the fort, with provision made atop the casemates for guns to be mounted *en barbette*. The entire gorge remained open.

Fort Calhoun was to be the first "tower fort" of the Third System, and was known as Castle Calhoun on the early drawings.[6] The fort was to consist of three levels of casemates, with an additional barbette tier of guns, arranged in a long, bent rectangle with rounded corners. Even with the relatively modest perimeter of 381 yards, the fort was designed to mount a formidable 216 guns. Coupled with the guns of Fort Monroe, almost 600 guns were to be available to defend the roadstead at Hampton.

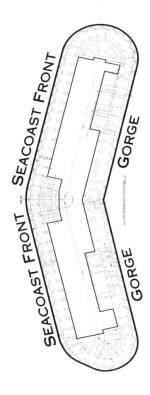

Figure 123: The "folded wing" design of Fort Calhoun was shared with Fort McRee in Pensacola, Florida. While approximately the same size, the interiors of the two forts - including the casemate designs - were quite different.

Figure 124: This rare photograph shows the seacoast front of Fort Calhoun when construction ceased. Unfortunately, most of this magnificent structure was destroyed to build gun batteries during later periods of coastal defense. *(Photo courtesy of the City of Hampton, Virginia)*

The ripraps at Hampton Roads consisted of a rocky shoal somewhat below the level of high tide. To allow construction of the fort, a massive mole was built of local stone, bringing the level of the land above that of high tide. The fort construction was begun in 1826 on this foundation.

Problems were evident from the beginning. As construction progressed, it became clear that the "island" was sinking. What was thought to be a solid, rock bottom was in reality a soft, rock-and-shell reef that was not anchored to bedrock. Many attempts were made by a succession of superintending engineers to stabilize the foundation, but their accounts read like a comedy of errors. Reports to the Chief of Engineers would, year after year, state that the foundation was now stable and construction would begin next year. In actuality, the island is still settling today.[7]

While Fort Calhoun was destined to never achieve its planned-for magnificence, it was a valuable fort with significant defensive capability during most of its active years. The massive stone casemates of the first tier were equipped with Totten embrasures and shutters, and cannon were mounted to defend the roadstead. The barbette tier also utilized Totten embrasures and mounted various guns, including both rifles and large Rodman smoothbores on the unfinished ramparts. On numerous occasions the guns of Fort Calhoun (by this time Fort Wool) fired on Confederate shipping and coastal batteries.

Only a small portion of the original fort remains. The entire area of the fort to seaward was demolished during the Endicott period and the granite walls replaced with concrete batteries. The portion of the Third System fort that remains, however, gives one a unique view of the cross-section of Totten embrasures and a good flavor for what the fort would have looked like when construction was halted.

Of particular interest is the craftsmanship displayed in the granite work. The size of the stones, the precision of the complex angles and curves, and the beauty of the architectural details leave the visitor in awe. The mix of granite for the main walls, piers, and floors blends well with the brick arches of the casemates.

Fort Calhoun is also the best place to study Totten Embrasures. The upper tier of the fort was partially completed when construction was halted, and the top of the Totten embrasures is

Figure 125: This current photograph shows the remaining portion of the Third System scarp wall. The settling problems that plagued the fort during construction continue to cause problems in the preservation of this beautiful example of granite work. *(Photo by author)*

134

exposed to view. This allows a plan view of an actual embrasure. The first tier embrasures are complete, so a completed Totten embrasure can be viewed at the same time.

The fort is owned by the city of Hampton, Virginia, and is accessible by tour boat from the Hampton waterfront. The pleasant boat ride takes the rider past Fort Monroe and through the channel that these two forts were to defend. Time is provided on the island for a ranger-led tour that explains both the Third System work and the later concrete batteries. This tour is supplemented by views of the largest naval base in the world, the base in Norfolk, Virginia. The trip is certainly time well spent.

Notes

[1] Transitional forts were the forts constructed following the War of 1812, but prior to Bernard's emigration and the formation of the Coastal Fortifications Board. These forts fall between the Second System and the Third System.

[2] Fort Calhoun was never completed, but was sufficiently completed to mount a significant number of cannon. See the description of Fort Calhoun for details.

[3] National Archives and Record Administration, Cartographic Branch, RG 77.

[4] This is Front 6, a secondary channel front to the left of the main channel front.

[5] The fort was originally named for Secretary of War John C. Calhoun. After the outbreak of the Civil War, it was considered an embarrassment to have a Union fort named for the famed secessionist. In 1862 the name was changed to Fort Wool in honor of John E. Wool, a hero of the Mexican War and a former commander of Fort Monroe.

[6] National Archives and Records Administration, Cartographic Branch, RG 77.

[7] Large cracks in the granite work have closed some areas to the public, and there is a growing concern for the future of the structure.

Figure 126: The massive stone casemates of Fort Calhoun are shown in the photograph above. The supports and main arches of the fort were granite, while the casemate arches were brick. *(Photo by author)*

The Defenses of
The Southern Atlantic Coast

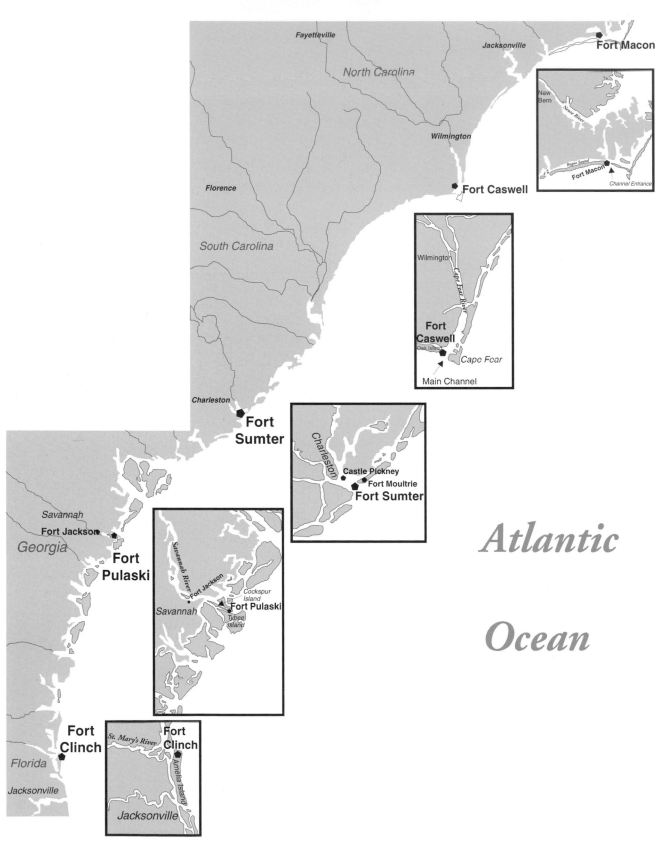

History

Of secondary importance to the Board of Engineers was the southern Atlantic coastal region. These areas were primarily agricultural, and were therefore of less strategic value than the more industrialized areas to the north and the main shipping centers on the Gulf coast. In Bernard's 1821 report, forts in this area were relegated to the Second Class which could "wait until the chief and more important points are secured...".[1] As the system was developed, these areas moved up the priority list and appropriate fortifications were designed.

The coast of North Carolina was protected from the Atlantic Ocean by a series of long, narrow islands known as the Outer Banks. Between these mostly sand islands and the shore was a series of shallow sounds, a transition area between the tidewater rivers and the ocean. Although there were numerous inlets between the islands, the shallow nature of the sounds did not allow deep-draft ships. Only two deepwater harbors existed along the shore, Beaufort and Wilmington.

The northernmost harbor, near Old Topsail Inlet, provided access to both the harbor at Beaufort and the Newport River, as well as to the railroad.

The next harbor south was at the mouth of the Cape Fear River, leading to Wilmington. In addition to this major harbor, the river provided the most significant interior communication in the state of North Carolina. Bogue Banks defined the deepwater entrance to the harbor on the south, and a series of small islands and shallows known as the Frying Pan Shoals defined the harbor entrance on the north.[2]

The two principal cities in the region were Charleston and Savannah. These cities were important merchant centers along the south coast, and both stood on important harbors. While protected by older forts from earlier periods, they still had a significant vulnerability to attack.

The St. Mary's River provided the major communication route for northeastern Florida and southeastern Georgia. The river mouth provided an anchorage, and the river itself controlled a large part of the inland region.

Finally, St. Augustine, Florida, was an important city with a good harbor. The Castillo de San Marcos, the oldest fort in the United States, guarded this harbor.

Third System Strategy

Each of these individual harbors were considered separately, with new-construction forts being designed for each critical location except St. Augustine. There, a water battery was added to the aging Castillo and the fort was renamed Fort Marion.

Being designed during the middle period of the Third System, these forts took on very interesting characteristics. They were specifically designed for their individual missions, as were most Third System forts, but the range of designs was more varied than in most other regions. Also, each of these forts had to be self-sufficient. While most Third System forts were built near other forts of the period, these forts were individually designated to protect a harbor, and the nearest fort was a considerable distance away.

These forts were, in fact, almost evenly spaced between the Hampton Roads area and the northern border of Florida.

To guard Beaufort Harbor, Fort Macon was constructed on the tip of Bogue Banks, overlooking Old Topsail Inlet. This location closed access to the river and harbor at a point near the ocean.

Fort Caswell was constructed on Oak Island at the mouth of the Cape Fear River, covering access to the river and the port of Wilmington. This fort was also located near the

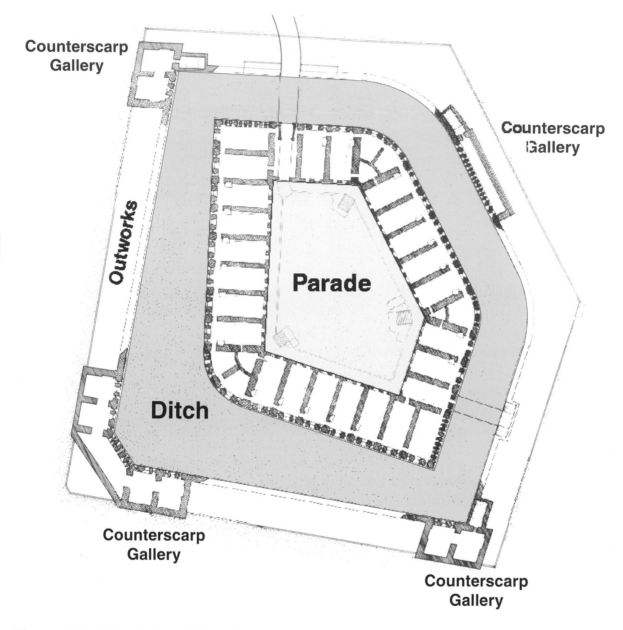

Counterscarp Gallery

Counterscarp Gallery

Outworks

Parade

Ditch

Counterscarp Gallery

Counterscarp Gallery

Figure 127: The design of Fort Macon was unique in the Third System. Seacoast cannon were mounted en barbette, with the casemates opening to the ditch with loopholes. A tall counterscarp wall surrounded the fort, with additional gun positions in the outworks. *(Sketch based on NARA Drawing)*

ocean and defended the coastal channel (now the Intracoastal Waterway) traversed by smaller shipping.

Two forts from previous periods, Fort Moultrie and Castle Pickney, guarded Charleston. While both were important forts, they were not adequate for the protection of such a critical harbor. To control this harbor entrance, the massive Fort Sumter, termed by Beauregard as a "Gibraltar," was constructed. While not as large or powerful as the strongest Third System forts, it was the most impressive Third System fort located adjacent to a populous city. This made the fort a symbol of Third System might, and prompted a high level of emotion regarding Federal defensive power.[3]

Savannah was protected by Fort Jackson, a non-casemated Second System fort on the Savannah River. This fort was located too close to the city to provide adequate protection, and did not mount a sufficient number of cannon. To provide a stronger and more distant defense for Savannah, Totten designed Fort Pulaski, a large-trace brick fort on Cockspur Island near the river's mouth. While originally designed to be as formidable as Sumter, the coastal soil prevented Sumter's vertical scale and required a larger-trace fort with only one tier of casemates.

The southernmost fort in this region, Fort Clinch, was constructed at the mouth of the St. Mary's River. This fort prevented the entry of the river, and defended the sheltered areas near the river's mouth where a hostile fleet could weather a storm.

Fort Macon

The cities of Beaufort and Morehead City in North Carolina were located near a large, sheltered harbor off Bogue Sound. The channel to that harbor and safe anchorage passed through Beaufort Inlet, previously known as Old Topsail Inlet. Guarding this inlet, on Bogue Banks, stood Fort Macon. Construction began in 1826 and the fort was completed in 1834.

Fort Macon was an irregular five-sided work with three seacoast fronts and two gorge walls. It was a massive brick fort unique in its design; it was substantially different from any other Third System fort.

The principal role of the fort was seacoast defense, but its location on a very long island, Bogue Banks, and its proximity to other land, made it susceptible to a sustained siege. These

Figure 128: The ditch of Fort Macon was well defended. Forward fire from the scarp galleries and reverse fire from selected points on the counterscarp was supplemented by howitzers located at strategic points in the counterscarp. The location of the howitzer embrasures and the curving scarp and counterscarp walls ensured that all points of the ditch were covered by enfilading fire. *(Photo by author)*

were the primary considerations in its design.

Seacoast defense was provided through the barbette tier of guns and a substantial battery on the covert way. Together, the fort was capable of mounting 51 seacoast cannon. While the fort was casemated around its entire perimeter, no cannon were to be mounted en casemate. This allowed the construction of a substantial counterscarp that could shield the scarp wall from siege guns.

Unfortunately, the barbette guns lacked traverses. That proved to be a problem during the Union siege of the fort, as there was no lateral protection from the Union shells.

The unique design of the fort was seen in the depth of the casemates. While the parade was relatively small, the trace of the fort was quite substantial. This was because the casemates were designed as significant barracks space and storage space, all in one tier. These deep casemates ended in loopholes from which small arms could fire into the ditch or, to some degree, onto the covert way should it fall. To provide an enemy less chance of firing into the loopholes from the covert way, Fort Macon had horizontal slits rather than vertical slits.

Some of the casemates were also designed with embrasures for carronades and howitzers, though none of these antipersonnel weapons were ever mounted in the fort.

The fort was unbastioned, but had substantial counterscarp works. The original design of the fort had only rifle galleries in the counterscarp, but a construction modification during Robert E. Lee's superintendence of construction placed howitzer casemates at three corners of the ditch. Since the central gallery provided forward rather than flanking fire, it remained as a rifle gallery. The howitzer casemates designed by Lee had one embrasure flanked by two loopholes. Above each embrasure was a chimney leading to a large smoke vent opening into the ditch.

Above the entire counterscarp was a large covert way. On the three seacoast fronts this covert way was fronted by barbette gun positions, while on the two gorge walls it was fronted by a banquette for small arms defense. Beyond the covert way on all sides was a long glacis.

Figure 129: The scarp galleries of Fort Macon provided forward fire both into the ditch and toward the rear of the covert way. *(Photo by author)*

The covert way was joined to the fort on one seacoast front by a bridge over the ditch, leading to a postern. This bridge went from the casemate level of the fort up to an area about halfway up the counterscarp wall. It terminated in a platform flanked by stairways to the covert way.

The counterscarp galleries were accessible through doorways from the ditch. Across from these doorways were posterns from the fort into the ditch. There were also stairways from the ditch to the covert way, again protected by heavy doors.

The main sally port of the fort was in a secondary seacoast front, in a position symmetrical to the bridge previously mentioned. This sally port was a two-chambered area closed with three sets of heavy doors. Loopholes built into the outermost chamber of the sally port defended the outer doors.

The facade of the sally port was brick, unlike the granite facade generally used. Built into the facade on either side of the sally port were loopholes opening into the guardrooms. The lone ornamentation on an otherwise plain gate was a granite coping with a small ledge below.

Leading from the sally port to the covert way was a wooden bridge, which in turn curved through a beautifully paved and revetted opening in the counterscarp wall. The pathway gradually tapered to the level of the glacis, and became a road. Original plans called for a drawbridge, but it was never implemented.

One very pleasant feature of the fort was the decorative ironwork seen in the stair railings and trim. These features added some architectural interest to an otherwise utilitarian structure. Also of interest were the curving walls of the fort. The masonry on these curves was smooth and flawless, giving a beautiful appearance to the brickwork.

A strange characteristic of the fort was the stairways leading to the counterscarp galleries. These stairways extended downward from the covert way to heavy wooden doors. Being closed on all sides, they formed a point of refuge for an attacker who gained the covert way, out of the fire of any guns of the fort.

Today, Fort Macon stands as a well-preserved example of a Third System fort. It is open to the public, managed by the North Carolina Department of Natural Resources. Several knowledgeable and historically aware guides lead tours and answer a variety of questions regarding the fort and its history. It is a very well managed program, and a very pleasant site to visit.

To reach Fort Macon, follow Route 70E east from New Bern toward Morehead City. Just before reaching Morehead City, turn south (right) on Morehead Avenue to Atlantic Beach. Turn east (right) on East Fort Macon Road and follow it to the end. You are at Fort Macon.

Fort Caswell

The Cape Fear River was North Carolina's only river that ran directly into the Atlantic Ocean. The Frying Pan Shoals, dangerous shallows that ran some 20 miles into the Atlantic, were the probable reason for the strange name of this waterway. Despite the danger, however, the river was an important waterway and provided the major communication with the inland areas of the state. More directly, it was the only connection to the port at Wilmington.

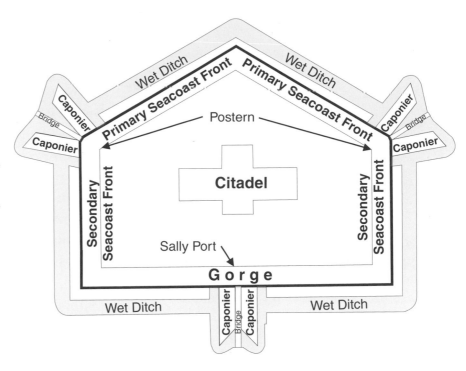

Figure 130: Fort Caswell was another unique design within the Third System. Use of a wet and a dry ditch - with six caponiers for the defense of the ditch - was not repeated within the system. Also unique was the cross-shaped citadel that was designed to provide fire to the rear of all portions of the ramparts.

To guard this waterway the Coastal Fortifications Board chose Oak Island, at the river's mouth. Oak Island formed a two-mile-wide channel with Smith Island (now known as Bald Head Island) at this point, a channel that could be readily defended by a fort on the shore. Construction on the fort began in 1827, and the fort was completed eleven years later.

Fort Caswell was a five-sided truncated hexagon, without bastions but with three pairs of caponiers. A cross-shaped citadel stood in the center of the parade. A substantial earthwork surrounded the entire fort during the Civil War.

Fort Caswell was designed as a seacoast defense fort, but was very vulnerable to a land-based siege from the western end of Oak Island as well as from the numerous nearby islands. For this reason, it was designed with all of its seacoast armament mounted en barbette. While not casemated, the scarp wall was backed by a rifle

Figure 131: A sally port of Fort Caswell, with the opening to what was once a caponier, is shown in this photograph. Unfortunately, only portions of the original structure remain. *(Photo by author)*

gallery that encircled the perimeter of the fort. Beyond the rifle gallery was a flat area of dry ditch, fronted with a wet moat. This moat, fed from a nearby creek, had brick-faced walls. Beyond the moat was the covert way, and later the substantial outworks.

The entrances to the fort were located at three points. The main sally port to the fort was in the middle of the gorge wall with two secondary sally ports at the salients between each primary seacoast front and its adjacent secondary seacoast front. The entrance to each sally port was flanked by caponiers, entered by tunnels through the ramparts. The sally ports were closed by drawbridges over the moat.

The caponiers provided defense of the dry ditch along the moat. They had loopholes along their entire length, and were positioned such that one caponier washed each wall. The interior of the caponiers was virtually identical to the interior of the rifle galleries.

The citadel provided barracks space as well as another level of defense. Built relatively low to the ground, it was entirely hidden by the ramparts of the fort. It occupied a large portion of the parade, and had loopholes in its walls. The cross shape provided flanking fire along all walls except the ends of the cross.

An interesting feature of the citadel was that it contained two levels of defense itself. Ringed by loopholes, the central interior walls also were provided with loopholes for a final defense if a portion of the citadel was taken.

The barbette tier of the fort provided positions for 64 seacoast cannon as well as positions for smaller land-defense guns. The large amounts of earth used in the construction minimized the ability of siege guns to do significant damage to the fort.

The archways of the rifle galleries are worthy of note. While designed of a typical elliptical arch design, the axis of symmetry of the arch was canted toward the interior of the fort. It is presumed that this is due to the angle of the force applied to the archway by the massive earthen ramparts. When viewing the archway endwise, it has a strange, asymmetrical appearance.

The design of the fort was unique among Third System forts. While the form of a truncated hexagon was common, the extensive use of caponiers was not. While structures of similar design to a caponier, or structures referred to as caponiers, were present in several Third System forts, only the Fort Adams, Rhode Island, redoubt and four forts, Fort Hamilton and Fort Tompkins in New York City, Fort Washington south of Washington D.C., and Fort Caswell, had "classic" caponiers. Also unique was the two-tiered ditch. No other Third System fort had a concentric dry ditch and wet moat.

Today, much of the fort has been destroyed. What is left is buried in sand dunes and beneath an Endicott period concrete battery, and it requires some imagination to picture the fort as it once was. The intrepid explorer can enter one magazine and two of the three structures that provided entry to the caponiers and a sally port. Also accessible are portions of the long rifle galleries. Visible beyond the fort on the seaward

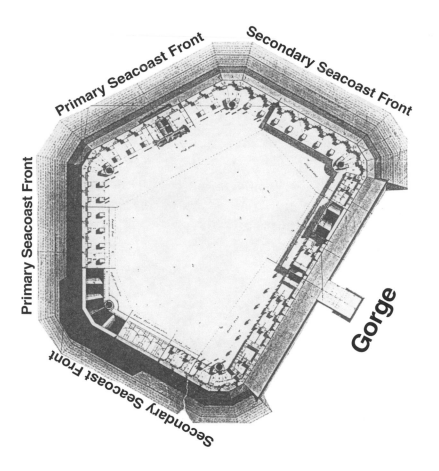

Primary Seacoast Front

Primary Seacoast Front

Secondary Seacoast Front

Secondary Seacoast Front

Gorge

Figure 132: Fort Sumter was a truncated hexagon, with no bastions or demibastions. Its location on a man-made island and extremely tall walls made extensive land defenses unnecessary. Machiacoulis galleries - wooden platforms extending from the ramparts - allowed firing on an attacker standing against the scarp. *(Drawing courtesy of NARA)*

Fort Sumter

Probably the most famous of all Third System forts is Fort Sumter, guarding Charleston Harbor. As the recipient of the opening shots of the Civil War, the fort was made a symbol for that war by both the Union and the Confederacy. Before these shots were fired, however, Fort Sumter was considered the embodiment of all fortification technology up to that time. Its massive appearance and the proximity to Charleston made it a showplace of the Third System. Indeed it was the seeming impregnability of the fort that caused the Confederacy to take whatever measures were necessary to prevent it from achieving its full armament and garrison.

The construction of Fort Sumter began in 1829, and was completed in 1860. At this time, only a small percentage of the fort's armament was in place, and a considerable amount of construction material was present in the fort.

side are the buried remains of two caponiers and portions of the counterscarp wall. Throughout all the remains, the beauty of the brickwork shows through the years of neglect and modification as a modern gun battery.

Fort Caswell is on the site of a retreat center for the Baptist Church, and its new owners treat the historic value of the fort with a great deal of respect. The site manager indicated that they hope that one day a museum can be created to commemorate the fort that once controlled entrance to the Cape Fear River. The author shares that hope.

The trace of the fort was to be of conventional design, a five-sided truncated hexagon, but it was to be built without bastions. Being the sole occupant of a man-made island only slightly larger than the fort itself, land defense was not a factor. All the might of the fort was to be dedicated to seacoast defense. To repel the small number of soldiers who might be able to slip ashore, the fort had wooden platforms that extended from the parapet at the midpoint of each face.[4] These platforms, called machicoulis galleries, provided firing platforms that could sweep each of the faces of the fort.

143

Figure 133: This painting by Seth Eastman shows the magnificent Fort Sumter prior to the outbreak of the Civil War. It was considered by many - including its attacker, P.G.T Beauregard - as the ultimate in the coastal defense technology of the day. Unfortunately, very little of this remarkable structure survived the Union bombardment and subsequent demolition for more modern coastal defenses. *(Photo courtesy MHI)*

The real power of the fort was the 135 guns bristling from the four seacoast fronts of the fort and from the barbette tier. These guns were arranged in two tiers of casemates and in an open tier atop the ramparts. The gorge wall had two tiers of loopholes to defend the wharf, as well as a tier of barbette guns above. Five circular stair towers joined the one-acre parade to each of these tiers.

The gorge wall and each of the two walls adjoining it were lined with impressive, three-story barracks buildings. These barracks buildings were similar in design to the barracks buildings that are still standing at Fort Delaware.

In the middle of the parade stood an impressive light, the "fort lantern," which provided interior illumination to the fort. Also on the parade was a hot-shot furnace that would supply the first-tier cannon. A wartime garrison of 650 men could be accommodated in this impressive structure.

The vulnerability of the fort was to land-based cannon. The unprotected masonry walls were designed to prevent the passage of ships, and were certainly up to this challenge. The fort was designed, however, to work in concert with the adjacent forts defending Charleston Harbor; it was not designed to withstand their bombardment. The weakest portion of the fort, the gorge wall, was to be protected by the batteries of Morris Island. Instead, this island was where both Union and Confederate besiegers placed their cannon, thereby inflicting the most severe damage to the fort.

A unique feature of the fort was that the second-tier casemates were set in slightly from the first-tier casemates. Rather than just a coping separating the levels, there was an offset in the construction of the piers. The purpose of this offset is unknown.

Figure 134: This model of Fort Sumter, located in the Fort Sumter National Monument museum, shows the magnificence of the one-time guardian of Charleston, South Carolina. *(Photo by author)*

Fort Sumter today is a mere shadow of the grandeur of the fort that once stood sentinel in Charleston Harbor. One casemate tier remains, but a large portion of the parade is now occupied by an Endicott-period concrete gun battery, Battery Huger. The walls of the fort that remained from the Union bombardment late in the Civil War were modified to allow the mounting of cannon in the 1870s, then cut down to the first tier and partially filled with earth to accommodate Battery Huger.

The interpretive program, however, is excellent and, with the remaining structures and narrative of the rangers, one can imagine the massive fort that many considered an impregnable defense, and that Confederate General P.G.T. Beauregard referred to as a "Gibraltar." In addition to an excellent museum at the fort, a larger visitor's center at Fort Moultrie tells the story of all of Charleston's defenses.

Fort Sumter is reached by tour boat from Charleston, South Carolina. The fort is very well managed by the National Park Service, who operate the museum and bookstore and provide guided tours of the fort.

Fort Pulaski

Originally conceived to be a near twin of Fort Sumter to its north, the soil system of Cockspur Island would not allow the weight of two tiers of casemates. The plans were modified, and Fort Pulaski was designed with a single casemated tier and a barbette tier of cannon. To compensate for the loss of one tier of cannon, the plan was expanded to increase the length of the curtains. Construction of the final design began in 1829, and the fort was completed in 1847.

To combat this soft soil, a very wide, complex system of cypress pilings and crosshatched beams was created as a foundation. On this grillage, tiers of brick were placed with the edges tapering to the base of the vertical walls. Inverted arches also assisted in spreading the weight of the walls over the entire foundation.

The fort was a five-sided truncated hexagon, with no full bastions and two demibastions protecting the gorge wall. Its primary mission was to control the entrance to the Savannah River, and it was designed to mount 146 guns on two tiers for that purpose.

The two seacoast fronts of the fort faced the river and two secondary fronts faced both river and marsh areas around the island. Firm ground was more than 1000 yards away, so these fronts were designed as unprotected masonry. This gave the cannon maximum versatility and the ability to fire flat-trajectory balls at water level.

The gorge wall, facing landward, had the requisite earthen protection. A large ravelin provided protection for the scarp wall and also provided additional gun positions to combat a siege. The gorge wall was also protected by two demibastions that extended into the wet moat, providing defense of the wall and the bridge leading to the sally port. The loopholes in the gorge wall provided further defense.

Figure 135: This photograph of the scarp of Fort Pulaski shows the damage caused by both smoothbore and rifled artillery. It also indicates the length of the curtains of this large-trace fort. *(Photo by author)*

The final land defense of Fort Pulaski was a wet moat that surrounded the fort. This seven-foot-deep moat presented a significant barrier to an attacker who would be vulnerable to riflemen in the gorge wall and the demibastions. The moat extended *around* the perimeter of the fort and ravelin, as well as *between* the fort and ravelin. This required the crossing of two moats, each with a drawbridge, to reach the sally port of the fort.

Unfortunately, Fort Pulaski was a victim of the progress of the technology of artillery. Designed to withstand the siege of cannon with a range of less than 1000 yards, the development of the large Rodman smoothbore cannon and the rifled Parrott Gun overpowered the design. These guns could be mounted on distant firm ground and still provide

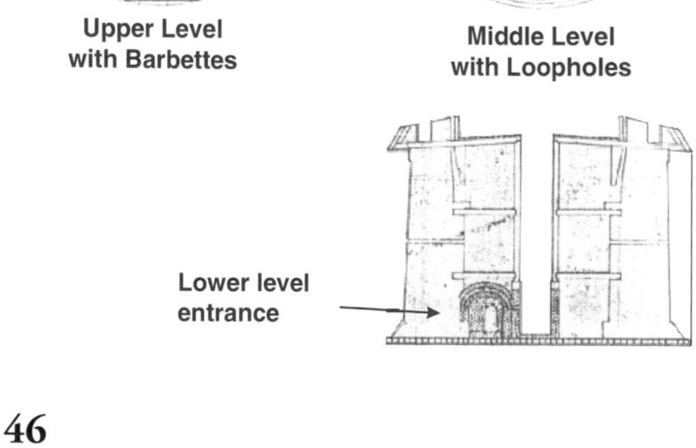

**Upper Level
with Barbettes**

**Middle Level
with Loopholes**

**Lower level
entrance**

Figure 136: The defensive tower on Tybee Island, shown in the drawing on the left, was constructed as a supplemental defense to Fort Pulaski on nearby Cockspur Island. Confederate forces abandoned the tower prior to the Union siege, paving the way for Union artillery batteries that eventually forced the surrender of the fort. *(Drawing courtesy NARA)*

146

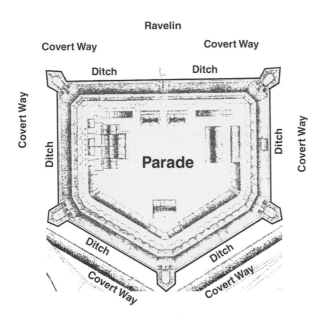

Figure 137: Above is the plan of Fort Clinch, one of two Third System forts using the Carnot Wall or detatched scarp concept. Some engineers of the day considered this design a revelation in military engineering, while others saw it as a passing fancy. Historians today are also divided on the concept. *(Drawing courtesy NARA)*

damaging fire on the unprotected masonry walls.

One of the more impressive sights to the Fort Pulaski visitor is the presence of rifled projectiles in the fort walls. These projectiles were used in the Union attack on the fort, and have been left intact from that day. The breach created by the Union guns was repaired by the Union forces after the battle, and a different color of brick makes these repairs obvious. The nearby areas of the walls that were not breached still contain the spent shot.

Fort Pulaski has an excellent interpretive program managed by the National Park Service, and has one of the finest museums and bookstores in the Third System. The fort is well worth

the scenic drive down the Savannah River from the city of Savannah. A stop at Fort Jackson along the route provides a good contrast of Second System vs. Third System forts.

Fort Pulaski can be reached by taking US-80 south from Savannah, Georgia. Turn into the Fort Pulaski National Monument area, the fort is just off the parking area.

Fort Clinch

Two Third System forts shared the same design, that of the Carnot Wall or detached scarp. Fort Clinch, guarding the St. Mary's River dividing Florida from Georgia, was one to these forts. Along with its twin,[5] Fort Gaines, this fort was built from a French design that allowed the loss of the scarp wall without destruction of the ramparts.

Fort Clinch was a five-sided truncated hexagon, with relatively small bastions at each corner. These bastions were joined to the fort through long tunnels under the ramparts, and were individually defensible. These tunnels also provided access to the chemin de ronde immediately behind the entrance to the bastion.

Another item of note is that the bastions were not identical in shape. The bastions on the seacoast faces had parallel flanks, while the bastions on the gorge had converging flank walls. The reason for this discrep-

Figure 138: This sketch shows a comparison of a bastion with flanks perpendicular to the curtain and flanks that meet the curtain at an oblique angle, such as those of Fort Clinch. The reduction in the size of the bastion is clear, as is the improvement in angle of fire of guns near the bastion flank.

147

Figure 139: The ramparts of Fort Clinch, well back from the Carnot wall on the right of the photograph, was the location where the heavy cannon were mounted. *(Photo courtesy NARA)*

ancy was that Totten chose to keep the angle between the flank of the bastion and the curtain constant. The difference in the 120° angle between the seacoast fronts and the 90° gorge angle was made up in the angle between the flank and the face of the bastions.

The principle of the detached scarp divided land defenses into two potential approaches: the coup de main and the siege. A coup de main consisted of a storming of the walls of the fort through a mass rush of people, known as the "human wave" in both the Korean and Vietnam wars. That would allow the relatively quick capture of a fort without the long, expensive process of a siege.

A siege was the protracted reduction of a fort through the emplacement of heavy guns to reduce the scarp of the fort, followed by the storming of the breach by infantry. A siege was also used to reduce the morale of the garrison by causing deprivation of supplies from outside the fort and by minimizing the sleep of the garrison through continuous bombardment.

The scarp wall of Fort Clinch afforded a solid protection against a coup de main. The tall, vertical masonry walls were a strong defense against storming, and were protected by a ditch and long glacis. The masonry was penetrated with loopholes for riflemen to fire on the attacking foe from a pathway immediately behind the scarp, the chemin de ronde. In addition to the defense from the scarp wall, the bastions that protruded from each of the corners of the fort provided howitzer embrasures for flanking fire down the ditch, a further discouragement of a coup de main.

If a protracted siege of the fort was attempted, the scarp wall became expendable. The reduction of the relatively thin scarp, with no earthen backing, was considered inevitable but did not significantly reduce the defenses of the fort. All heavy guns were mounted en barbette atop the rampart, some distance behind the masonry scarp. The earthen ramparts provided a "soft" material to absorb the impact of the shot and shell of the siege guns, and could maintain the defense of the fort even with the scarp destroyed.

Figure 140: The chemin de ronde of Fort Clinch provided a place for riflemen to defend against a coupe de main or other infantry assault. *(Photo by author)*

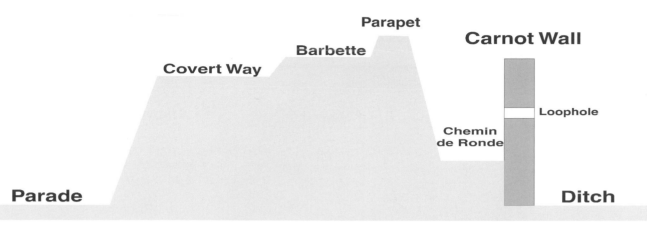

Figure 141: This sketch of a detached scarp fort shows the two distinct barriers to an attacker - the Carnot Wall and the parapet. It is a further refinement on the scheme of defense in depth.

The bastions of the fort were another manner. The theory of the Carnot wall was based on solid-faced bastions that could withstand heavy bombardment while their flanks continued to provide defense of the ditch. Totten, however, for a currently unexplained reason, placed the main magazine of the fort in a landward bastion. Even though the faces of the bastion were very thick, it seems quite a gamble. The hope would be that an attacker would not realize the magazine was in this exposed location.

The seacoast defenses of the fort were limited in the number of guns that could be brought to bear on the channel because of the lack of casemated gunrooms. This limited the fort to a single barbette tier containing 70 guns.

Today, Fort Clinch remains in pristine condition. No massive concrete structures were poured in the fort during the Endicott period, so the parade and ramparts remain as they were during the Third System. The strategic value of the fort was reduced by conquests further north along the coast, and Confederate troops withdrew without an attack by Federal forces. This left the fort free of the damage which would have been sustained had a siege of the fort occurred.

While never officially completed, the fort stands today as it was left by the Union forces, near enough to completion to be able to receive a garrison. Only the armament is missing from the walls of this interesting fort.

Fort Clinch can be reached by taking Exit 129 from I-95 just south of the Florida-Georgia state line, north of Jacksonville, Florida. Follow State Route 200 east to Fernandina Beach. Turn left on Fort Clinch Road, at the entrance to Fort Clinch State Park. Follow Fort Clinch Road to its end, the old fort is just off the parking area.

Notes

[1] ASP-MA, Vol II, p. 304-313.

[2] Later, a second entrance to the Cape Fear River was available to shallow-draught vessels. This new entrance was defended during the Civil War by the earthen Fort Fisher, located on Federal (Confederate) Point on the east shore of the river. During the planning of the Cape Fear defenses for the Third System, however, the deep-water inlet was the only one considered.

[3] It was, to some extent, this appearance of invulnerability and Federal might that lead to the opening shots of the Civil War.

[4] Fort Sumter, Anvil of War, U. S. National Park Service, Harper's Ferry, VA.

[5] While not identical, these two forts were the most alike of any forts in the Third System. The differences were insignificant in terms of both appearance and defensive capability; they were virtually indistinguishable in design.

The Defenses of the Florida Strait

History

Following the Louisiana Purchase, New Orleans became the key to trade — not only on the Gulf coast, but with the West as well. Trade routes up and down the Ohio, Missouri, and Mississippi Rivers all terminated in that bustling city, increasing the importance of the already established link between the Atlantic coast and New Orleans. This vital link passed through the Florida Strait, a 90-mile-wide passage between undefended Key West and the Dry Tortugas on the north, and Spanish-controlled Cuba on the south.

While it was obvious that a fort, or even a series of forts, could not defend a 90-mile-wide channel, a fleet could either defend or blockade a strait of that size with ease. That fleet, however, would need safe anchorage for shelter from Gulf storms, and a nearby depot for supplies.

In that part of the Gulf, only one deep-water anchorage of a size to accommodate a fleet existed, off Garden Key in the Dry Tortugas. That location, however, was too remote from primary sources of supply to provide a supply depot. Key West, on the other hand, was nearer primary supply sources and had become one of the largest cities in Florida, as well as being the wealthiest. It therefore became clear that two separate sites needed to be fortified: an anchorage at Garden Key, and a supply depot at Key West.

Third System Strategy

The acquisition of Florida in 1821 opened the door to fortifying these critical locations. On Garden Key, a work of staggering proportions was planned, surpassed in size only by Fort Monroe in Hampton Roads, and unsurpassed in the amount of armament it could mount. For Key

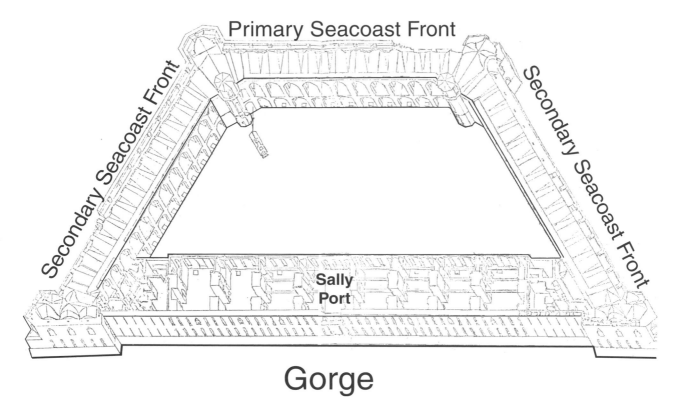

Primary Seacoast Front

Secondary Seacoast Front

Secondary Seacoast Front

Sally Port

Gorge

Figure 142: Fort Taylor was a four-sided truncated hexagon. The long gorge opened with loopholes, while the three seacoast fronts were casemated for large cannon. *(Drawing courtesy of NARA)*

West, a much smaller work was planned, but still one of substantial armament. The Key West fort was begun first, followed two years later by the fort on Garden Key.

To support the Key West fort, two towers were constructed, controlling the two "backdoor" landing sites on the island. These towers were larger and more elaborate than a conventional Martello tower. They consisted not only of the main tower, but also a casemated battery and a substantial scarp wall.

The choice of the two islands was proven correct during the Civil War. Federal fleets based at these two locations controlled access to the Gulf, capturing blockade-runners seemingly at will. Trade between the Atlantic and Gulf states of the Confederacy was reduced until it was virtually nonexistent.

The site at Key West mounted armament from Civil War times continually through the Cuban Missile Crisis in the 1960s, more than

ten years after the disbandment of the United States Coast Artillery and more than 100 years after the construction of Fort Taylor. The naval supply depot it protected is still in use today.

Fort Taylor

Overlooking the main anchorage of Key West stood Fort Taylor, once an impressive work of the Third System. Similar in construction to its sister fort in the Dry Tortugas, Fort Taylor had a much smaller trace and was equipped with far less armament. The fort was, however, a masterpiece of construction and an intimidating factor to anyone with ill intentions toward Key West. Construction began in 1845 and the main fort was completed in 1866. The coverface was not constructed.

Fort Taylor was a four-sided truncated hexagon, with three seacoast fronts and a long gorge wall. While the primary mission of the fort was seacoast defense, its location on one end of a large

Figure 143: In the Nineteenth Century, Fort Taylor was a sight to behold, as is evidenced by this painting by Seth Eastman. Along with similar forts Jefferson and Sumter, this mighty fort was a symbol to the world of American coastal defense. *(Photo courtesy MHI)*

island required that it be capable of withstanding a significant siege. Accordingly, its land defenses were to be considerable. The entire gorge was designed to be masked by a huge, casemated coverface that was not constructed. This coverface would have been fronted with sand to absorb the impact of direct artillery fire, protecting the gorge wall of the fort from siege guns.

The coverface would have been a freestanding structure, separated by water from both land and the fort, with a drawbridge connecting it to the fort. It would have been capable of mounting 48 guns for siege defense.

Behind the location of the coverface rose the gorge wall of the fort, with its upper tier of 49 barbette guns. The lower two tiers were fronted with loopholes looking toward the coverface. At

each end of the gorge was a bastion, where flank howitzers provided additional protection to the wall.

The three seacoast fronts of the fort were each 225 feet in length and were designed for 14 casemated guns per tier, with an additional 15 guns mounted en barbette. This would allow 130 heavy guns to bear on the channel, an impressive amount of armament. Bastions at each corner provided the minimal land defense required for these fronts. Like Fort Jefferson, circular stair towers at the corners of the fort protected day-use magazines.

The gorge contained a three-story barracks building to house the garrison and several storerooms to hold the supplies of the fort. Additional storage would have been provided in some of the casemates of the coverface. The two strange-shaped bastions along the gorge provided both flanking fire along the gorge wall and forward fire toward the coverface.

Today, Fort Taylor is a shell of what it once was. Modification of the fort to allow construction of concrete gun batteries has left only a single tier of casemates, many of them filled with sand. Excavation of the casemates must be done with great caution, as live ammunition has been found amid the sand. It is ironic that the upper levels of the fort were removed to accommodate the Endicott-pe-

Figure 144: The once-majestic Fort Taylor is now a mere shadow of its former self. Modified during later periods of coastal defense, it now has only one casemated tier remaining. *(Photo by author)*

riod Battery Osceola, Chief Osceola being a principal foe of Zachary Taylor.

A unique feature of the current Fort Taylor becomes apparent when viewing the concrete of the Endicott gun battery. Iron cannon from the fort were used as fill when the concrete was poured, and many of the cannon are visible protruding from the concrete.

Stabilized by the State Park Service and with a great deal of volunteer energy, Fort Taylor's story is told once again. An excellent museum has been constructed within the fort, and displays have been created to depict the majesty that was once Fort Taylor.

The Martello Towers

Protecting the anchorages on the south shore of Key West, and supporting the defense of Fort Taylor, were two defensive structures known as East Martello Tower and West Martello Tower. While the official names for these structures were "Fort Taylor Tower No. 1 and Advanced Battery" and "Fort Taylor Tower No. 2 and Advanced Battery," the name Martello Tower was used by the engineers and has stayed with the structures. These towers, however, were very different from a classic Martello Tower.

At each location, an outer structure with a masonry scarp and a square inner tower were constructed. This outer structure was asymmetric – the seacoast front had conventional casemates with embrasures while the landward fronts had curved revetments with an interior counterfire gallery.

The casemates of the seacoast front, very similar in design to the water battery of Fort Monroe, Virginia, had a single casemated tier of cannon with no barbette tier. The seacoast defenses consisted of a long front facing the water with positions for ten guns, and two short fronts with two gun positions each. These casemates were open in the rear, opening to the interior

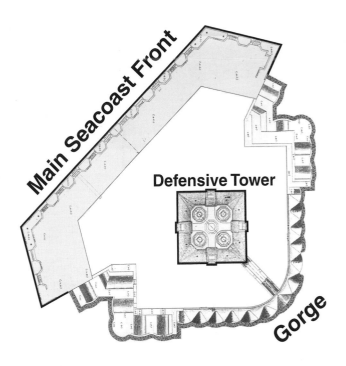

Figure 145: Known as East and West Martello Towers, these defensive structures embody the principles derived at the Bay of Martella, but not the classic design of a Martello Tower. *(Drawing courtesy NARA, labels by author)*

courtyard or parade.

The landward defenses had a solid masonry wall penetrated only by the sally port. This wall consisted of a series of curved revetments on the exterior, and a straight wall on the interior. At the ends of the wall, providing fire throughout the area between the outer structure and the central tower, were counterscarp galleries. Additionally, a caponier extended from one corner of the central tower to the gorge angle of the outer structure. This provided additional enfilading fire for the landward side.

In the approximate middle of this structure was a square, three-story tower. This tower had a single tier of very tall casemates, with a wooden platform dividing it into two stories. The upper story opened with loopholes to the inner courtyard. It also had a sally port and a postern that connected directly to the caponier.

The third story of the tower was a barbette tier with emplacements for four guns on 360° mounts.

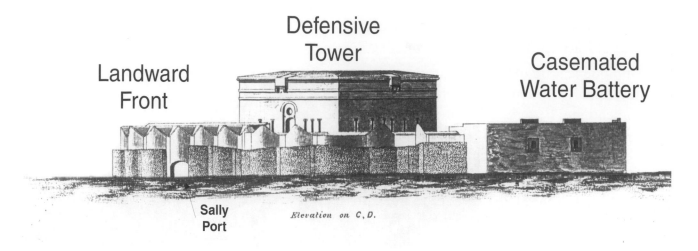

Defensive Tower

Landward Front

Casemated Water Battery

Sally Port

Elevation on C, D.

Figure 146: The directional nature of the defenses around the tower are shown in this elevation drawing. The water battery had open-backed casemates while the landward front had counterscarp galleries. *(Drawing courtesy NARA)*

This allowed the guns to provide additional firepower to seaward, or to provide heavy guns in an elevated position to combat a siege.

These unique fortifications can be interpreted in two ways. First, the can be considered a tower with a seacoast battery. This is implied in the name on the engineering drawings, and fits with the concept of a defensive tower. The problem with this interpretation is that the tower provided less than one-fourth of the defensive might of the fortification!

An alternative interpretation is that the fortification is a redoubt or a closed battery, with the tower acting as a citadel. The presence of loopholes controlling the rear of the outer structure and casemates supports this concept.

Figure 147: The water battery of the West Martello Tower is shown in the above photograph. The somewhat overgrown tower stands in the center rear of the casemated battery. *(Photo courtesy Dale Manuel)*

Whichever interpretation is used, these unique structures provided a very functional defensive scheme with a significant number of seacoast guns in a very small trace.

The East Martello Tower is located on South Roosevelt Boulevard at the southeast corner of the island. The West Martello Tower is located near the corner of Atlantic Boulevard and White Street, in the south-central area of the island.

Fort Jefferson

When approaching the Dry Tortugas, some 68 miles due west of Key West, a massive, shadowy form is seen in the distance. As the form becomes clearer, the huge, vertical walls of Fort Jefferson begin to take shape. The view becomes more awesome as the fort is neared. Entering the sally port and walking onto the parade, a visitor cannot help but marvel at this incredible fort.

Probably the most impressive of all Third System forts was Fort Jefferson on Garden Key in the Dry Tortugas Islands. Begun in 1846, the perimeter of the fort was more than one-half mile, and the parade was over 17 acres. In area, the fort ranked third behind Fort

Figure 148: The amazing Fort Jefferson was designed to be the most heavily armed fortification in the history of the United States, mounting 450 cannon. While the fort never reached this level of armament, it served its role as a fort and later coaling station with a grandeur not matched by any other fortification. *(Photo by author)*

Monroe and Fort Adams.[1] What set Fort Jefferson apart was its vertical scale. While the other giants of the Third System were limited to one tier of casemates,[2] Fort Jefferson sported two tiers, each with larger vertical dimensions. The height of the parapet was 50 feet above the base of the walls.

Designed by Joseph Totten, Fort Jefferson was a regular hexagon that had been "squashed" in one direction to better fit the shape of the island. This left the fort with two parallel sides 325 feet long and the remaining four sides 477 feet long. There was a tower bastion at each corner of the fort, behind which was a day-use magazine protected by a circular-stair tower. These stair towers provided communication between all levels of the fort.

The mission of Fort Jefferson was purely seacoast defense, but it did have minor land-defense capability. The provision for land defense included a wide moat (formed by a sea wall on two sides and a portion of two of the other sides) with a drawbridge and the six tower bastions.

Each bastion defended the scarp with six howitzer embrasures per flank.

The remaining might of the fort was dedicated to seacoast cannon. Some 450 guns could have been mounted en casemate and on the barbette tier, making the fort one of the most heavily armed in the history of the United States. Totten embrasures with Totten shutters protected gunners when loading their cannon, and hot-shot furnaces served the first-tier casemates. Between the second tier casemates and the parapet were a tier of "false embrasures," indentations in the brickwork that made the fort look — to ships on the sea — like it boasted four tiers of cannon rather than the three tiers that actually existed.

Fort Jefferson also had the most pleasing design of living accommodations in the Third System. Designed to house 1,500 men in time of war, the fort had two three-story barracks buildings, one for officers and one for enlisted men. Two other buildings were built for higher-ranking officers. These four buildings were separate

Figure 149: The extensive, open parade of Fort Jefferson is complemented by two tiers of casemates and tier of barbette cannon. The size of the fort is overwhelming to the vistor. *(Photo by author)*

from the casemates and therefore did not have the dampness and ventilation problems so common in Third System barracks. The buildings were strictly barracks buildings, so they had full-sized windows rather than the rifle slits common in defensive barracks or citadels.

Fort Jefferson also had the largest magazine of any Third System fort. The massive structure sat on the parade just behind one wall of the

Figure 150: While necessarily utilitarian in nature, many Third System forts had decorative touches that further demonstrated the skill of the craftsmen. This brickwork along the top of the wall at Fort Jefferson is a classic example of these touches. *(Photo by author)*

fort, and included innovative designs to assure that the powder was kept safe and dry. This magazine supplied the day-use magazines on each of the casemate tiers as well as the magazines built into the traverses on the barbette tier.

The barbette-tier traverses are the best preserved of the Third System. Placed between gun batteries, they provided protection for gunners should explosions occur on adjacent portions of the ramparts, and to keep solid shot from bouncing along the ramparts.

An impressive water-collection system used piping within the casemate piers to transport water to the cisterns. The cisterns themselves were built so tightly that they were in use well into the twentieth century.

Today, Fort Jefferson stands much as it did during the Third System. Cared for by dedicated and historically conscious National Park Service rangers, the interpretive program is very well done. The signs that guide visitors on a self-guided tour are among the best of any Third System fort.

The only problem with a visit to the fort involves access. It can be reached by boat (private boat, or charter boats operating out of Key West) or by a seaplane service operating out of Key West. However difficult the arrangements, Fort Jefferson is a "must see." Bring water, however, because there is no drinking water (or food, etc.) available in the *Dry* Tortugas.

Notes

[1]The evaluation of the size of a fort is an art rather than a science – the size depends on how it is measured.

The classic measurement methods were the perimeter of the scarp wall or the area of the parade. Forts with massive outworks integrated into their design were understated by this method. On the other hand, forts with outworks a substantial distance from the main work would be overstated if the area of the entire complex were used. This leads to ongoing controversy regarding the relative size of the larger Third System forts.

[2]Fort Adams, defenses of Newport, Rhode Island, has two tiers of casemates on the seaward side, but the second tier is at the level of the parade. The vertical scale of Fort Adams in not nearly as impressive as Fort Jefferson.

Figure 151: The incredible size of Fort Jefferson makes the classic photograph of arches dimminishing in the distance especially impressive. As in most Third System forts, the casemates had a set of arches between the cannon, and a second set of arches for communication behind the extreme of the carriage. *(Photo by author)*

The Defenses of Pensacola Bay

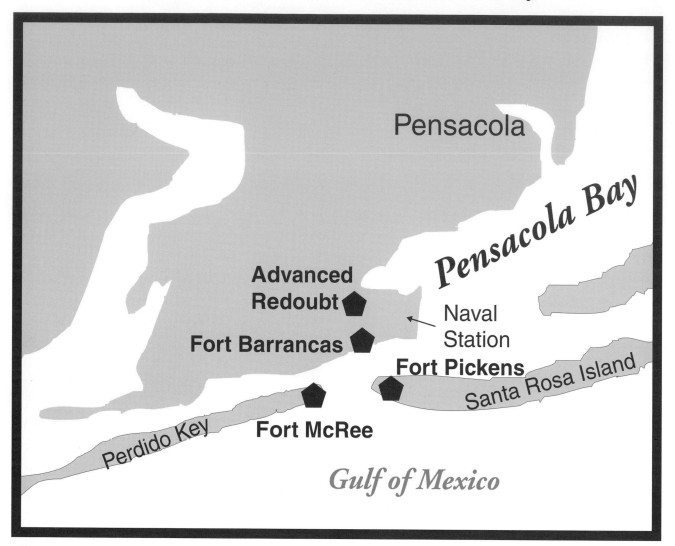

History

Since Florida was in Spanish possession when the first report of the Board of Engineers was written, no defenses of the area were listed in that report. In June of 1821, the Spanish vacated Pensacola, leaving it in American hands. The forts left by the Spanish were in very poor condition, with the only inhabitable fort being the small, wood-revetted Fort San Carlos and its water battery. With the city nearly void of defenses, the Board was sent to Pensacola to make a proposal for its defense. The Board decided on two forts, one on Santa Rosa Island and one at the site of the Spanish Fort San Carlos.

Pensacola was an important city, and was chosen as the capital of West Florida. The harbor became most important, however, when Pensacola was finally chosen over Key West for the site of the naval yard and depot for the Gulf Coast. This, coupled with the ability of the harbor to shelter a fleet, gave priority to the efforts of the Fortifications Board. The fact that Pensacola rated *four* Third System forts related to the importance placed on the Navy Yard, and the need for significant land defenses. These were required because of the large number of locations where an attacker could land his forces.

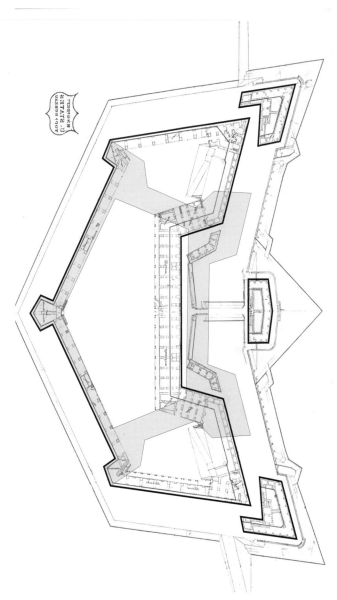

Figure 152: The design of Fort Pickens was born in controversy. The dark lines indicate the orignial Totten design for the fort, while the shaded area is the modified Bernard design. *(Sketch from NARA drawings)*

Third System Strategy

The water approaches to Pensacola harbor were straightforward in terms of defense. A barrier island controlled the main channel for a significant portion of its length, and a nearby point across the channel mouth, on a second barrier island, could provide crossfire. Additionally, fire could be brought to bear on the main channel,

as well as the harbor in general, from an area midway along the north shore.

The land approaches to the Navy Yard were not difficult, either. The Navy Yard was to sit at the end of a peninsula defined by Pensacola Bay on the south and Bayou Grande on the north. The old Spanish Fort San Carlos was located on a bluff above the bay at the narrowest point on the peninsula.

A grouping of four forts was designated to defend the area: two for the primary defense of the water approaches, one of mixed mission for water defense and control of the land approaches, and one for purely land defense. The largest of these forts was also designed to be the "headquarters" fort for the Gulf Coast.

The channel was guarded by this headquarters fort, Fort Pickens, and by the smaller tower fort, Fort McRee, on Foster's Bank. These two forts provided crossfire on any ships attempting to enter the harbor. Supporting this crossfire was the forward fire of Fort Barrancas and its water battery. They provided bow-on fire on ships entering the bay, as well as broadside fire on ships proceeding toward the harbor.

Fort Barrancas and the Advanced Redoubt provided Land defense. This defense was supplemented by a large earthwork connecting these forts, and extending beyond the Advanced Redoubt to the edge of Bayou Grande.

Fort Pickens

Fort Pickens was unique in that it was designed by two different engineers, *half of the fort designed by each.* This was not collaboration in the design of the fort, but the result of a conflict between the two principal fort designers of the period, Simon Bernard and Joseph Totten.

The conflict began when Totten prepared the plan for the defenses of Pensacola Harbor and began construction prior to receiving the approval of the plans from his superior, Bernard.

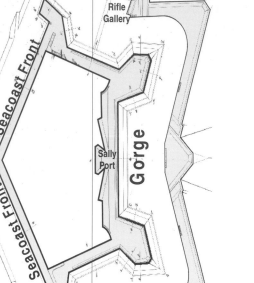

Figure 153: The final design of Fort Pickens was far less elaborate than the original, but was still a formidable work. The long seacoast fronts and massive gorge bastions provided a strong defense from land and sea. (Sketch from NARA drawing)

Bernard disagreed with Totten's approach, believing that the Santa Rosa Island fort could be made somewhat smaller and less complex, and the money saved could be applied to an additional fort across the channel on Foster's Bank.

Since construction on the fort had begun in 1829, a great deal of the money to be saved would be wasted in the rework of the foundations and the time delay in getting the new project approved.[1] In addition, Bernard had to take some care in dealing with Totten to prevent his humiliation in being overruled. To this end, Bernard decided on a compromise position. The seacoast fronts of the fort, already under construction, would proceed with the Totten design. The remaining three fronts, however, would be redesigned by Bernard to reduce the complexity of the fort and

to incorporate some of Bernard's preferences in design.

This compromise was not the end of the debate. Totten wrote a lengthy letter to the Chief of Engineers defending his reasoning in the design of the fort. While conceding that Bernard's design was satisfactory, he stated that his design was "no less adequate" to the defense of the harbor. While not attempting to overrule Bernard, Totten thus assured that "his side of the story" was told and that he was allowed to save face.

Under these circumstances the "hybrid" fort was built. It was to be the headquarters fort for the Gulf Coast, and was therefore the largest of all Gulf Coast forts. Located on what was the western end of Santa Rosa Island, the fort provided the primary defense of the channel leading into Pensacola Bay.

The fort is an all-brick, irregular five-sided work with two primary seacoast fronts, two secondary fronts, and a gorge. While the island currently extends almost one mile beyond the seacoast fronts, when the fort was built it was very close to the end of the island. The same natural forces that destroyed Fort McRee have caused the shoreline to move that distance.

Figure 154: The ravelin in advance of the gorge of Fort Pickens was far less extensive than the masonry outworks originally conceived, but its large size made it very impressive. (Photo by author)

160

Figure 155: Fort Pickens, minus a bastion due to an accident in a later period, stands guard near the tip of Santa Rosa Island. *(Photo courtesy Terrance McGovern)*

The seacoast fronts of the fort, designed by Totten, were over 1000 feet long, providing both casemated and barbette cannon to control the channel. Wide, shallow arches housed two cannon per casemate on these fronts, with a barbette tier of guns above. A small bastion, called the tower bastion,[2] joined the two curtains.

The narrow beach area beyond the fort walls on this side of the fort made a land attack from that direction unlikely, minimizing the need for land defenses. The tower bastion provided the required defenses, and also allowed the mounting of large barbette guns atop the bastion. To provide additional firepower on the channel area, the seacoast faces of the tower bastion were casemated to house heavy cannon.

At each end of the seacoast front was an irregularly shaped bastion, a mixture of the demibastions that Totten designed and the full bastions of the Bernard modification. The seacoast faces of these bastions were casemated for heavy cannon, while the landward faces were loopholed for small arms. The flanks of the bastions were casemated for howitzers.

The remaining two bastions were of Bernard's design, medium-sized conventional bastions. They replaced two very large demibastions, thus greatly reducing the overall size of the fort.

In addition to reducing the trace and area of the fort, Bernard greatly reduced the complexity. He replaced a fully casemated gorge wall

Figure 156: The long seacoast fronts of Fort Pickens, designed by Totten, are still the most impressive part of the fort. *(Photo by author)*

with an earth-backed curtain, and eliminated a tenaille, a caponier, and three masonry structures in the outworks.

Each of Bernard's landward bastions provided four howitzer embrasures to wash the gorge wall. The shorter secondary-front curtains were washed by three howitzer embrasures per bastion.

These secondary fronts were significantly shorter than the seacoast fronts, and each casemate contained a gunroom and living quarters. The cannon mounted there were of smaller caliber than on the seacoast fronts, and bore on the bay to the north and the gulf to the south. The

support. Buttresses were also added to the counterscarp wall as a preventive measure.

Access to the barbette tier of the fort was provided by beautiful curved stairways at each corner of the parade. At the junction of the seacoast fronts, two stairways led to the terreplein with an arch between them opening into the tower bastion. The other stairways joined with wedge-shaped masonry structures to protect the powder magazines within the bastions.

An interesting feature of Fort Pickens was the presence of tunnels underneath the landward bastions. These tunnels served a dual function: as a countermine, they could detect and thwart

Figure 157: The long sweeping arches of the casemates on the seacoast fronts were designed for two cannon per casemate. A second tier of cannon would stand on the barbette tier above. *(Photo by author)*

south curtain also contained the sally port and its flanking guardrooms.

The gorge wall was the most vulnerable to a siege, as it faced the bulk of Santa Rosa Island, the land approach to the fort. This curtain was not casemated, but rather was backed with a substantial sand fill forming a large place d'armes. Barbette guns would provide fire against the siege force, supplemented by gun positions on each of the large bastions.

Unfortunately, the sand fill proved too much for the masonry walls. The scarp wall began to bow outward, and buttresses had to be added to the outside of the gorge wall to provide

an attempt by an attacker to mine the bastions of the fort; as mining galleries, they could be used to collapse the bastions of the fort should they fall to attackers.

An extensive outwork protected the gorge wall and the two large bastions. This outwork consisted of two blunt-ended salient places d'armes, one at the salient of each bastion, and a V-shaped place d'armes at the middle of the gorge wall. Four brick-revetted traverses divided the covert way, with zigzag passageways along the banquette. Access to the covert way was provided by granite stairways along the counterscarp wall.

The outwork was terminated at each end by a rifle gallery that was entered through a door opening to the ditch. The north gallery provided additional flanking fire to guard the sally port, while the south gallery cooperated with the bastions to defend the south secondary front.

Today, Fort Pickens is well-preserved by the National Park Service and is open to the public. It has, however, undergone major modifications. Some of these modifications have been to adapt its use in later periods, but the most extensive modification was accidental.

In the latter part of the nineteenth century, a concrete gun battery was built on the parade of Fort Pickens. Earthen fill was added to protect the battery, and the walls of the fort were reduced in height on one seacoast front and one secondary front of the fort. This reduction in height not only removed the parapet, but also stripped the terreplein down to the masonry arches.

At this same time, the unintentional "modification" took place. Powder for the new guns was being stored in one of the bastions, and adjacent to this bastion was a storage area for the blocks and tackle used to move the heavy guns into position. A fire started in the area where the blocks and tackle were stored, and the hemp rope burned quickly. Although a bucket brigade was formed to fight the fire, it was soon out of control and the fort was abandoned. When the fire reached the powder storage area, an explosion occurred that showered bricks as far as 1-1/2 miles away. The bastion and portions of the adjacent curtains were completely removed!

Despite these modifications, and to some extent because of them, Fort Pickens is a very good place to visit. There is enough of the old fort remaining intact to understand what it looked like, and the areas where portions of the structure were exposed help the visitor to see the methods used in the construction of the fort. Where the bastion was removed, a cross-section of the curtain wall remains. The area where the terreplein was removed reveals the drainage system and the construction methods used to form the top of the arches.

Fort Pickens is part of the Gulf Islands National Seashore, and is therefore operated by the National Park Service. An excellent tour program and an extensive visitor center supplement the fort itself. Books on period forts, histories of the area, and other subjects of historical significance are available, as well as gifts and souvenirs for all ages.

Fort Pickens is reached by traveling south from Pensacola on US 98, crossing the long bridge over the western end of the harbor. Follow Pensacola Beach Road across a second bridge to Santa Rosa Island, then turn west on SR-399, Fort Pickens Road. Following this road to the end, you will pass through the outworks of the old fort. Turn right just beyond the fort to reach the parking area.

Fort McRee

The only Third System fort that is gone without trace is Fort McRee, once the western

Figure 158: The magazines of Fort Pickens were protected by the strange-looking structure pictured above. This massive stone structure was covered with earth to absorb the impact of artillery and prevent damage to the magazine. A passageway between the structure and the magazine provides an air gap for further protection, ventilation, and communication. *(Photo by author)*

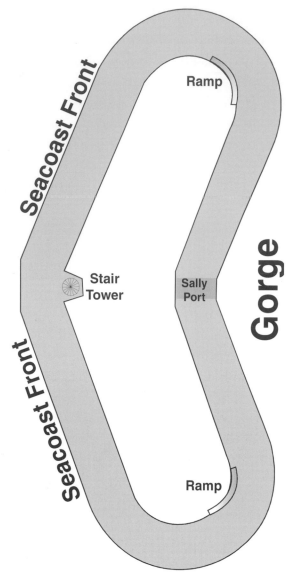

Figure 159: Similar in size and shape to Fort Calhoun, the interior of Fort McRee was quite different. Immediately south of the fort - above in the drawing - stood a separate water battery.

A significant source of confusion has existed in relation to the name of this fort. Originally named Fort McRee in honor of William McRee of the Corps of Engineers in 1840,[3] the fort was referred to as Fort McRae in both official and unofficial correspondence. One hundred years after its official naming, the War Department attempted to clear up the confusion in the fort's name. After extensive researching of records, the original name of Fort McRee was restored and it was confirmed that Lt. Col. William McRee, an original member of the Board of Engineers, was the namesake of the fort.

Naming the fort after Colonel McRee adds an interesting twist to the history of the Third System. Totten and Chase were the instigators of the name of the fort, and their choice seems to point out some of the conflict they had with Bernard. One of the first forts named after Bernard's return to France was to bear the name of his arch rival, who had resigned from the Corps of Engineers rather than serve under a foreign engineer.

Begun in 1838, the trace of Fort McRee was shared with Fort Calhoun at Hampton Roads. It was a long rectangle with rounded ends, "folded" in the middle. This gave two long sea-coast fronts, two rounded land-defense ends, and two obliquely angled gorge walls. The sally port was at the junction of these gorge walls.

The remarkable feature of Fort McRee was the construction of the casemates. Similar in design to Fort Schuyler and Fort Adams, the large casemates were designed to hold four cannon on two tiers. The division of the tiers was by a heavy-beamed wooden floor. Above these casemates was a barbette tier of cannon.

It can be speculated that these extremely large arches, with no intervening masonry, resulted in a weaker structure. A combination of the cannon fire against the fort's walls, and the burning of the timber inside the fort caused the loss of structural

guardian of the entrance to Pensacola Harbor. The fort was located on Foster's Bank, opposite Fort Pickens, but a combination of tidal action and hurricanes have caused its remains to become lost. Work is ongoing in attempting to locate the remains of the fort, but so far the projected locations are theories. A universal accord has not been established, but technological advances may assist in this process. When the site is established, it is hoped that an archeological excavation will follow.

Figure 160: The interior of Fort McRee during the Civil War is shown in this historic photograph. *(Photo courtesy NARA)*

integrity. The forces of nature finished the demolition begun by Union cannon.

The fort was designed to be very heavily armed for its size. Forty-four seacoast cannon could have been mounted *en casemate* on the two fronts of the fort, with an additional twenty-four heavy guns on the barbette. The curved ends of the fort had provision for an additional twelve guns each, with fourteen embrasures facing the gorge. The barbette tier of the ends and gorge could mount additional cannon for land defense.

Communication between the tiers was provided by a circular stair tower at the angle of the seacoast fronts, and by a straight stairway at each end of the fort. Hot-shot furnaces were located on the parade in the center of each seacoast front.

The fort, located on a very narrow island, was devoid of outworks for land defense. The gorge wall was unprotected masonry, and there was no ditch. The gorge embrasures and barbette positions provided the only defense against a land-based assault.

The only outwork, located immediately south of the fort, was a large water battery. This battery was not casemated, but instead utilized the detached-scarp concept used in Fort Gaines and Fort Clinch. A Carnot wall surrounded the battery, with a chemin de ronde and the sloping earthen ramparts. All guns in the battery were mounted en barbette. The battery offered a further thirteen heavy-gun positions for the defense of the channel.

Today, visitors can stroll the beaches of Perdido Key across from Fort Pickens where, rumor has it, portions of the ruins are visible following a storm. Ruins of three concrete batteries are visible, causing some confusion to the casual observer. Differing opinions place the location of the fort beneath the sand dunes and beach, or off shore under the western portion of the entrance to the bay. Further efforts will be required to solve the mystery of Fort McRee's location.

Fort Barrancas

Guarding the north shore of Pensacola Bay stood Fort Barrancas and its water battery, Bateria de San Antonio. This small brick fort provided forward fire on ships entering the bay, provided secondary protection of the bay should ships be able to run past the guns of Forts Pickens and McRee, and provided the southern anchor of the land defenses of the Navy Yard. Construction began in 1839 and the fort was completed in 1844.

These varied missions drove a design that was unique within the Third System. First, Fort Barrancas was one of the rare hilltop forts of the System. Because of the land-defense mission, it had to be located on the high ground it was required to defend. Immediately below the fort on the hillside toward the bay stood the old Spanish water battery for Fort San Carlos. While not at the water line as would be preferred, the presence of this battery so close to the new fort begged for its usage.

Using the existing structure as a foundation, the curved scarp was raised to 15 feet 2 inches above the parade of the battery, and the gorge

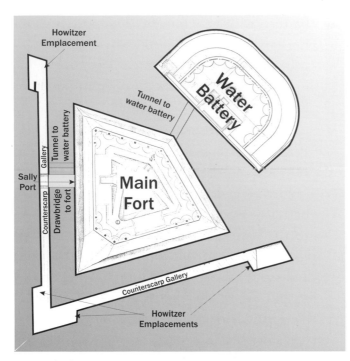

Figure 161: Fort Barrancas is a combination of a modified Spanish water battery and a new Third System fort. The kite-shaped fort and counterscarp galleries on two sides is similar to Fort Livingston south of New Orleans. *(Sketch from NARA drawing)*

wall was raised almost 10 feet above the level of the parapet. Earth was used to raise the terreplein appropriately, and barbettes were installed for mounting the heavy guns. The final task was to construct a tunnel that connected the battery to Fort Barrancas above.

In addition to the thirteen heavy guns of the water battery, Fort Barrancas mounted fourteen seacoast cannon to bear on the channel. These guns were all mounted en barbette, and were reached by ramps from the small parade in the middle of the fort. The remainder of the fort was designed for its land-defense mission.

The two long walls of the kite-shaped fort pointed toward the probable route of a land attack, with the north wall roughly perpendicular to the earthworks that connected with the Advanced Redoubt. The masonry walls of the fort were well shielded by the glacis, but there was no covert way or banquette at the top of the

glacis. Rather, the glacis terminated at the vertical counterscarp wall, making a formidable obstacle for the attacker. Fire down the glacis, both cannon and small-arms, would be provided from the ramparts of the fort. On reaching the top of the glacis, the attacker would also be under the small-arms fire of the rifle galleries surrounding the perimeter of the fort.

A drawbridge that was backed by the standard two-ply oak doors with iron studs sealed the only entrance to the fort. This left the only route into the fort through the ditch. The ditch was defended not only by the forward-fire rifle galleries, but by the most impressive counterscarp gallery in the Third System. This V-shaped gallery extended around the two landward sides of the fort, and provided loopholes at a lower elevation than those of the scarp. At the point of the "V", two howitzer embrasures swept each leg of the ditch. Further howitzer embrasures were located at each end of the "V", and swept the walls above the water battery.

Access to the rifle galleries was through the main sally port. The sally port also provided the entrance to the tunnel that led to the counter-

Figure 162: The scarp gallery of Fort Barrancas is shown above. Note the vertical smoke vents immediately above each loophole. *(Photo by author)*

Figure 163: The interior of the counterscarp gallery of Fort Barrancas is shown above. These long galleries provide reverse fire on the two landward sides of the fort. *(Photo by author)*

scarp galleries. This tunnel extended completely under the level of the ditch, with no evidence of its existence provided to an attacker. The sally port was also flanked by a guardroom that supplied the only "living space" within the fort. This area, and the adjoining scarp galleries, were independently defensible should the parade fall to an attacker.

An interesting design feature of the fort was the use of the natural angle of the sand to provide the rear of the rifle galleries. It cannot help but be assumed that the problems with the potential collapse of one wall of Fort Pickens due to the pressure of the sand inspired the engineers

to carefully consider the forces applied to the walls when designing Fort Barrancas. The rear wall of the rifle gallery was only shoulder-high, with the remainder of the wall formed by exposed sand.

The angle of the sand sloping to the top of the arch minimized the force on the interior wall. An additional feature is the curvature of the wall toward the sand fill. This convex shape spread the force of the sand away from the center of the wall, its weakest point, toward the stronger portions of the wall where it joined the transverse arches.

The magazines of the fort were of some interest. Main magazines were located on either side of the sally port behind the rifle galleries, in the rear of the water battery, and at the "V" of the counterscarp gallery. Secondary magazines were located at the ends of the counterscarp galleries, behind the howitzer emplacements, and a service magazine is located beneath the terreplein of the water battery.

Today, Fort Barrancas is a well-preserved example of a mixed-defense fort. Extensive work has been done by the National Park Service to stabilize the structure, and it is very well maintained. The fort is located on the Pensacola Naval Air Station, and is open to the public. The National Park Service manages the fort, as well as a bookstore/display area. This unique structure is a must-see for anyone interested in forts of this period.

To reach Fort Barrancas from Pensacola and points east, follow Barrancas Avenue southwest from the downtown area. Turn south on Navy Boulevard, and enter the Pensacola Naval Air Station. Follow this road as it becomes Duncan Road and then Hulse Road. Turn east at the end of the road on Radford Boulevard. You will pass Fort Barrancas on your right. Continue to the Blue Angels Parkway – the Naval Air Museum is straight ahead – and turn east (right).

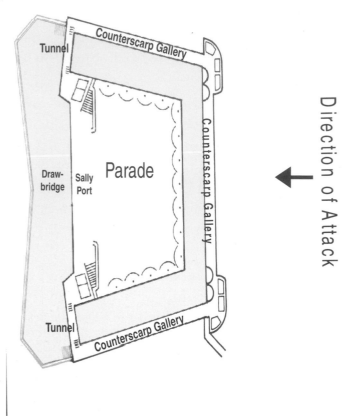

Figure 164: The Advanced Redoubt had a very directional nature. Both the fort and its outworks were aimed at the approach up the peninsula, although the rear of the fort had significant defenses as well. *(Sketch based on NARA drawing)*

The entrance to Fort Barrancas is on the right.

From Points west, follow SR-297, Gulf Beach Parkway, to the Blue Angels Parkway. Turn right, continuing east on the Blue Angels Parkway. Enter the Pensacola Naval Air Station, and continue past the Naval Air Museum. The entrance to Fort Barrancas is on the right.

Advanced Redoubt

The "Advanced Redoubt of Fort Barrancas" was neither in advance (toward an attacker) of Fort Barrancas nor was it, by classical definition, a redoubt. A redoubt was an unbastioned work, while the Advanced Redoubt had two demibastions. It was the mission of the fort, however, that caused the author to treat this as a

separate Third System fort.[4] Construction began in 1845, and the fort was completed in 1859.

As mentioned previously, the Navy Yard sat at the end of a peninsula defined by Pensacola Bay on the south and Bayou Grande on the north. At the narrowest point of this peninsula stood Fort Barrancas and the Advanced Redoubt, once connected by a continuous earthwork. The mission of the Advanced Redoubt was to hold the northern end of this earthwork and provide support down half its length, with the remainder of the defense provided by Fort Barrancas.[5]

This positioning placed the Advanced Redoubt parallel to Fort Barrancas, equidistant from an attacker. The classical positioning of a redoubt was in advance of the fort, to serve as an early warning of attack. The Advanced Redoubt could not have served such a function.

The Advanced Redoubt was unique in its mission: it was the *only* Third System fort with no seacoast defense mission. It was designed and constructed only for land defense.

The Advanced Redoubt was a trapezoid with two parallel walls. One wall was slightly longer than the other three, causing the sides of the fort to "flare" out. While not a seacoast defense fort, it did have a distinct "gorge," in this case a curtain less susceptible to land attack than the three "faces." This gorge wall had no counterscarp galleries but did have flanking fire from two demibastions. Additionally, the terreplein was fronted by loopholes in this wall rather than having barbette-type gun emplacements.

The scarp wall at the level of the terreplein on the flanks of the demibastions had a crenellated embrasure which allowed the howitzer to fire at a steeper downward angle than if it were firing over the parapet. The only other use of a crenellated embrasure in the Third System

Figure 165: The Advanced Redoubt had two demibastions protecting a center-pivot drawbridge in the center of the gorge wall. In addition to howitzer embrasures in the flanks of these demibastions, the faces contained loopholes for forward fire. *(Photo by author)*

was guarding the main sally port of Fort Adams in Newport, Rhode Island.

The sally port opened with an interesting center-pivot drawbridge that rotated down into a recess inside the scarp wall. Also of interest was that the sally port was open to the sky, unlike the casemated sally ports in most other Third System forts. This open area led through an archway onto the parade of the Redoubt.

The three faces of the fort had positions for 15 heavy guns, designed for land defense. Beneath these barbette guns was a rifle gallery that encircled three sides of the fort. This rifle gallery fired out over the counterscarp wall, covering both the covert way and the glacis. The rifle gallery used the same recurved walls and open-sand slopes as were used in Fort Bar-

rancas.

An interesting feature of the Advanced Redoubt was the foundation. Built on very swampy soil with a high sand content and variable water-table levels, a set of arches was constructed beneath the rifle gallery. These arches supported the structure, and the sand floor sloped upward. While not well documented, it is believed that this area would contain sand at low water and a mixture of sand and water at high water.[6] By allowing the self-leveling of water and sand, independent of water level, undue stress on the outer walls was eliminated.

Access to this area was through a hatch in the floor of the rifle gallery. The arched chamber, never intended for communication, only for structure, was closed by brick walls at either side of the sally port to prevent entry from the ditch.

169

Immediately opposite the rifle gallery, again on three sides of the fort, was a substantial counterscarp gallery. This gallery, like the one at Fort Barrancas, was accessed under the ditch, in this case by two tunnels. At the corners of the gallery, howitzer embrasures swept the ditch. Magazines were located behind the casemates.

The outworks of the Advanced Redoubt were simple, consisting of a covert way and a breast-height wall. The only adornment was the presence of four traverses, located on the two secondary fronts. This would have prevented an attacker from firing down the length of the parapet from the glacis on the face of the fort.

It is interesting to note the strong directional nature of the Redoubt's defenses. The main ditch protected the north, south, and west sides of the forts, where the counterscarp galleries were located. A much shallower, separate ditch guarded the east side of the fort. The traverses on the outworks were earth-faced to the west, with exposed masonry revetments to the east. While certainly not defenseless from the east, the Redoubt was far more vulnerable than to the expected attack from the west.

Today, the Advanced Redoubt is being well maintained by the National Park Service, but is generally not open to the public. While on the property of the Pensacola Naval Air Station, the fort is actually part of the Gulf Islands National Seashore. Special tours of the Advanced Redoubt are given, and it is open on some weekends. The exterior of the fort can be visited at any time. Information on the Redoubt is available from the Fort Barrancas Visitor's Center, and from the well-informed NPS personnel at both Fort Barrancas and Fort Pickens. Tours of the interior are scheduled through the Fort Barrancas visitors' center.

The Advanced Redoubt is reached by turning right (east) on Blue Angels Parkway from the Fort Barrancas entrance. The Advanced Redoubt is a short distance on the left.

Notes

[1] Note that this was after the Fort Gaines fiasco, and Congress approved each fort project individually. The change in the size of Fort Pickens and the addition of Fort McRee would require Congressional approval before construction could proceed.

[2] While this bastion had the shape of a tower bastion, it had only one casemated tier and one barbette tier – not the multiple tiers of a classic tower bastion.

[3] The name is given in General Order No. 14, Army Adjutant General's Office, 16 March 1840.

[4] Great exception is taken by some who would group this structure as simply a redoubt of Fort Barrancas. If the reader so wishes, it makes little difference in the text, and the number of Third System forts can be reduced to 41.

[5] The Redoubt did not stand on the shore of Bayou Grande, but was approximately 100 yards from the shore. This last 100 yards was quite swampy, and was defended by a short earthwork that extended from the Redoubt to the shore.

[6] This phenomenon has been observed by National Park Service Rangers.

The Defenses of Mobile Bay

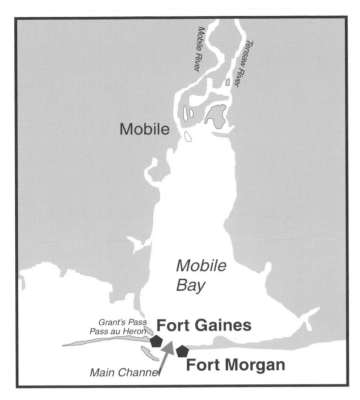

History

Near the top of the priority list when the Coastal Fortifications Board was first convened was the defense of Mobile Bay. There were three main reasons for the strategic value of the bay: 1) It provided a safe harbor for a large fleet to weather storms on the Gulf; 2) Access to the bay controlled access to the river system at the north end of Mobile Bay. This included the Mobile River and the Tensaw River which led to the two major inland waterways, the Alabama River and the Tombigbee River; and 3) A sheltered waterway, now known as the Gulf Intracoastal Waterway, connected Mobile Bay with New Orleans. For these reasons protection for the bay was designated as "First Priority" and construction of the forts was to begin immediately. While they were among the earliest of the Third System forts, construction began after the New Orleans and Hampton Roads forts.

While Mobile Bay was very large, its mouth was relatively narrow. Approximately three miles across, it was defined by Mobile Point on the east and Dauphin Island on the west. While two channels led into the bay, only the eastern channel was deep enough to allow deep-draft ships to pass. A "back door" to the bay through Pass au Héron and Grant's Pass was a narrow, shallow-water connection between the Gulf and the Bay.

Third System Strategy

The geography of Mobile Bay made its defense straightforward. Two identical, medium-sized forts were designed, one located on each side of the bay's mouth. Together the guns of these forts would command the entire entrance to the bay. Lower on the priority list was a defensive tower to defend the "back door" approach. This tower could be supplemented by earthworks should the need arise.

While the construction of both forts began expeditiously, construction of the fort on Dauphin Island was soon halted.[1] Work on the Mobile Point fort continued without interruption. The development of shallow-draft steam vessels and their adaptation as warships in the 1830s caused a reevaluation of the situation at Mobile Bay. The strategic value of the Dauphin Island fort was reconsidered, and a new fort was designed to guard the western channel. The completion of this second fort consummated Mobile Bay's defenses, as the "back entrance" through Pass au Héron was considered to be in need of only an earthwork should an attack appear likely.

Fort Morgan

On the eastern side of the channel leading to Mobile Bay, occupying Mobile Point, stood Fort Morgan. Guarding the mile-wide eastern

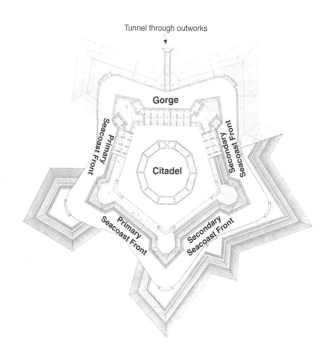

Tunnel through outworks

Gorge

Citadel

Primary Seacoast Front

Secondary Seacoast Front

Primary Seacoast Front

Secondary Seacoast Front

Figure 166: Fort Morgan had the tradtional bastioned pentagon shape common in early Third System forts. Extensive outworks, also common early in the system, complemented the fort. *(Drawing courtesy NARA)*

channel, the fort was of moderate trace and designed for a relatively small number of cannon. It was, however, a classic fort of the early Third System. With construction beginning in 1819, it was one of the first forts of the system.

The fort was designed as a regular pentagon, with moderately large bastions at each corner. Two primary seacoast fronts bore directly on the channel, while two secondary fronts defended the Gulf and Bay approaches, respectively. The gorge faced the isthmus that connected Mobile Point with the mainland. This isthmus provided the only land approach to the fort.

The curtain walls of the fort were fully casemated, and each flank of each bastion contained two casemates with embrasures for two howitzers. Each of these flanks was entered independently, with no interconnection within the bastion. The body of the bastion was filled with earth, a classic approach as the salient of a bas-

tion was considered a fort's most vulnerable area.

Each of the casemates of the fort had an embrasure for a seacoast cannon, flanked by two loopholes. This approach indicated a strong priority for the defense of the ditch from a land-based attack. While this was understandable on the landward side of the fort, the pattern was repeated on the seacoast fronts. It is presumed that this is because of the width of the land outside the outworks, allowing an attacker to move around the fort.

In the initial design of the fort, caponiers were designed to assist in the defense of the ditch. These caponiers, however, were eliminated from the design before construction began, and the defense of the ditch was left to the bastions and the curtain wall embrasures and loopholes.

The principal seacoast cannon were to be mounted en barbette on the two primary and two secondary fronts. The entire barbette tier of the fort was completely paved with brick. This rare approach provides a very attractive view for the visitor to the fort.

In addition to barbette batteries and the casemate batteries, seacoast cannon were mounted in a small reduit in advance of the primary seacoast bastion. This reduit also contained a hot-shot furnace to heat solid shot before firing at wooden ships.

Between the flanks of the two landward bastions, against the parade wall, were the main powder magazines. These magazines had air vents opening to the parade, with offsets in the vents to prevent a spark from entering the magazine.

The locations of the magazines were carefully chosen. The thickness of the earth-filled bastion protected their exterior walls, and land-based cannon could not impinge on their parade walls. Shipboard cannon, with much less accuracy, were the only threat. Those cannon would have to fire with incredible accuracy to

Figure 167: The traditional shape and outworks of Fort Morgan are shown in this modified aerial photograph. Only the citadel, shown outlined in the grass of the parade, is missing from the configuration of the fort during the ninteenth century. *(Photo by author)*

reach the small exposed area between the heavy stairways and the massive citadel occupying the parade.

The ten-sided, three-tiered citadel was the largest in any Third System fort. It was built tall enough to control the ramparts from the third tier, and to catch the sea breezes through the loopholes that perforated the walls. Although numerous, the small slits did not catch a sufficient amount of fresh air to adequately ventilate the barracks area, and it was deemed an unhealthy accommodation. Despite the lack of ventilation, the interior courtyard provided some of the most pleasing architecture of the Third System. Large, columned entrances opened onto paved porticos, forming an ornate and very pleasant piazza.

Fort Morgan's location on a very long peninsula, coupled with the fact that it was built early in the Third System, led to the construction of considerable land defenses. In addition to the defenses of the ditch mentioned previously, the fort mounted heavy cannon on the barbette tier of the gorge. These cannon could menace an attacker from a considerable distance, and would provide defensive fire against siege guns.

Placing the sally port in the northern secondary front also increased the strength of the gorge. The sally port had two chambers, with the outermost chamber sealed by solid wooden doors.[2] This chamber, if breached, was defended by four loopholes high in each wall. Loopholes in the doors to the rear chamber provided additional defense. This rear chamber opened to the parade and to the two adjacent casemates.

The outworks that completely ringed the fort provided further land defense. The design of the outworks was in the classic style. A long

173

glacis sloped to a breast-high wall that was only slightly lower than the scarp. Behind the breast-high wall was an earthen banquette, with a slope down to a wide covert way. A masonry counterscarp wall dropped to the ditch. Periodically along this wall, stairways and ramps led from the ditch to the covert way.

The entry path through the outworks was unique to Fort Morgan. The initial plan of the fort depicted a curving, masonry-faced pathway through the outworks leading to the sally port, similar to the entry ways of Fort Pike and Fort Wood. This pathway, however, was not constructed. Instead, the entryway was a long, straight tunnel under the outworks, closed by heavy doors at each end. While there were no flanking guardrooms to defend the tunnel, it is suspected that the doors at the end of the tunnel toward the ditch were either loopholed or of a latticework design.

Fort Morgan had two very curious features. First, no ramps were provided from the parade to the ramparts, only pairs of very steep stairways. This meant that soldiers providing balls and powder to the barbette guns would have to run up these steep stairs with their heavy loads, a very tiring task even when one was not being shot at by the enemy. The original design showed one sweeping stairway (perhaps replaced by a ramp at some locations) toward the parade from each bastion; but, when constructed, two steep stairways were used at each bastion instead. Adding to the curiosity was the presence of long ramps and sweeping stairways to the parapet of the outworks, where few if any cannon would be mounted!

The second curious feature was the presence of posterns leading to the ditch from each face of each bastion. These posterns would provide weak points in the face of every bastion in the fort. Following construction, these posterns were carefully closed to conceal the fact that they

Figure 168: The gorge of Fort Morgan was particularly impressive due to the height of the walls. While the fort had only one tier of casemates, the ramparts were very tall. *(Photo by author)*

once existed, but their presence was very clear from inside the bastions. One postern was left open, and remains open today.

A remarkable feature of the fort was the smooth curve on each counterscarp wall. This magnificent brickwork, the very ornate granite facade on the sally port, and the ornate piazza inside the citadel made Fort Morgan a masterpiece of architectural form as well as being carefully designed to fulfill the requirements of function. Of all the Third System forts, Fort Morgan appears to have been the most ornate.

This magnificent structure is in very good condition, and has a large portion of its extensive outworks intact. The condition of the outworks allows the visitor a clear perception of the way the glacis and counterscarp work together to protect the scarp wall from land-based cannon, and the parapet, covert way, traverses, and places d'armes are clearly visible. Even though they are truncated on the western end by a more modern concrete gun emplacement, Fort Morgan's outworks are the best preserved of any Third System fort.

Currently, Fort Morgan is well managed by the Alabama Historical Commission. The structure is in very good condition, though a concrete gun battery, Battery Duportail, occupies a significant portion of the parade. A pathway around the battery allows access to the seacoast casemates, and the original structure has been preserved. The citadel is completely gone, though a line of brickwork in the parade traces its outline.

An excellent museum is located in a modern structure outside the fort, and traces the history of Mobile Point and its fortifications. Thorough information on the fort's design and construction leads to a very good treatment of Fort Morgan's role in the Civil War. Information on the later periods of seacoast defense at Mobile Point completes the display. A collection of books and memorabilia are available in a small gift shop within the museum.

Fort Morgan is reached most directly by following SR-59 south to Gulf Shores, Alabama. Follow SR-180, Fort Morgan Road, west approximately 22 miles to the fort.

The alternative route is to take the Fort Morgan Ferry from Fort Gaines on Dauphin Island. The fort is near the ferry dock.

Fort Gaines

Midway through the Third System, Totten experimented with a new type of fort design, totally unlike any of the other Third System forts. He used this design on two forts,[3] Gaines and Clinch, which were essentially twins. Fort Gaines, guarding the western side of the entrance to Mobile Bay from Dauphin Island, was the first of these two forts to be constructed.

The original plan for Fort Gaines was to be the twin of Fort Morgan across the channel. The controversy described in Chapter One suspended construction, however, and when Congress supplied funds in 1853, Totten decided to abandon the original plan. In its place, he designed a new fort utilizing the latest in French fort-design theory, that of the detached scarp.

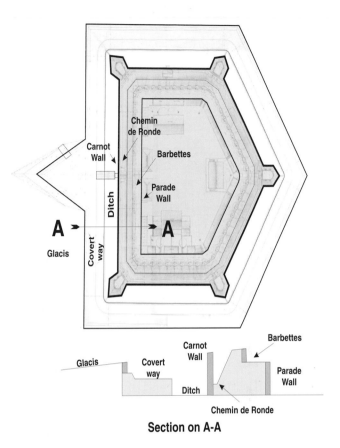

Figure 169: The plan of Fort Gaines is shown here, with a sketch of a section view. This design was shared by Fort Clinch on the Florida-Georgia border. *(Sketch based on NARA drawing)*

This new concept consisted of a thick masonry scarp surrounding the fort, backed with earth to approximately half its height. This perimeter wall, called a Carnot wall, ranged in thickness from four to eight feet of solid masonry (brick in both American forts). The half-height earthen fill provided a chemin de ronde, or walk around, fronted by loopholes for small-arms fire. Behind the chemin de ronde, the rampart sloped steeply upward to form the parapet. A breast-high wall fronted the barbettes where the heavy guns were mounted. This left an earthen parapet that was structurally independent of, and well behind, the scarp.

175

This design concept was based on the progressive stages of an attack on a fort. The first stage of attack would be an attack by warships. When attacked by ships, the chemin de ronde would not be manned, and the heavy barbette guns would provide the response of the fort. Any damage to the scarp would be expected to be minimal, as by this time it had been shown that ships could not effectively compete with fort-based cannon. The attacker would have to rely on a land-based attack.

zers mounted in the flanks of the bastions. Heavy guns atop the bastions would provide further support, but the barbette guns of the fort would not be used while the chemin de ronde was manned.

The certain failure of a coup de main would leave the attacker with no option but to mount a protracted siege. In a siege by heavy land-based cannon, the destruction of the scarp would be

Figure 170: This modified photograph shows Fort Gaines as it appeared in the nineteenth century. The ramparts for the heavy cannon and the chemin de ronde are clearly visible. *(Photo by author)*

based cannon. The attacker would have to rely on a land-based attack.

The first stage of a land-based attack would be an attempt at a coup de main, or infantry attack. The Carnot wall would provide the primary defense, with forward fire from small arms fired through the loopholes. This would be supplemented by flanking fire from the howit-

inevitable. With the detached scarp, however, this scarp wall is sacrificial; its destruction does not substantially weaken the fort. The heavy guns of the fort would continue to respond, and the crumbled scarp wall would provide a further barrier to attacking cannon.

The scarp having been destroyed, the final stage of the attack would be an infantry assault.

This would involve climbing the steep slope of the parapet, while under small-arms fire from the banquette. Even if this final assault was successful and the parade was reached, the battle was not over. Each of the bastions of Fort Gaines was designed as an individually defensible structure, connected to the parade by a long tunnel. Openings were also provided to the chemin de ronde from the rear of the bastions, but these would be expected to be closed by the rubble of the fallen Carnot wall. The bastions would require further assault against the small-arms and howitzers in the casemates, and the small arms and heavy cannon on the ramparts.

One other structure in the fort was designed to be individually defensible: the latrine! While structurally this was designed to hold out against an invader for some time, the quality of life for the soldiers confined there would not be very good!

The principal disadvantage in the detached scarp design was that all heavy cannon were mounted en barbette. This precluded multiple tiers of cannon, limiting the potential firepower of the fort. It also left all cannon exposed to shells exploding overhead, and to the effects of shot and shells from siege mortars.

A very curious feature of Fort Gaines was the location of the magazines. In all previous Third System forts, the magazines were well protected from enemy fire. The salients of the bastions, on the other hand, were earth-filled because of their prominence and therefore their vulnerability to enemy fire. In Fort Gaines, Totten put the magazines in the salient of the bastions where they were the most vulnerable!

The only casemates of Fort Gaines were in the bastions, and on the parade along one secondary front. The casemates in the bastions provided the traditional function of giving flanking fire to protect the scarp, while the remaining casemates housed storerooms and cooking ovens.

Figure 171: Long passageways connected the bastion to the parade, making it very easy to defend the bastion should the remainder of the fort fall. *(Photo by author)*

These casemates were under the ramparts of the fort, but were well behind the scarp wall.

Today, the Dauphin Island Park and Beach Board run Fort Gaines. There is a very good interpretive program with costumed rangers and informative signs. Reenactments are performed periodically, and often a blacksmith is on duty within the fort. The fort also has a nice bookstore/gift shop that provides historical information and souvenirs.

The structure of Fort Gaines was modified by the construction of a concrete gun battery on its parade. Modifications for the battery and its support have obscured most of the two primary seacoast fronts, but most of the fort is intact. The visitor can experience the unique style of fort design used in Fort Gaines, and enjoy several period cannon that remain at the site. It is a very pleasant fort to visit.

Further modifications have been made to the fort to enhance safety and comfort for the visitor. This included the addition of railings throughout the fort and adding walkways in some locations. Unfortunately, some of these modifications obscure the original appearance of the fort, but they do allow the visitor access to virtually all areas of the fort.

Fort Gaines can be reached by following the Dauphin Island Parkway south, exit 22 from I-10. Follow the parkway, SR 163, south to Dauphin Island. Turn east on entering the island, and follow the perimeter road to the fort.

Alternatively, the fort can be reached by taking the Fort Morgan Ferry from Fort Morgan on Mobile Point. The fort is just southeast of the ferry dock.

Notes

[1] See "The Evolution of the Board of Engineers" in Chapter One for details of the Dauphin Island controversy.

[2] These doors, like most in Third System forts, consisted of multiple layers of oak with the grain running in different directions in successive layers.

[3] He also used the design on the external battery at Fort McRee, Pensacola, Florida.

Figure 172: The extremely steep stairways of Fort Morgan remain a curiosity to historians. The original design showed shallower stairways alternating with ramps to the terreplein, but the design was changed during construction. The outworks retained the shallow stairways and ramps - only the interior of the fort was changed. *(Photo by author)*

The Defenses of New Orleans

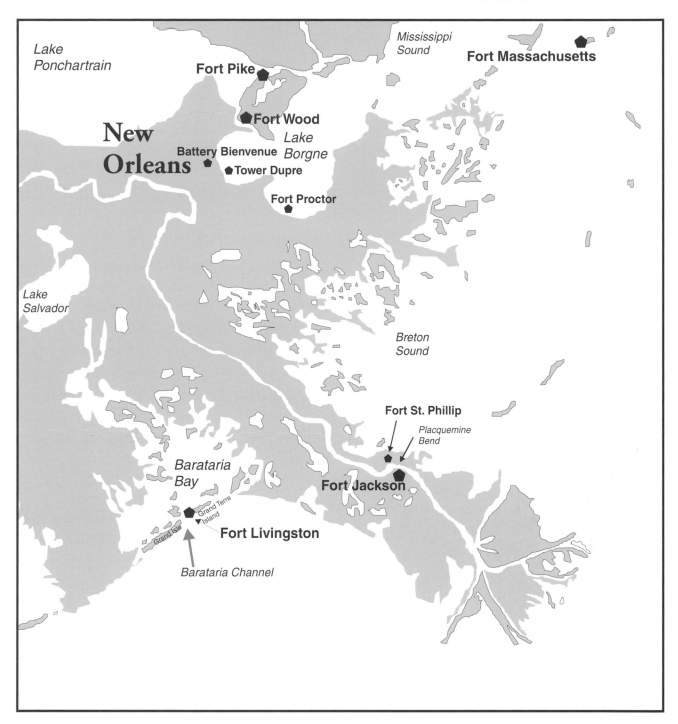

History

Immediately following the appointment of the Coastal Fortifications Board in 1816 and its initial review of the coastline, two areas were determined to be urgently in need of permanent fortifications. These were to be acted upon im-

mediately, rather than waiting for the completion of a detailed study and a set of overall recommendations. The first of these areas to be addressed was the defense of New Orleans.

The problem in designing a defense for New Orleans was the large number of options for an invading force. The most straightforward approach, and the one that required the most impressive works, was directly up the Mississippi River. This approach not only provided an opportunity for the capture of New Orleans, but also allowed navigation of the principal western waterway. At the time of the analysis, Fort St. Philip, a small, dilapidated French fort, "protected" this approach; it was the only permanent fortification in the area.

A second approach to New Orleans was through Lake Borgne and into Lake Pontchartrain. While there was no access to the Mississippi River from Lake Pontchartrain, it provided an ideal place to bombard the city, and countless areas to stage a land attack supported by ships. An invader thus capturing New Orleans could lay siege to the Mississippi River forts; isolated from reinforcements, their fall would be inevitable. Two narrow passages existed between Lake Borgne, opening on the Gulf, and Lake Pontchartrain: The Rigolets and pass Chef Menteur.

Of somewhat lower priority was the protection of Lake Borgne itself. The western shore of the lake provided opportunities for ships to land troops for a land attack on the city, and the western edges of the lake brought the city within range of shipboard cannon. That area was where the British attacked during the War of 1812.

Also, Barataria Bay, to the south of the city, provided access to Lake Salvador that bordered the city. This lake, while not as ideal as Lake Pontchartrain, provided a location from which the city could be bombarded and troops could be landed. There were also many passages that connected Barataria Bay with the Mississippi River, some upstream of the Fort St. Philip site at Plaquemines Bend (also known as Plaquemines Turn).

Western approaches to New Orleans involved passage through shallow bayous and swamp areas, not suitable for transporting an army. Thus the area to the west of New Orleans held its own natural defense and did not require fortification.

A final area critical to the defense of New Orleans was the anchorage off Ship Island, used by the British to stage their attack during the War of 1812. That was the only deep-water anchorage near New Orleans, and the island bordered the main ship channel to the city.

Third System Strategy

To combat these options, the Board designed the largest number of new fortifications in the Third System. In total number of forts, both new and renovated, New Orleans was second only to New York City, the nation's largest metropolitan area. Five new forts, two towers, and one battery were constructed, and one existing fort (St. Philip) was renovated.

Politically, the defense of New Orleans was very easy to "sell." Not only would Louisiana back any proposals for the defense of that area, but also all of the western states that depended on the Mississippi River for commerce knew the importance of the control of the waterway. The nation's largest western and southern city, New Orleans traded with virtually all the cities on the Eastern Seaboard and her commerce was critical to the economy of the entire nation. Bernard, referring to the defense of New Orleans in his 1826 report, stated, "The value of the stake is now too great, is too rapidly augmenting, and is too justly appreciated for the nation to suffer its safety ever again to hang on the doubtful issue of a battle."[1]

Work began immediately on the most vulnerable area, Pass Rigolets. That work was followed immediately by work at the sister pass, Chef Menteur, and at Fort Jackson across from the old French fort, St. Philip. By the time of the 1821 report, those three forts were under construction, and two more New Orleans forts

Figure 173: Fort Pike is a crescent, with demibastions at the corners of the curved face and a full bastion at the junction of the two straight walls. The arc-shaped citadel can be clearly seen on the parade. *(Photo by author)*

were "indispensable to the defense" and were to commence immediately. Those two additional forts were at Bayou Bienvenue and a replacement for Fort St. Philip. In the works of the Third Class, New Orleans rated one fort and one tower. The fort was to be located on Grand Terre Island, and the tower was to be at Bayou Dupré.

In 1822, the fort at Bayou Bienvenue was downgraded to a battery, which was begun in 1826. Although the replacement for Fort St. Philip remained as a fort of the highest priority from 1821 on, it was never constructed. In the 1850s, the old French fort received substantial renovation, but a new fort never took its place. The tower at Bayou Dupré began construction in 1829, with the fort at Grand Terre beginning construction in the middle-1830s. The tower at Proctor's Point in Lake Borgne was begun in 1856, but was never completed. Unique to this structure was the use of steel beams in the construction, rarely used in the construction of the body of the fort during the Third System.[2]

The final fort protecting New Orleans would be constructed much later. Not comprehended in any of the Bernard studies, the fort at Ship Island was first projected by Totten in 1851, but at that time a design had not been completed. Debate had taken place as to whether one fort or several forts were needed to defend this channel and anchorage used by the British in 1814, or if attempting to defend this large an area was pointless.[3] Construction finally began in 1859, but the fort was not completed when construction ceased in 1866.

Fort Pike

The isthmus leading to Pass Rigolets, between Lake Borgne and Lake Pontchartrain, is now covered with homes and cottages, almost obscuring the low brick structure located at its tip. By looking over the earthen mounds originally designed to protect the masonry walls from an enemy siege, however, a classic example of an early Third System fort can be seen.

Fort Pike was, in fact, the first fort designed and constructed in the Third System. Its design, engineered by Simon Bernard and drawn by Guillame Tell Poussin, was intended for use at three locations: at Pass Rigolets, a short distance down the shore at Pass Chef Menteur, and guarding the entrance to Barataria Bay on Grand Terre Island. Pass Rigolets was considered to be the top priority of the three sites, and construction began in 1818 under the superintendence of J. G. Totten.

Fort Pike had two main goals: to prevent entry into Lake Pontchartrain by an enemy fleet, and to deprive an enemy of a strong point from which it would be difficult to dislodge him. The locale, however, was not suited to a large militia and a small fort was considered most appropriate. One of the smallest of the System, Fort Pike has a perimeter of only 308 yards and was designed for a wartime garrison of 400 men. The fort was shaped like a piece of pie,[4] with one bastion at the junction of the straight sides and a demibastion at each intersection of the arc with a side.

It was well understood that ship borne cannon were much less accurate than cannon mounted on land, and therefore no earthen protection was required for the seaward face of the masonry walls. Along that curved face, Fort Pike mounted 13 guns *en casemate* and 11 guns *en barbette*. They provided the primary seaward armament of the fort, with the remaining guns used primarily for land defense. These remaining guns were a combination of howitzers and heavy cannon. The howitzers were mounted in casemates along the two straight walls, providing forward fire, and in the flanks of the bastion and demibastions, providing flanking fire. The heavy cannon were mounted en barbette, along the parapet of the straight faces, the bastion, and the demibastions.

An interesting feature of the fort, typical of Bernard designs of this period, was the use of "tunnel casemates." Instead of having casemates with large openings to the parade, Fort Pike's

Figure 174: The interior of Fort Pike, as seen in this photograph, provided a small parade that was dominated by the citadel in the foreground. *(Photo by author)*

182

casemates opened through long tunnels, providing protection for the rear of the gunners. That would prove beneficial should the fort be simultaneously attacked from multiple sides and would provide protection from shells exploding on or above the parade, but would make life noisy and smoky for the gunners.

The landward side of the fort was designed to sustain its defenders in event of a prolonged siege. That type of defense required both the protection of the masonry from siege cannon, and obstructions to make a massed attack more difficult. Fort Pike provided both of those through an impressive array of outworks.

On approach to the fort, an attacker was confronted by *two* wet moats, with considerable earth-and-brick works outside the inner moat. Drawbridges provided access across both moats, and a curved pathway led through the outworks between the bridges. If an attacker crossed both moats, breaching the earthworks between, he was faced with the curtain of the fort. A demibastion at one end and a full bastion at the other protected the straight walls of the fort; both designed to accommodate flank howitzers. Also, each straight wall contained casemated emplacements for cannon to fire across the moat.

Once the curtain was breached and the fort itself fallen, the garrison could fall back to an eight-sided brick citadel on the parade. In addition to containing barracks, this citadel had loopholes for riflemen to make their last defense. It was tall enough to control the ramparts of the fort, preventing the attacker from turning the fort's guns on the remaining defenders. The fort contained two cisterns to provide the garrison with water in event of a siege, one at the junction of the two straight faces and one between the citadel and the center casemate of the curved face.

Of particular interest was the drain in the center casemate. This drain connected to the brick-lined trenches around the parade, and led through the center of the casemate to a spout emptying into the moat. It also connected to the overflow for the cistern, allowing an exchange of water in the cistern to keep it fresh.

A small village located beyond the outworks provided barracks space for the garrison during peaceful times, a significantly healthier situation than living inside the fort. The poor ventilation, coupled with the marsh-type environment surrounding the structure, made the interior of the fort a less-than-ideal home, especially during the summer months. The buildings in the village were constructed of wood so that they could be easily burned, preventing an enemy from making any use of the structures and maintaining a clear field of fire across the glacis.

The all-brick fort was constructed on a foundation of cypress logs and cemented shells on the unstable coastal soil. A seawall divided the ditch from the pass on the curved front of the fort, protecting the foundation from tidal action.

In 1849, plans were drawn to add a second level of casemates, but those plans were never implemented. A second level was, however, added to the citadel, raising it above the parapet and allowing better ventilation in the quarters. An interesting (but unconfirmed) story is that the fort was originally constructed without smoke holes in the top of the casemates, and these had to be drilled through the structure after the first cannon firings!

Today, the structure is in the care of the Louisiana State Parks Board, and is open to the public. The fort itself is very presentable, and the majority of the outworks are still present. Its current condition is worsening: two visits separated by three years have indicated a marked increase in the size of several structural cracks. One bastion is in significant danger of losing its salient, though a 1995 study indicates that the

Figure 175: Virtually identical to Fort Pike, Fort Wood has slightly smaller casemates. These were a result of improvements in casemate design that allowed an equal traverse of a cannon in a smaller space. *(Photo by author)*

structure is stable. Currently, brickwork is being repaired on both the fort and the citadel. There remains concern, however, that without structural repairs, a major part of our history could disappear.

A museum is located in the center room of the citadel, and a very caring staff is happy to share the history of the fort with visitors.

Fort Wood

Fort Wood, named for War of 1812 veteran Eleazer Derby Wood, is a twin to Fort Pike at the Rigolets entrance to Lake Pontchartrain. Originally known as the Fort at Chef Menteur, it was named Fort Wood in 1827. The name was changed in 1851 to Fort Macomb, in honor of Major General Alexander Macomb of the Corps of Engineers. The change in the name was to minimize the possibility of confusing this fort with Fort Wood on Bedlow's Island in New York City - now the base for the Statue of Liberty.

The isthmus that divided Lake Borgne from Lake Pontchartrain had two passes approximately five miles apart. Those passes were critical to the defense of New Orleans because they would allow an enemy fleet access to the city, and therefore control of the Mississippi River. While the passes were of equal strategic value, the pass at Rigolets was deeper; therefore, that fort took priority. The fort at Chef Menteur was the second of the Louisiana forts of the Third System to be completed.[5]

Construction began on the fort in 1822, and the structure was completed in 1827. While armed and garrisoned at various times during the Civil War by both Union and Confederate forces, it was never attacked. Its location not being significant to later periods of fortification,

Figure 176: The seacoast front of Fort Wood, shown in the above photograph, allows the entire pass to be covered by a relative short trace. Cannon in the casemates would be joined with cannon on the barbette tier to prevent the passage of a ship through this strait. *(Photo by author)*

Figure 177: The straight faces of Fort Wood were protected by howitzer embrasures in the flanks of the demibastion and full bastion. Further defense was provided by two wet ditches with substantial earthworks between the ditches. Casemates in the curtain and barbette positions atop the ramparts would provide cannon for support. *(Photo by author)*

it was happily left intact as a legacy to the early Third System on the Gulf Coast.

While Fort Wood was a "twin" to Fort Pike, it was not an identical twin. Fort Wood is slightly smaller, though it had the ability to mount the same number of guns. The major change was the downsizing of the casemates, principally by reducing the size of the walls between the gun positions. That allowed the same number of casemates on a shorter front. Also of note was the reduction of the height of the ramparts by two feet. That made for lower-ceiling casemates, but the height was still adequate for manipulation of the cannon. The shape of the ceiling of the casemates was also different. Rather than a continuous arch, as seen in most Third System forts, there was an 18-inch-wide secondary arch that was structurally attached to the scarp wall, followed by the casemate arch, which was structurally separate.

The sally port of Fort Wood was different from Fort Pike in that once inside the first chamber, three equal-size arches opened to a tunnel to the parade and to the casemates on either side. While Fort Pike had a similar chamber, only small doors opened to the flanking casemates.

The citadel at Fort Wood was identical to the citadel at Fort Pike, but the smaller area of the parade causes the citadel to come much closer to the straight walls of the fort. The distance was maintained, however, between the citadel and the curved face.

Despite these differences, the overall design of the fort was the same as Fort Pike, with a curved landward face with casemates for thirteen cannon and casemates in the bastion, demibastions, and straight faces for nine howitzers. The barbette tier was very similar to Fort Pike, but the pintles were arranged for a somewhat different selection of guns. It appears that Fort Wood was designed for more armament toward seaward than Fort Pike, but with fewer cannon toward the landward faces. This slightly changed the shape of the parapet.

Fort Wood today is in quite good condition. While little or no work has been done toward preservation of the fort in many years, the amount of settling, and therefore cracking of the masonry, is significantly less than at Fort Pike. The principal reason for this appears to be the presence of land between the walls of the fort and Chef Menteur pass, while at Fort Pike the tidal action works on the wall and its foundation. Of great concern, however, is the building of a marina immediately adjacent to the fort on the west. Wave action from the boats works on the west wall of the fort, and only a wooden barrier tempers the wake which impinges on the walls.

While the fort is structurally sound, the outworks are almost nonexistent. Only the brickwork adjacent to the main entrance to the fort is still standing, and it is in marginal condition. Due to a lack of maintenance effort, the site is covered with weeds and underbrush, and the snakes rule the site. It is currently closed to the public, pending funding to stabilize and staff the site. It is under the jurisdiction of the Louisiana State Parks Board.

Figure 178: Fort Jackson was a conventional pentagon with bastions, with outworks around all except the river side of the fort. A ten-sided citadel stood in the center of the parade. *(Sketch based on NARA drawing)*

Fort Jackson

The area most critical to the defense of New Orleans and the inland commerce of the country was the Mississippi River. Guarding the direct approach to this waterway was the French Fort St. Philip, which had fallen into disrepair. This fort was located at Plaquemines Bend (also called Plaquemines Turn) in the Mississippi River, where sailing ships had to decrease speed to navigate the sharp turns in the river. This slowing caused the ships to be under the guns of the fort much longer than they would have been if the fort had been located on a straight section of river.

Giving a high priority to the location, Bernard proposed the construction of a new fort opposite St. Philip, followed by the replacement of the French fort by a second new structure.[6] The latter was never realized, though repairs were performed on Fort St. Philip to increase its defensive capability and to allow the mounting of more modern guns. The major defense of this area was to be provided by the new pentagonal fort designed to mount 97 cannon.[7]

Fort Jackson was one of the early pentagonal forts of the Third System, with construction beginning in 1824. It was designed by Bernard, with the details and drawings provided by Henry L. Smith,[8] rather than the more familiar Poussin. Casemates were employed on the two seaward faces of the fort to increase firepower, but no casemates were used in the three landward faces. This increased the strength of the walls against a landward siege, as it would be nearly impossible to breach the 20-foot-thick earthen ramparts. The 25-foot-high walls were of red brick, and guns were mounted *en barbette* around the 650-yard perimeter.

Large bastions were located at each corner of the fort, reached by a long tunnel from the parade. These structures were casemated for howitzers in the flanks, but the faces were earth-filled to provide a better defense against siege guns. Those "tunnel bastions" were independently defensible should the fort fall to an attacker, a supplement to the defensive citadel which occupied the parade.

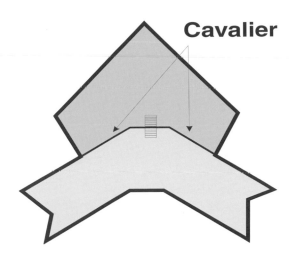

Cavalier

Figure 179: The bastions of Fort Jackson were unique within the Third System. The level of the terreplein of the bastion was significantly lower than the terreplein of the curtains. These levels were divided by a breast-high wall, called a cavalier, that allowed the defenders to control the top of the bastion should it fall to an attacker.

The treatment of the top of the bastions was unique to Fort Jackson. The parapet, with the barbette mounts behind it, followed the interior trace of the fort when it reached the bastions. At the center of each bastion was an opening in the parapet with steps leading downward through an archway and short tunnel to the top of the bastion. A second parapet followed the trace of the scarp wall of the fort, with a banquette for small-arms fire behind this parapet. That would provide additional protection to the scarp wall of the fort, by small arms, from the top of the bastion rather than just from the flank howitzers.

Further protection against a land attack was provided by a wide, water-filled moat. Filled by the adjacent river, the depth of the moat varied with tidal fluctuations, but it provided a substantial obstacle to an attacker. Outside the moat were three demilunes, connected and supplemented by substantial brick outworks. These demilunes were connected to the fort by wooden bridges which could be

Figure 180: The seacoast fronts of Fort Jackson, facing the Mississippi River, were casemated for large cannon, with barbette positions for even larger cannon above. The flanks of the bastions provided howitzer positions. *(Photo by author)*

Figure 181: The casemates of Fort Jackson are quite deep, but do not have a reduced-size tunnel connecting them to the parade. Note the magazine at the intersection of the two curtains, behind the bastion. *(Photo by author)*

burned should the demilune fall. Small posterns provided access to the parade from the bridges.

To support the structure in the soft soil, an exotic foundation scheme was employed. A layer of cypress 2 x 4s topped two layers of cypress logs. That structure was then covered with willow mats to complete the foundation.

The remains of a drainage system can be found on the ramparts of the bastions. It is assumed that this drainage system led to a cistern, and that the overflow of the cistern emptied into the moat. It is clear that each bastion had a brick-lined drainage pipe that flowed into the moat.

Preparations for Fort Jackson began in 1822, but the climate was inhospitable to the Northern craftsmen. Disease was rampant during the humid, mosquito-infested summer months, and numerous delays were encountered. In 1824, the Chief of Engineers reported "The sickness was still greater at Fort Jackson, on the Mississippi, and proved fatal to a number of workmen and military convicts employed at hard labor."[9] This problem recurred throughout the construction period, with some years more favorable than

others. Finally, in 1832, the fort was considered complete. The final cost was $554,500.

Today, Fort Jackson continues the battle it has fought with the encroaching Mississippi River, and with the dense flora of the region. A levee along the river shore and near-constant attention by the Plaquemines Parish Commission Council are doing an excellent job of preserving the work. An Endicott battery covers a portion of the parade and one face, but a great deal of the original work has been preserved. A museum occupies a guardroom and the fort's powder magazine, and offers an exceptional slide program depicting the history of the fort.

Fort Livingston

When Bernard originally conceived the defense of Barataria Bay to the south of New Orleans, he planned to use a fort of the same plan as Forts Pike and Wood, forming the only set of "triplets" in the Third System. Showing that fort

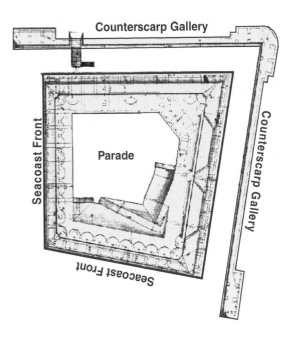

Figure 182: Fort Livingston shared the same kite shape and two-sided counterscarp galleries with Fort Barrancas, but it is there that the similarity ended. The parade, ramparts, and interior functions were completely different. *(Drawing courtesy NARA)*

in the "Third Class" (lowest priority for construction) in his 1821 Report, it was elevated to the Second Class in 1822 and to the First Class in 1826. While slipping back to the Second Class in 1832, land procurement began in 1833 and construction "was commenced" in 1835. Progress, however, was not forthcoming. Little

was done in the first five years due to the lack of an officer to take charge of the project. In 1840, Captain of Engineers J. G. Barnard was placed in charge of the construction and work began immediately.

The fort begun by Barnard was, however, very different from the one originally designed for the site. Joseph Totten had taken over the Board of Engineers on Bernard's return to France, and was putting his stamp on the design of the newer forts. The new Fort Livingston was a kite-shaped (trapezoidiform) structure with an impressive array of counterscarp works on two sides. Like the counterscarp galleries of Fort Barrancas in Pensacola, the ends of the galleries extended past their opposite walls and wash the two otherwise-unprotected faces of the fort with howitzer embrasures. Embrasures for four howitzers were also located at the intersection of the two galleries, providing flanking fire along the walls.

Like the original design, Fort Livingston was constructed with the seaward faces unprotected and a full glacis protecting the landward sides. Because of the height of the glacis and the land-defense mission of this portion of the fort, the casemates to the landward side were opened with loopholes to the ditch rather than embrasures for cannon. All of the seacoast cannon of the fort would be mounted *en barbette* around the entire terreplein.

Figure 183: Fort Livingston has suffered heavily from hurricanes and coastal erosion. Only two of the four sides remain, and the amount of land between the fort and the water varies according to season and tide. On some visits the water was against the wall of the fort, while at other times there was a large beach between the fort and the Gulf. *(Photo by author)*

Figure 184: The parade of Fort Livingston must have been beautiful in the nineteenth century. The barracks rooms surrounding the parade had ornate stonework around brick pillars, opening into a courtyard that collected breezes from the Gulf. *(Photo by author)*

The two seaward faces of the fort were backed by earth, forming a huge place d'armes. Atop this place d'armes stood the barbette cannon defending the channel. The place d'armes was reached by long, earthen ramps from the parade.

Designed for 60 guns and a wartime garrison of 600 men, Fort Livingston was one of the most lightly armed forts of the Third System. Like the similar Pensacola forts, Fort Barrancas and the Advanced Redoubt, the majority of the fort was consumed by the casemated rooms that comprised the ramparts, the middle of the fort shared between a small parade and the place d'armes.

The rooms facing the parade formed an ornate "piazza" which occupied the majority of the parade. Those rooms were divided from the rifle galleries by lath-and-plaster walls, and were provided with decorative granite lintels over the parade entrances.

The sally port of the fort entered the parade adjacent to the junction of the two landward faces through a drawbridge over the dry ditch. The center-pivot design of the drawbridge is shared with the Advanced Redoubt in Pensacola. The difference was in the way the bridge crosses the outworks. In all other Third System forts, an opening in the outworks allowed a relatively shallow-sloped bridge into the fort. Fort Livingston, however, had no such concession. With only the removal of the parapet at the beginning of the bridge, the rifle galleries continued under the bridge, and the bridge sloped steeply from the top of the counterscarp to the casemated sally port.

Of particular interest in the construction of the fort was the use of a concrete-and-shell filling for the walls. While all walls were faced with multiple courses of brick, this mixture provided a significant portion of the mass of the walls. That construction technique was shared with the Advanced Redoubt in Pensacola.

Today, Fort Livingston exists as an unoccupied ruin. Encroachment of the coastline and two hurricanes removed both seaward faces and has greatly damaged one end of each landward face. Fortunately, however, Grand Terre Island is once again growing and the walls of the fort are again protected by a substantial amount of land.

Figure 185: Fort Massachusetts had the only circular scarp of the Third System, albeit truncated at the gorge wall. Forts Pike and Wood had portions of a circle and Fort Popham was parabolic in shape, but only Fort Massachusetts followed a similar trace to Second System Forts Clinton and Williams. *(Photo by author)*

The parade of the fort is very swampy, with many of the quarters under water. Insects and snakes abound, making access difficult. The terreplein of one wall is quite accessible, and provides excellent views of the fort and the surrounding area. Large sections of the counterscarp galleries are also still intact.

Grand Terre Island is accessible only by boat, and the ruins, governed by the Louisiana State Park Board, are closed to the public. Views of the fort are available, however, from Grand Island State Park across the channel. While a hike down the beach is required, this pleasant walk yields views of the once-impressive guardian of Barataria Pass.

Fort Massachusetts

The main ship channel to New Orleans passed near a series of barrier islands off the Alabama-Mississippi coast. That channel passed very close to the western end of Ship Island, and the island sheltered a deep-water anchorage. It was this anchorage that the British used in 1814 to launch their attack on New Orleans.

The construction of a fort on Ship Island was a matter for debate for many years. Proposed numerous times by congressmen from Mississippi, the technical merit of a fort at this location was generally rejected by the Board of Engineers. A principal argument was that it would require multiple forts to control the harbor, and that other suitable harbors existed in the area. That meant that to close all harbors to an invader, many more forts were required.

In 1845, with the annexation of Texas, Totten became interested in fortifying Ship Island. A depot was needed for coaling and resupplying of ships in that section of the Gulf, and Ship Island was an ideal location. Plans were made for a fort on Ship Island and Martello towers for the passes between the Malheureaux Islands. While supporting those defenses, Totten stated that priority must be given to the Dauphin Island fort, Fort Gaines.

The Mexican War consumed the finances and manpower priorities of the War Department before any work began, but in 1847 Ship Island was declared a military reservation. The project

Figure 186: The parade of Fort Massachusettes is very small, owing to the thickness of the ramparts and the shape of the fort. The exceedingly tall casemates make the parade seem even smaller. *(Photo by author)*

was finally approved in 1857 after significant controversy,[10] and construction began in 1858. Little was done that year, but after the death of the original superintending engineer,[11] Lieutenant Prime was given the responsibility and construction began in earnest.

The fort was doomed to another hiatus in construction, this one caused by the Civil War. While the engineers were working on the fort, the Mississippi Militia seized the fort in the name of that state and the Confederacy. The engineers departed, and the Confederate Army took possession. Due to the indefensible nature of the fort in its early stages of construction, earthworks were erected atop the low walls, and guns mounted in the earthworks. In late 1861, the Confederates left the fort and the Union Army returned. The fort was brought to a very defensible condition, though it has never been considered "complete."

The name "Fort Massachusetts" seems strange for a fort located on the south coast of Mississippi. The fort was actually named for the Union warship, USS Massachusetts, that provided the cannon for the fort.

Fort Massachusetts was located on the western tip of Ship Island, overlooking both the ship channel and the anchorage. One of the smallest of all Third System forts, it was designed for 37 guns on two tiers. The seaward front of the fort comprised almost two-thirds of a circle, joined in the gorge by a front with two demibastions. Minimal land defense was provided, with the major mission of the fort being control of the channel and harbor.

While the fort had no moat, the sally port was equipped with a drawbridge which spanned an eight-foot by eight-foot by eight-foot-deep pit at the entrance. This pit was bounded by the sally port walls on each side, and by the raised bridge on the fort end. Rifle slits in the guard-rooms defended both the pit and the lowered bridge. Howitzer embrasures in the demibastions defended the area beyond the gorge wall, as did loopholes in the face of the gorge.

Since construction of Fort Massachusetts was concluded near the end of the Third System, the design of the fort encompassed the latest innovations in both fort design and artillery. The casemate embrasures were equipped with Totten Shutters, and barbette mounts were designed to hold 15-inch Rodman cannon and 100-pounder Parrot Rifles.

The fort also made use of concrete for the structure, an innovative approach in that time period. The concrete was faced with brick on both the inside and outside of the walls, but the bulk of the wall thickness was the concrete fill. That saved a great deal of brick and even more labor in the construction of the fort.

Fort Massachusetts also had an innovative water system, very similar to the one at Fort Jefferson in the Dry Tortugas. The system employed piping in the columns of the casemates, leading to the cistern below a guardroom. Slate was used for the piping and for lining the cistern, but unfortunately lead was used to seal between the pieces of slate. What level of lead poisoning was experienced as a result of the water system is unknown.

Today, Fort Massachusetts looks very much like it did when construction was halted. The National Park Service has done an excellent job of preserving the fort, and it sports a high quality interpretive program. The fort can be reached by a very pleasant boat ride from either Biloxi or Gulfport, Mississippi.

Tower Dupre

Guarding Bayou Dupre, a shallow inlet joining Lake Borgne with the Mississippi River just north of the peninsula ending in Proctor's Point, is Tower Dupre. Similar in shape to a classic Martello Tower, Tower Dupre was hexagonal rather than round. It also departed from the classic Martello design in that the entrance to the tower was on the first level, rather than the second. The first level was ringed with loopholes, while the second and third levels had cannon embrasures. A shallow-pitched hexagonal roof sat atop the structure. On the roof was a lookout platform with a railing, with a flagstaff in the center.

In 1844, plans were drawn to place a six-gun barbette battery in advance of the tower, but these plans were not realized.

Currently, Tower Dupre is privately owned, and is one level shorter than its original design. It is also now completely surrounded by water, standing a significant distance off shore.

Battery Bienvenue

During the War o 1812, the British approach to New Orleans involved moving troops from Lake Borgne to the Mississippi River. The route used was through Bayou Bienvenue, or

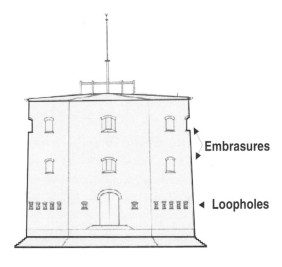

Figure 187: Tower Dupre was similar in design to a classic Martello tower, far more so than other Third System defensive towers. It had one tier of loopholes for small-arms defense and two tiers of cannon. *(Drawing courtesy NARA)*

Embrasures

Loopholes

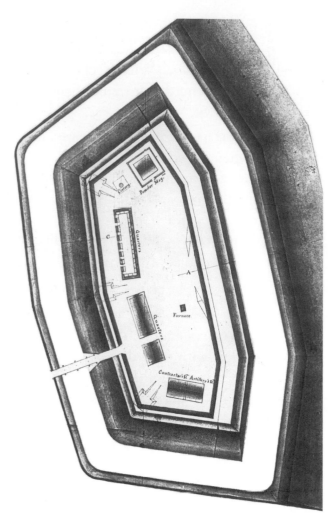

Behind the terreplein was a sizable parade, with two barracks, a storehouse, and a magazine. The rear of the battery was closed with two angled masonry scarp walls, the sally port located in the center of one of these walls. Two medium-length curtains connected the secondary fronts with the gorge fronts.

Today, the battery lies in ruins, and is overgrown with vegetation. Accessible only by boat, the battery and its surrounds are said to be populated by numerous snakes, some poisonous. The intrepid visitor, therefore, must use due care when visiting the battery. Also present, still standing proudly atop the barbette tier, are three original Rodman cannon on iron carriages – a real treat!

Proctor's Tower

At Proctor's Landing, in the southern portion of Lake Borgne, a shallow bayou connects to the Mississippi River. This site also provides

Figure 188: Battery Bienvenue protected the route through the Louisiana bayous that the British used in their move toward New Orleans during the War of 1812. It was a quite large barbette battery with an ancillary barracks and magazine. *(Drawing courtesy NARA)*

"welcome bayou." While only suitable for very shallow draft vessels, a secondary defense at this location was considered necessary.

Battery Bienvenue was a cross between a barbette battery and a fort. The battery had no casemates and no bastions – the minimal land defenses consisted of a masonry scarp and earthen counterscarp fronting a ditch. The mission of the fort was to control the bayou, and the long seacoast front and two short secondary fronts provided emplacements for barbette cannon.

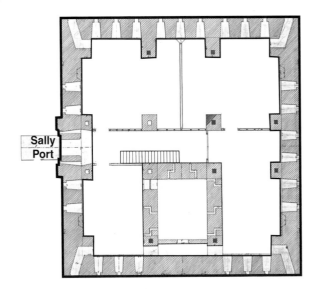

Figure 189: Proctor's Tower was a defensive tower controlling a landing point on the shore of Lake Borgne. The square tower was never completed.

194

Figure 190: A relatively large portion of Battery Bienvenue still remains - with at least three seacoast cannon visible. Also remaining are portions of two support buildings for the battery. *(Photo by author)*

a landing with firm ground all the way to New Orleans. The last New Orleans defense in the Third System was designed to guard this landing.

Known officially as the Tower at Proctor's Landing, it has gone by many names. Fort Proctor and Proctor's Tower were two common variations, and Fort Beauregard and Beauregard's

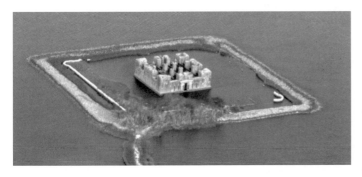

Figure 191: The uncompleted tower near Proctor's Landing still stands in Lake Borgne. Access to the structure is very difficult. *(Photo by author)*

Castle were used as well. The latter two names came into play because P.G.T. Beauregard superintended the construction of the tower.

The defensive tower was typical of the square, multistoried towers of the late Third System. Surrounded by a seawall defining a moat around the perimeter of the tower, the first two levels were to contain loopholes for small-arms defense, while the third, barbette tier would hold seacoast cannon.

Construction of the tower halted, however, after only a portion of the first story was constructed. It stands today, off the shore of Lake Borgne, in its partially constructed state. While accessible only by boat, it is visible from shore. To view the tower, follow Route 39 south through Chalmette – site of the War of 1812 battlefield – and continue on to Route 46. Follow Route 46 to Shell Beach – there is a rocky jetty at the end of the road. Proctor's Tower is visible from the jetty.

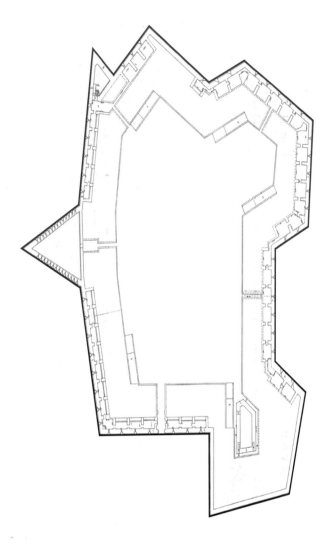

Figure 192: Fort St. Philip, a colonial fort that was modernized during the Third System, stands opposite Fort Jackson on the southern reaches of the Mississippi River.

Notes

[1]ASP-MA, Vol. III, p. 295.

[2]Parkerson, Codman, <u>New Orleans: America's Most Fortified City</u>, The Quest, New Orleans, LA, 1990.

[3]See Bearss, Edwin, Historic Resource Study: Fort Massachusetts, National Park Service.

[4]The plan of the fort was in the shape of a sector of a circle, modified to include the two demibastions and the full bastion.

[5]ASP-MA, Annual Reports of the Chief of Engineers.

[6]Bernard's original plan called for the repair of Fort St. Philip. In the 1821 Report, he stated that Fort St. Philip was beyond repair, and that a new fort would be needed to replace it. This position was maintained until it was clear that funding for the replacement of the fort was not to be forthcoming, and the compromise position of repairing Fort St. Philip was revived.

[7]ASP-MA, Vol. III, p. 299 (1826 Report). This was changed to project 156 guns in 1836.

[8]National Archives, Cartographic Branch: Drawer 88, Sheet 16.

[9]ASP-MA, Vol. , p. 713.

[10]See Chapter One for the controversy with the Leadbetter Board regarding Ship Island fortifications.

[11]Alexander died of yellow fever while obtaining materials and stockpiling for the construction of the fort.

Figure 193: Portions of the scarp of Fort St. Philip are intact, such as this seacoast front facing the Mississippi River. *(Photo courtesy NARA)*

The Defenses of San Francisco Bay

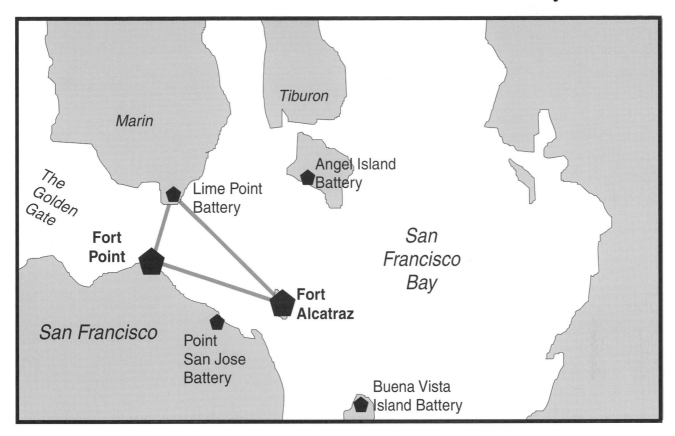

History

In 1848, following the Mexican War, the entire area of Upper California was ceded to the United States. With world politics still in turmoil, the defense of the nation's new coastline was predominant in the thoughts of the War Department. Joseph Totten, now Chief Engineer of the Army, commissioned a team of three engineers under his command and three naval officers to survey the "whole extent of the Pacific Coast...(to ascertain which harbors, etc.) will need defense by fortifications and other means." Elsewhere in their charter, it was stated that "works of defence and a site for a naval depot would be decided upon."

Brevet Lieutenant Colonel John L. Smith led the team, which included Major Ogden and Lieutenant Leadbetter from the Army, and Commanders Goldsborough, Van Brunt, and Blunt from the Navy. The survey was accomplished and a preliminary report drafted when, in 1851, Totten constituted a Board of Engineers. By this time, the "Gold Rush" was in full swing and the value of San Francisco had increased to the point that it had become the most significant city in the West. That increased the urgency of defending the area, and political pressure to begin a project was becoming strong. Totten could no longer wait for the final survey before beginning fortification design.

Four months later, a preliminary report was written. That report designated three locations for "batteries" guarding San Francisco, and "works" to defend three other areas of the Pacific coast. Two of the sites designated in San Francisco received forts, and two of the latter three defenses were constructed.

Third System Strategy

San Francisco Bay could only be reached by entering the "Golden Gate," which lay between two projections of land, Fort Point[1] on the south and Lime Point on the north. That rocky strait was about one mile across, easily controlled by the coastal guns of the day. Advances in the technology of warships,[2] however, dictated that many guns bear on the strait for as long a portion of the channel as possible, and the rocky cliffs on both points minimized the area available near sea level for mounting the guns.

Another consideration in defense of the bay was the infamous San Francisco fog, which rolled in over the coastal range most evenings. Visibility dropped to near zero, and a brave warship may have been able to pass through the straits undetected. For that reason, batteries were needed "for the near defense as to deter an enemy from approaching or lying dear enough to destroy" San Francisco.[3] In addition, San Pablo Bay provided interior communication all the way to Sacramento and this vital waterway had to be kept free of invading ships. Three straits provided access from beyond the Golden Gate, all of which could be controlled from Alcatraces Island. The island also provided for the "near defense" mentioned above, and was chosen as the site of the secondary defense for the bay.

Thus designed, San Francisco Bay would be defended by three forts: two at the Golden Gate and one on Alcatraces Island. That was commonly known as the "triangle defense" of the bay. The idea of batteries was discarded for two reasons. First, the growth of the city and its increase in importance dictated that the defenses be substantial. Second, the results of the survey determined that only small areas were available near the water,[4] greatly limiting the number of guns that could be mounted in a barbette battery. As a result, vertical tiers were required to provide sufficient firepower to guard the channel.

In addition to the "triangle defense," three batteries were constructed to assist Fort Alcatraz with the secondary defense of the bay. Those batteries, varying in size, were located on Angel Island, Buena Vista Island, and on the shore near the city itself.

Fort Point was slightly less steep than Lime Point and was on the San Francisco side of the channel. Additionally, there were problems in obtaining the rights to the land at Lime Point. Fort Point was therefore chosen as the site of the first work protecting the entrance to the bay. Alcatraz was to be next but, due to the cheaper and quicker construction methods employed, was actually the first defense to mount guns. When the final survey was completed, Fort Point was increased in size over the original estimate. That greatly increased the number of guns to be mounted there and diminished the need for the Lime Point fort.

Lime Point was finally utilized in the 1870s when brick-faced earthworks were constructed on both points as a supplement to the two existing forts. By this point in time, land defense was less of an issue than the vulnerability of masonry to large-bore cannon. Additionally, masonry-revetted earthworks were far less expensive to construct than full-masonry forts, and fortifications budgets were very limited in the post-Civil War era.

Two points at the mouth of the Columbia River were fortified. The north side of the river, at Cape Disappointment, three batteries were placed on hilltops overlooking the river entrance. On the south side of the river, a large, closed battery was constructed, called Fort Stevens.

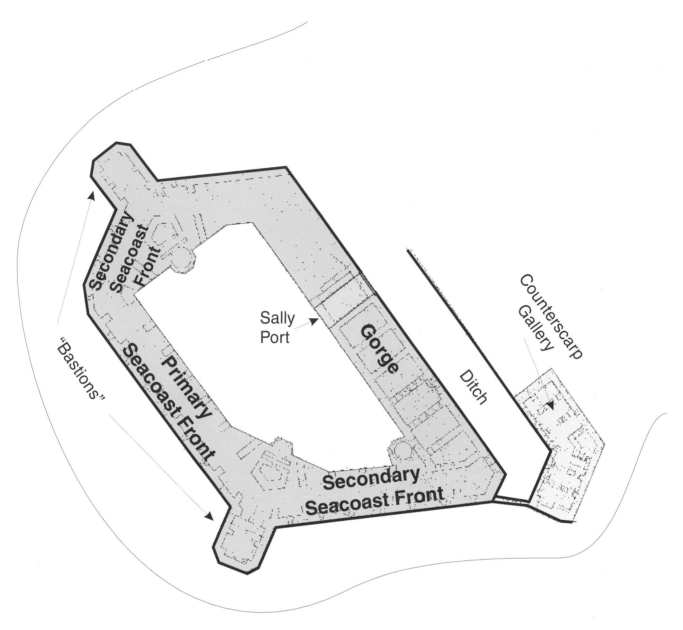

Figure 194: Fort Point, guarding the entrance to San Francisco Bay, was designed to make maximum use of a small amount of land blasted from the shore of the bay. The four tiers of seacoast cannon easily made up for the relatively small trace of the fort. *(Sketch based on NARA drawing)*

Fort Point

One of the most impressive and well-preserved examples of a late-Third-System fort is Fort Point. Located beneath the Golden Gate Bridge, it was spared through the farsightedness of the bridge's designer, who added a special arch in the southern end of the bridge to span the fort. The 45-foot-high walls contained three tiers of casemates and supported a fourth tier of bar-

bette guns. Designed for 126 cannon, it was a formidable work of small trace, representative of the designs[5] and construction methods near the end of the Third System. Construction began in 1853 and the fort was completed in 1861.

The point of land on which the fort stood originally held a Spanish fort, causing the projection to be referred to as Fort Point. When the Third System fort was constructed there was a substantial delay in its being named. In the

Figure 195: Prior to the construction of the Golden Gate Bridge, Fort Point dominated the entrance to the bay. Note the Rodman cannon on the barbette tier. *(Photo courtesy NARA)*

absence of a name, the Corps of Engineers referred to the structure as "the fort at Fort Point." This was naturally shortened to Fort Point, a name that has held to this day.[6] During the late 1800s, the military reservation in this portion of The Presidio, including the Third System work, was named Fort Winfield Scott. This name was applied to the older work for a short time, but the original name (or corruption thereof) of Fort Point reasserted itself with the passage of years.

The original trace of the fort was to have been an irregular pentagon, designed to utilize as much as possible of the small point of land on which it rests. Receipt of a more complete survey of the surrounding area resulted in the lengthening of the fort through the addition of two "bastions." Those bastions were not shaped like conventional bastions, nor were they designed

to perform the function of a bastion. They were elongated projections from the fort that allowed the mounting of two additional cannon per tier on each flank, and one cannon per tier on the face of each bastion. Additionally, two cannon were mounted *en barbette* on each bastion, using 360-degree-swivelling, center-pintled carriages. These additions to the design increased the potential armament of the fort by 32 cannon.

Although the fort appears to present a strong land defense to the casual observer, it was relatively weak by Third System standards. The principal weakness was due to the presence of a large rock cliff with a flat plateau immediately adjacent to the fort. While slightly lower than the fort's walls, that area and the even higher area behind it would allow an enemy to nullify any activity on the north side of the barbette tier and in many of the seaward casemates.

200

To counter this vulnerability to the landward, two redoubts were designed. Those diamond-shaped redoubts were to be located on the two highest points of The Presidio, each point approximately one mile from the fort. Unique to the design of these redoubts was the use of circular rifle positions beyond two points of the diamond. The redoubts were not constructed.

The fort did have some land-defense capability, however. The cannon on the barbette tier would make life very difficult for an attacker coming along the cliff, and howitzers mounted in the southern casemates of the east bastion controlled the road leading to the fort. The three tiers of casemates on the gorge wall of the fort were penetrated by loopholes, allowing riflemen to provide a substantial amount of volley fire in the ditch. Additionally, a counterscarp gallery was constructed at the southwest corner of the fort, with howitzers protecting the gorge wall.[7]

Original plans called for a dry ditch along the gorge, but the encroachment of water from the bay turned the original excavations into a moat. The proximity of this moat to the magazines convinced the superintending engineer to discard the idea of a ditch altogether. A view of the facade of the sally port reveals the holes where chains to lift the drawbridge were to be installed, but the bridge was never needed.

The design of the sally port was typical of Third System forts, with outer doors made from two layers of wood. The outer layer had the grain of the wood running vertically, while the inner layer had the grain at 45 degrees from vertical. This would cause significant problems for someone trying to use an ax to breach the door. To further complicate the attempts of an ax-wielding attacker, iron studs were evenly spaced along the surface of the door.

Figure 196: This historic photograph shows the interior of a fully armed Fort Point. Rodman cannon point both seaward and landward from the barbette tier, and the rear of carriages can be seen in the rear of the casemates. *(Photo courtesy NARA)*

Once inside this outer door, loopholes high in the wall allowed defenders in the flanking guardrooms to fire on the passageway to the fort. Inner doors closed the back of the sally port, with an X-patterned lattice in the top half of each door allowing defenders within the fort to fire the length of the passageway.

To delay the success of a major siege, however, the area to landward would require further defenses. Extensive outworks were planned for this area, but they were never constructed. Those outworks included the two very elaborate diamond-shaped redoubts, mentioned previously, that would sit on two knolls behind the fort. Extensive earthworks and covert ways were to connect the redoubts and to extend to the edges of the plateau, sealing this rear approach to the fort.

The efficacy of the existing defenses was never tested, though there was some concern that pro-secessionist forces in San Francisco would attempt to seize the fort. The fort commander took special precautions, but it is certain that even with less-than-complete armament and a small garrison, Fort Point could have easily resisted such an attempt.

In contrast to any weakness in land defense, to the seaward Fort Point was a formidable work. Its four tiers of guns controlled all seaward approaches to the Golden Gate, and the opposite shore was well within the range of these guns. The rough water and strange currents in the channel would minimize the ability of a ship-of-war to mount an attack from the seaward, and the dense packing of the fort's cannon assured the defeat of the intruder.

The only vulnerability was to a ship passing undetected through the strait. The dense fog that sometimes obscured the entire channel, coupled with darkness, could allow an intruder to slip past the defenses into the bay. Even if an enemy ship entered the bay, however, Fort Point did not present a viable target. Some of the larger guns on the barbette tier could swivel through a full 360 degrees, while many guns on the lower tiers (including the face and one flank of the eastern bastion) could be brought to bear on the bay side of the fort.

The interior of Fort Point was in most ways utilitarian, but the facade of the barracks along the gorge wall had some very pleasing architectural features. Each of the floors had a full-length balcony, supported by iron Corinthian columns. Beams along the front edge of the balcony provided structural support as well as a decorative touch. The underside of the balcony maintained the familiar arched form, with iron beams supporting each end of the arches.

The balconies were joined to each other and the parade by decorative iron stairways. While the railings were quite plain in design, the treads were crosshatched for traction and the risers sported a decorative diamond pattern.

Granite piers on all the first-tier casemates and a granite facade facing the parade accented the extensive brickwork of the fort. Additionally, each tier had a granite coping extending beyond the brickwork.

The embrasures of the fort were of the Totten design, complete with iron throats and Totten shutters. The loopholes of the first tier, however, were unique. In order to minimize the ability of an attacker to fire into a loophole while maintaining a wide field of fire for the defender, a complex double-taper design was used. When viewed from the exterior, the loophole was a vertical slit. From the interior, however, the slit was horizontal. That horizontal slit tapered inward from the sides, giving a wide horizontal traverse of the weapon. At the same time, the slit widened in the vertical axis. That allowed the defender to aim his weapon upward or downward while minimizing his vulnerability.

The loopholes of the upper tiers were the conventional vertical slits. Those were enlarged to windows shortly after the first garrison arrived and began to suffer from the poor ventilation in the barracks building.

Today, Fort Point still stands as a proud guardian of the Golden Gate. While the massive bridge above overshadows its brick walls, the visitor who climbs to the barbette tier cannot help but appreciate the vertical scale of the masonry fort. Preservation and restoration work by the National Park Service gives the Fort Point visitor the feeling that time has been turned back to the days of breech-loading cannon and sailing ships.

Fort Point is considered by many to be a signature-piece of the late Third System. It is certainly the best-preserved example of a completed tower fort that is open to the public. The architectural style, similar to the larger Fort Sumter, and the excellent interpretive program make it a "must see" for San Francisco visitors. Costumed interpreters and an excellent bookstore complement the restoration.

Fort Point can be reached by taking the "Viewing Area" exit at the south terminus of the Golden Gate Bridge. Exit the parking lot to the south, and follow the road to the bottom of the hill. Turn left into the driveway marked "Fort Point," and follow the driveway to the end.

Alternatively, a very nice walking trail leads from the viewing area for the bridge down to the fort. The return trip, however, is a little more arduous than the descent.

Fort Alcatraz

The fort with the least similarity to other Third System forts was the "Fort on Alcatraces Island,"[8] more commonly referred to as Fort Alcatraz. This uniqueness was due primarily to the lack of a traditional curtain wall defining the perimeter of the fort. For this reason, many have considered it as not a "real" fort, but a combination of batteries. It did, however, have a masonry scarp around much of its perimeter and had many other attributes of Third System forts. It was called a fort by both its occupants and the Corps of Engineers, and will be dealt with here as a Third System fort.

On surveying the island, the Corps of Engineers found that the rock cliffs created a quite adequate scarp in many areas. Construction began in 1853 with selective blasting of the rock created a steeper slope in areas that could be more easily scaled, leaving a natural wall around the perimeter of the island. This natural wall was supplemented with vertical brick walls in many locations, forming a traditional scarp and a solid revetment for the gun emplacements. This was supplemented by masonry walls in areas that were most vulnerable, and a breast-height wall wherever guns were to be emplaced. A sheltered cove on the east side of the island had a relatively flat area adjacent to it that would allow for the construction of a pier and dock area. The fort, then, was the entire island, except for the small dock area.

A road was blasted between the area where the wharf and permanent dock would be located and the area atop the island. The first defensive construction on the island was the creation of a guardhouse and sally port controlling access along this road. While the guardhouse was relatively small and mounted only three howitzers, the roadway it was defending was relatively narrow. Two howitzers were emplaced to defend this road, while the third howitzer swept the scarp beyond the guardhouse. The sides of the roadway were made steeper, and faced with brick-and-mortar walls to cause attackers to "bunch up" in front of the guardhouse, increasing the effectiveness of the howitzers. On the approach to the guardhouse, a formidable cliff rose to the west and the land dropped away in an equally steep cliff to the bay on the east side of the roadway.

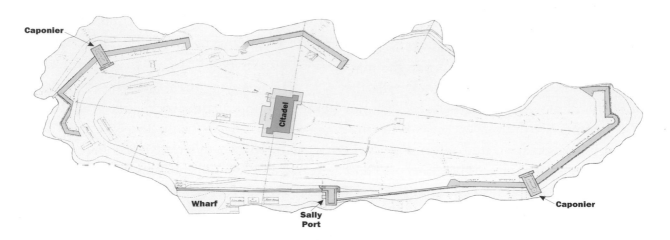

Caponier

Citadel

Wharf

Sally
Port

Caponier

Figure 197: Fort Alcatraz and Alcatraz Island were inseparable. Portions of the island were modified through blasting to create a natural scarp, while other portions were faced by a conventional masonry scarp. The principal scarp walls are shown on the sketch above. *(Sketch based on NARA drawing)*

In addition to the howitzer embrasures, rifle loopholes were constructed in the scarp wall in advance of the guardhouse, as well as in the sides of the sally port. Finally, a dry ditch was dug — blasted would be more accurate — and a drawbridge installed across it. Thus, the only reasonable approach to the top of the island was well defended.

Later, it was decided that the dock area itself required more extensive defenses. The construction of a heavily armed "defensive barracks" immediately opposite the wharf prevented an enemy from landing at the dock, thus eliminating the opportunity for the establishment of any type of foothold on the island. When completed, the battery eliminated the need for the guardhouse as a defensive structure, and its function was changed to accommodate the now-expanding mission of the military prison.

The heart of Fort Alcatraz was the series of barbette batteries that almost completely encircled the island. Breast-high walls and barbette-type gun emplacements covered most of its circumference. A shallow ditch was blasted immediately in front of where the base of these walls would be located, but the unstable rock

of the island would not support the weight of the brickwork and the large-bore cannon. The wall was thickened, and extended to the base of the ditch, which gave it exceptionally good support. While the "scarp" had a slightly lower effective height using this method, the steep, rocky slope provided a suitable deterrent to assault.

On the northeast and southwest angles, caponiers were constructed to protect the breast-high walls and cliff areas. These structures resembled small bastions more than caponiers,

Figure 198: The masonry scarp of Fort Alcatraz is shown here, with various seacoast cannon mounted en barbette. *(Photo courtesy NARA)*

204

providing the traditional role of either a bastion or a caponier – flanking fire along the scarp. Their positions at an angle of the scarp allowed the cliff and scarp wall to be swept with howitzers, as in a traditional fort. In addition, however, these structures rose above the level of the batteries and provided flanking fire down the length of the gun emplacements. The top of each caponier was covered with earth, and provided a prime location for a sentry.[9]

Atop the center of the island stood a massive three-floor citadel, 200 feet long by 100 feet wide, with iron-shuttered loopholes, a dry ditch, and two drawbridges. Loopholes on the lowest level opened into the dry ditch, while the second level provided access across the drawbridges. Loopholes on the third level were wider than on the first two levels, providing good ventilation to the occupants. It is speculated that these would be bricked to normal width on suspicion of attack or the onset of war.[10]

By design, the citadel overlooked the rear of all of the barbette batteries, and provided a last line of defense for the fort. The citadel also provided the primary housing for the post in the early days, but it was not large enough to house the larger number of troops who were later assigned to the fort. Wooden barracks buildings that had no defensive capability, but provided more comfortable living quarters, supplemented it.

By 1867, the works were impressive. Mounting 108 cannon, it was the largest fort on the Pacific coast, and controlled the central area of the entrance to the bay. Although it was classified as a secondary defense, its importance rivaled that of Fort Point and it was the place where all ships were required to "register" on passing through the Golden Gate.

Little is left of this magnificent fort today. Modifications during the years when it was a

Figure 199: The caponiers of Fort Alcatraz were positioned such that they defended the scarp, and also controlled the terreplein should it fall into the hands of an attacker. *(Photo courtesy NARA)*

military prison, then a civilian prison, have camouflaged many of the remains. The beautiful granite work of the citadel entrance can be seen, however, in the entrance to the main cell-house of the prison. The architect preserved this archway for posterity by designing it into the more modern cell house structure.[11]

The sally port and guardhouse are obvious to even the casual visitor, and the howitzer embrasures and the loopholes are well preserved. Later additions and modifications change the overall look of this structure, but with closer inspection the original structure can be discerned.

Throughout the island are the remains of brickwork that marked the excellent craftsmanship of the era. The intrepid visitor can see the remains of the north caponier near the generator station, though the upper levels were removed during the prison period.

Beneath the cell house lies the dry moat and the lower level of the citadel, but they are off limits to visitors. It is remarkably well preserved, with many of the iron-shuttered loopholes still present. Storerooms across the ditch are intact, as are many of the interior rooms of the citadel.

Interpretation of the "fort period" of Alcatraz Island has increased. Tours of the military mission of this island are given throughout the year, and several park rangers are very knowledgeable about this portion of the history of Alcatraz. A set of particularly good displays, including an excellent model of the island in the height of its mission as a fort, is located in the Visitors Center.

A trip to Alcatraz guarantees the visitor some of the most magnificent views of the San Francisco Bay area, as well as a truly enjoyable boat ride through time to the days when "The Rock" was a Third System fort.

Fort Alcatraz is reached by tour boat leaving from Fisherman's Warf in San Francisco. Reservations are strongly advised, and must be made well in advance during peak tourist seasons.

Notes

[1] Fort Point was so named because it was the point of land occupied by the Spanish Castillo de San Joaquin, which, at the time of the American occupation, was in ruins.

[2] Those advances included steam power, higher speeds, and iron armor. All of them diminished the effectiveness of coastal guns.

[3] Final Report of the Board of Engineers for the Pacific Coast.

[4] In actuality, the small areas near the water had to be created by blasting away the promontories at Fort Point and Lime Point.

[5] Fort Point is considered a "tower fort," popular late in the system. The increased speed of ships, the use of steam power to replace or augment sails, and the eventual use of ironclads led to the need for more armament guarding a channel. Limitations in the size of the trace of a fort drove designers to use more tiers of cannon.

[6] The name Fort Point is applied to both the fort and the site on which the fort was built. This provides some confusion, but by examination of the context, the reader can determine to which a reference is being made.

[7] This gallery is gone with very little trace. Depending on the drifting sand on that corner of the fort, the foundations appear and disappear. The construction of a bridge pier during the building of the Golden Gate Bridge required demolishing this structure.

[8] This fort was also referred to as the "Post on Alcatraces Island" in official correspondence, though several original drawings refer to it at Fort on Alcatraces Island. Its garrison knew it as Fort Alcatraz.

[9] An excellent photograph in John Martini's *Fortress Alcatraz* shows a sentry at his post atop a caponier.

[10] The windows in the gorge wall of Fort Point were enlarged to provide good ventilation, with the proviso that in event of attack they would be secured by rebricking the interior portions of the loopholes. This is the basis for speculation regarding the Fort Alcatraz citadel windows.

[11] It is interesting to note the openings in the facade where the chains of the citadel drawbridge once passed through the granite.

Epilogue:
Why the <u>Third</u> System?

This magnificent series of forts has been known by many names, but the name I prefer, and continue to use, is the Third System. Why the Third System? I'll attempt an answer for my prejudice:

Guilliame Tell Poussin, the French designer who drew the original plans for a large number of Third System forts, referred to the system as the Bernard System, after his mentor. Bernard was the visionary who conceived of the approach to coastal defense implemented in the system, and he had a hand in the design of more of the forts than any subsequent engineer. His dealings with the heirachy of the Army, with all elements of the Navy, the State Department, and Congress allowed the initiation of the system and put it well upon its way to completion.

Bernard, however, was only involved in the system for fifteen years of the fifty-one-year project. Fewer than half of the forts had begun when he returned to France, and he saw the completion of a very small number of forts. It was the efforts of subsequent engineers which were responsible for the majority of the building of the Third System. For these reasons, the name "Bernard System" is discarded.

Many American engineers and subsequent historians prefer the more chauvinistic name, the Totten System. Joseph Totten was with the system for longer than anyone else, a full forty-eight of the fifty-one years. He was involved in the design and construction of virtually all the forts in the system, and was the principal designer of many of the forts. Additionally, it appears appropriate that an American system of forts be named for an American general.

Totten, however, was not the originator of the system. While involved from the early days, he was not in a leadership role but following in the tutelage of Bernard. While Totten was involved throughout the period, many other engineers played very significant roles in the implementation of the system, and to name it after a single individual denigrates their contribution. "Totten System" is therefore rejected.

The name originally given the system by Bernard was the "Permanent System." Unlike earthwork-and-wood fortifications that were by nature impermanent, and unlike hastily erected masonry works, this system was to be a well planned, carefully designed and executed system that would provide defense to the shores of the nation *ad infinitum*. These forts, like the many-hundred-year-old fortifications in Europe, would exist "forever."

History has shown that this system of defense, like all its predecessors, would not last forever. By the end of the century it was considered obsolete, and by the middle of the next century all types of coastal fortifications were considered obsolete. Since history has shown the system not to be permanent, that eliminates "Permanent System" from the alternatives.

This leaves us with the Third System. It is questioned whether we can consider the previous efforts as "systems," and can two previous systems actually be pinpointed rather than three or four? The name Third System comes from Totten, who did feel comfortable with defining two previous systems. We have not, in our clear vision of hindsight, been able to give evidence of there **not** being two previous systems, so we can feel at least somewhat comfortable with the name "Third System."

After all, Shakespeare said it best: "What's in a name? ...A rose by any other name would smell as sweet."

Appendixes

Appendix A: Glossary *

Angle of Traverse: The angle through which a cannon can be rotated. The pintle location, embrasure size, and carriage design influence this angle.

Banquette *(bahn KET)*: A raised earthen or masonry platform behind the parapet on which riflemen can stand when firing.

Barbette *(bar BET)*: A platform behind the parapet on which a cannon is mounted, such that it can fire over the wall. Also, the upper tier of a fort without overhead protection. (See also, En Barbette)

Bastion *(BAST yun)*: A projection in the enceinte, made up of two faces and two flanks, which allows flanking fire along the adjacent portions of the enceinte. Bastions are generally, but not always, located at the angles of the enceinte.

Battery: A position for a group of guns, either within a fort, in the outworks of a fort, or standing as an independent work. Usually a battery is under the command of one officer.

Canister: Containers filled with iron balls, usually ranging in size from three-fourths inch to two inches in diameter. On firing, the canister splits open, discharging the shot in a shotgun-like pattern.

Caponier *(cap un YAIR)*: A covered passage, normally constructed across a ditch, to provide protected communication. Also a small, vaulted outwork designed to provide flanking fire along a ditch or, in the absence of a ditch, along the enceinte. A caponier may or may not be attached to the scarp wall.

Carnot Wall *(CAR noh wall)*: A detached scarp; a scarp wall which is separated from the ramparts of a fort by a chemin de ronde.

Casemate *(CASE mate)*: A vaulted, bombproof room of masonry construction, often used to provide a firing position for a cannon. In the Third System, they generally provide the mass of the ramparts and the flanks of the bastions. They are also found in the faces of bastions, in internal structures, and in counterscarp galleries and other outworks. They provide overhead protection, and allow tiers of guns to be stacked. Casemates may also provide firing positions for small arms, and may be used for quarters, kitchens, storage, and other sundry functions. They were sometimes called gunrooms.

Cavalier: An obstruction – in the Third System, a masonry wall – that separates the terreplein of a bastion from the terreplein of the body of the fort.

---

* This glossary contains the definitions of fortification terms **as used during the Third System**. Many of these terms have different or expanded meanings if used in a different context. The pronunciations shown are the original French, as taught at the U. S. Military Academy in the early nineteenth century. Many have been anglicized, most notably redoubt and portcullis, and the anglicized pronunciation is the one in common use.

Chemin de Ronde (*SHEH min deh RON dah*): A pathway around the interior of the scarp wall of a detached-scarp fort, serving as a firing platform for riflemen.

Citadel (*SIT ah dell*): In the Third System, a stronghold inside the body of a fort that serves as a defensive barracks and a last line of defense.

Cordon (*cor DON*): A masonry projection from the top of the scarp wall, usually at the base of the exterior slope, that inhibits scaling the scarp wall and protects the face of the scarp from drainage. When no exterior or superior slope exists, the cordon is often called a coping.

Countermine: A tunnel going outward from the fort, used as a defense against mining the fort walls. A countermine generally has areas in which explosives could be placed to cave in the mine of a siege force or to bring down a bastion of the fort if the bastion falls to an attacker (see also, Listening Gallery).

Counterscarp: The outer wall of the ditch.

Counterscarp Gallery: Casemated or vaulted areas behind the counterscarp wall that allow reverse fire into the ditch. They generally contained howitzer emplacements at the corners, with loopholes in the remaining walls. Access is from the ditch or a tunnel under the ditch.

Counterfire: Defensive fire toward the fort, i.e., into the rear of an attacker. Also known as reverse fire.

Counterfire Gallery: Casemated or vaulted areas that allow reverse fire into the ditch. A counterscarp gallery is a type of counterfire gallery.

Coup de Main (*KOO dah MIN*): An assault of a fortification by storm, rather than by siege. A coup de main, if successful, would allow the possession of a fort in a very short time period compared to that required by a siege.

Coverface: An earthen or earth-and-masonry outwork made up of two faces, placed before a bastion, a ravelin, or the scarp to protect the masonry of the fort from siege guns. A coverface often mounted cannon en barbette. Also called a counterguard.

Covered Way, *or* **Covert** (KUV ert) **Way**: A walkway, hidden from the view of an attacker, provided with a parapet, a banquette, and sometimes barbettes to cover the glacis. While usually around the counterscarp, a covered way may provide communication between outworks. Its primary functions are to provide an outer line of defense, provide communication, and serve as a place for sorties to assemble.

Crenel: An open-topped embrasure at the top of a wall. A crenel is defined by two adjacent merlons.

Crownwork: An outwork consisting of two demibastions joined by curtains to a central bastion.

Curtain: The portion of the scarp wall between bastions.

Demibastion (*DEH mee BAST yun*): A half-bastion; a bastion with only one face and one flank.

Demilune: Literally, "half moon." The French name for a ravelin. In the Third System, also the name of a semicircular outwork, generally used for land defense.

Ditch: A low area, either wet or dry, which inhibits the passage of the enemy to the scarp wall. The ditch is located between the scarp and counterscarp wall. A wet ditch is usually referred to as a moat.

Embrasure *(em BRAY shur)*: An opening in a wall through which a gun may fire.

En Barbette: The practice of mounting cannon such that they fire over a wall rather than through an opening (embrasure) in that wall.

En Casemate: The practice of mounting cannon in a casemate such that they can fire through an embrasure.

Enceinte *(awn SENT)*: The body or mass of a fort.

Enfilading fire: Fire directed perpendicular to the advance of an attacker, sometimes called a cross-fire.

Exterior Slope: The slope on the exterior side of the rampart, usually earthen, that connects the superior slope with the scarp, the berm, or the ground. The exterior slope is usually the steepest slope of a parapet.

Face: The exterior portion of a bastion or outwork between its salient angle and a shoulder. In the Third System seacoast forts, the front or fronts facing onto the water in which the primary armament of the fort is mounted.

Flank, or Cheek: The portions of a bastion lying between the face and the adjoining curtain. The flank of a bastion provided the primary fire along the curtain and, often, the face of the opposite bastion.

Flank Howitzer: A howitzer designed to fire down the length of the ditch, usually from the flank of a bastion.

Front: A side of a fort. On an unbastioned fort, a front is measured from corner to corner. On a bastioned fort, it is measured from the salient of a bastion to the salient of the opposing bastion, including the curtain wall between the bastions.

Glacis *(glah SEE)*: The gentle slope beyond the covert way, cleared of all obstructions, which an attacker must traverse to reach the fort.

Gorge: The open portion of a bastion toward the parade. Also, the rearward-facing front of an outwork or irregular fort. In Third System seacoast forts, the front or fronts away from the water, where the primary entrance to the fort is usually located.

Grillage: A web of timbers, often placed in perpendicular layers, used as the foundation of a fort. Cedar was the most popular wood to use to form a grillage.

Hornwork: An outwork, consisting of two demibastions connected by a curtain.

Howitzer: A short-barreled cannon. In Third System forts, howitzers were generally used for antipersonnel missions and generally fired canister shot. Note that in field artillery, a howitzer often fired explosive shells.

In Advance: Toward an attacker, or toward the likely route of an attacker.

Listening Gallery: A tunnel extending beyond the scarp of a fort that is used to detect the sounds of the mining operations of a siege force.

Loophole: A narrow embrasure through which a rifle or musket can fire. Sometimes called a rifle slit.

Machicoulis Gallery: A platform that extends from the ramparts of a fort above the ditch, allowing defenders to fire downward along the curtain of the fort.

Magazine: A place for storage of powder inside a fort. The main (or storage) magazine stored the bulk of the powder, and service (or day-use) magazines stored powder for immediate use near the guns.

Merlon: A rectangular projection from the top of a wall. Crenels and merlons alternate on a crenellated wall.

Militia Artillery: A group of reserve soldiers who were trained in artillery drill. Militia artillery was used to supplement the regular garrison in most Third System forts.

Moat: Another name for the ditch, usually implying a wet ditch.

Outworks: Works located within or beyond the ditch, i.e., supporting works outside the enceinte of the fort.

Parade: The open area in the center of a fort, usually used for drilling troops, for barracks area, etc.

Parados: An earthen berm or mound, sometimes supported by masonry, on the parade of a fort that shields the rear of the casemates. A parados protects gunners from reverse fire and from shells exploding on the parade.

Parapet: A low wall along the top of the rampart, generally masonry or masonry-revetted earth, which protects the terreplein from observation and fire and over which troops and artillery may fire.

Place of arms *or* **Place d'armes** (PLAHSS deh ARMS): A gathering place for counterattacking forces, generally located at the salient or reentrant angles of the covered way. In the Third System, a non-casemated earthen salient of the fort was referred to as a place d'armes.

Portcullis *(port cue LEE)*: A wooden or iron gate that bars access but not sight, often on the inner side of a sally port. This allows the attacker to be trapped within the sally port while under fire from the defenders.

Postern *(POST ern)*: Literally, back door. A secondary entrance leading through the ramparts and either into or over the ditch. Posterns often connect to exterior batteries or other outworks.

Rampart: The full thickness of the walls of a fort, including the casemates.

Ravelin *(RAV eh lin)*: A V-shaped outwork placed in advance of a curtain so that its gorge is aligned with the counterscarp. A ravelin provides protection to the scarp and may contain additional batteries. In Third System forts, ravelins were sometimes constructed on the gorge front to mask the masonry curtain and sometimes constructed on a seacoast front to provide additional cannon positions beyond the scarp.

Redan *(reh DAHN)*: Any V-shaped, open back outwork other than a ravelin.

Redoubt *(reh DOOT)*: A small, enclosed fortification without bastions, generally functioning as an advance work for a fort or as part of a line of fortifications. A redoubt normally does not contain facilities for a permanent garrison.

Reduit: A strong point, the last line of defense. In Third System forts, a small redoubt incorporated in other outworks.

Reentering *or* **reentrant:** An inward-pointing angle in the trace of a fortification.

Reentering *or* **reentrant place of arms:** A place of arms located at a reentering angle of the covered way.

Retrenchment: A defensive structure placed across a bastion, usually at the throat, to assist in the defense of the salient.

Reverse fire: Fire toward the fort by the defenders, i.e., fire into the rear of the attackers. Counterscarp and counterfire galleries provide reverse fire.

Revet: To face an embankment, usually with masonry or wood, to sustain it.

Revetment: A defensive work consisting of a revetted earthen embankment.

Salient: An outward-pointing angle in the trace of a fortification. For example, the salient of a bastion.

Salient place of arms: A place of arms located at a salient angle of the covered way.

Sally Port: A postern. In the Third System, the main entrance or entrances to a fort, generally located in a gorge wall.

Scarp, or **Scarp Wall:** The inner wall of a ditch, or the wall immediately in front of the rampart. The perimeter wall of the fort.

Scarp Gallery: A casemated or vaulted area inside the scarp wall that opens to the ditch with loopholes, thus providing forward fire into the ditch.

Shell: A projectile fired from a cannon or mortar that has a hollow interior, generally filled with explosives.

Ship-of-the-line, or capital ship: A large warship. A ship-of-the-line was generally a three-masted sailing ship with three of four decks of cannon. These large ships were the principal warships of a fleet prior to the use of ironclads.

Shot: A projectile fired from a cannon made of solid iron. Shot has more momentum than shell, but does its damage through momentum only. While most shot was spherical, the shot fired from rifled cannon were cylindrical, generally called a bolt.

Shoulder: The place on a bastion where the face and the flank meet.

Siege: The methodical reduction of a fort. A siege generally consists of: 1) separating the fort from external support and supplies, 2) eliminating the ability of the fort to counterattack, 3) creating a breach in the enceinte, and 4) exploiting the breach, usually by storm.

Sortie: A counterattacking force. Also, the act of counterattacking.

Storm: The assault of a fort or other work by a massed attack of infantry.

Superior Slope: The top surface that reaches the crest of a parapet, slanting downward toward the glacis. The slope is generally such that defenders can cover all the ground outside the ditch, but is usually the shallowest slope of a parapet.

Tenailles *(ten EYE)*: An outwork placed in the ditch between bastions, intended primarily to protect the scarp from artillery fire. In Third System forts, tenailles have casemated demibastions with an earthen mass between the casemates. This mass is revetted with masonry.

Tenaille Trace: A sharply angled outline of a fort, allowing adjacent walls to provide enfilading fire. A fort with a tenaille trace is generally referred to as a star fort.

Terreplein *(TARE a pleh)*: The area atop the ramparts behind the banquette upon which barbettes are often constructed.

Throat: The narrowest part. *Of a bastion*, the narrow portion between the flanks, nearest the parade. *Of an embrasure*, the narrowest portion of the opening.

Totten embrasure: An embrasure reinforced with iron, developed by J. G. Totten. These embrasures provided for a smaller opening and a wider angle of traverse. Totten embrasures usually, but not always, utilized Totten Shutters.

Totten shutters: Iron doors that close an embrasure between cannon firings. J. G. Totten developed this intricate system.

Tower bastion: A bastion, generally of small trace, with multiple tiers of casemates. Tower bastions provided multiple embrasures for flank defense while maximizing the length of the curtain, and sometimes provided embrasures on the salient of the upper tier(s).

Trace: The line defining the exterior of the enceinte, or body, of a fort. A trace is often referred to by the geometric figure that defines it, for example, a pentagonal trace for a fort with five sides.

Traverse *(trah VERSE)*: An earthen or masonry-revetted earthen mound constructed on a terreplein, or elsewhere, to provide protection against enfilading fire and minimizing damage from exploding shells. Traverses also allow defense of portions of the ramparts when other portions have been stormed, and often house bombproofs and magazines. Traverses are often constructed between gun positions. Also, the arc of stone and/or iron on which the rear wheels of guns travel. The individual stones are generally referred to as **traverse blocks,** and the flat iron is generally called a **traverse iron** or **traverse rail**. *See also, Angle of Traverse.*

Water Battery: An outwork or independent battery positioned to fire over a body of water.

Work, or Works: A defensive structure. Works generally refer to batteries, redoubts, or towers – something less than a fort.

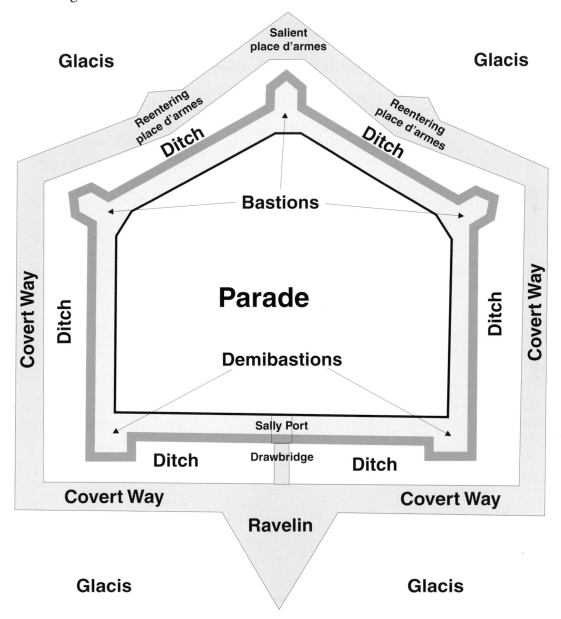

Fortification elements often found in Third System forts
Plan View

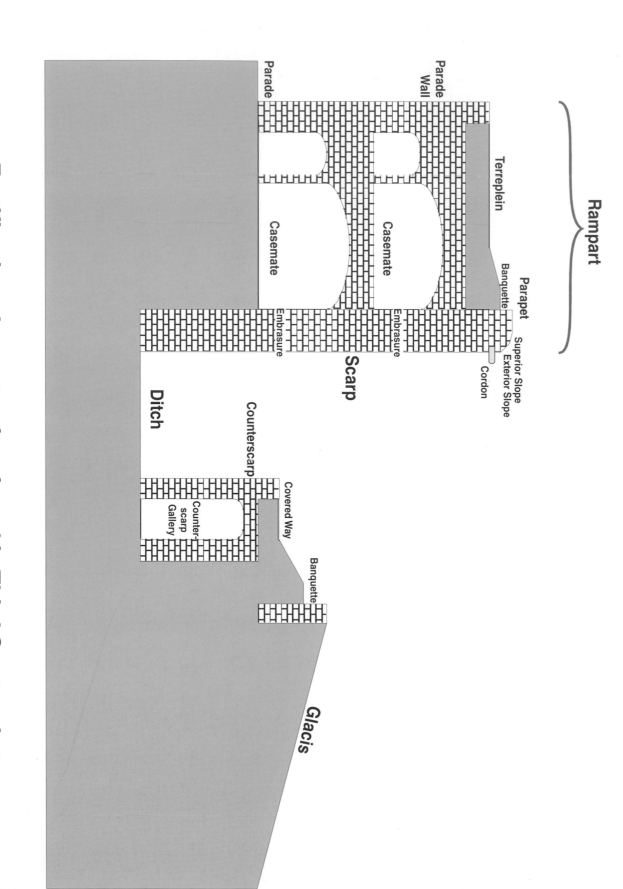

Fortification elements often found in Third System forts

Section View

Parade

Parade Wall

Casemate

Casemate

Terreplein

Banquette

Parapet

Embrasure

Embrasure

Superior Slope

Exterior Slope

Cordon

Rampart

Scarp

Ditch

Counterscarp

Covered Way

Counter-scarp Gallery

Banquette

Glacis

Appendix B
Fort Names

Third System forts were generally referred to first as a place name (e.g., Fort at Throgg's Neck) or as the name of a pre-existing fort that the Third System fort was to replace (e.g., new Fort Adams). Somewhere in the design/construction cycle, a name was given to the fort. Often, for political (e.g., Fort Calhoun becoming Fort Wool) or other reasons, the name of the fort was changed – sometimes multiple times. Some forts did not receive a name during the Third System (e.g., Fort at Clark's Point), but were given unofficial names by the garrison (Fort Taber). Others received their names after the Third System (e.g., Fort Hancock).

For the consistency and ease of reference, a name was adopted for each fort in the Third System. Generally, this was the first official name for the fort. If the fort was not named during the Third System, the first common-use name for the fort was used. However, the author took license in a few cases. Fortress Monroe was the first official name for Fort Monroe, and Castle Calhoun was the first official name for Fort Calhoun. Both of these names were replaced with the second official name, using the more accurate *fort* nomenclature. For the rationale used in the choice of individual fort names, please see the description of that fort in Part II of the text.

Following is a list of common names of Third System forts, referenced to the name used in this work. It also indicated the chapter in Part II of the book that contains a detailed description of the fort.

Name	Name in this work	Chapter
Battery Weed	Fort Richmond	Defenses of New York City
Battery Bienvenue	Battery Bienvenue	Defenses of New Orleans
Castle Calhoun	Fort Calhoun	Defenses of Middle Atlantic Coast
Castle McRee	Fort McRee	Defenses of Pensacola Bay
Fort Adams	Fort Adams	Defenses of Southern New England Coast
Fort Advanced Redoubt	Advanced Redoubt	Defenses of Pensacola Bay
Fort Alcatraz	Fort Alcatraz	Defenses of San Francisco Bay
Fort Beauregard	Proctor's Tower	Defenses of New Orleans
Fort at Chef Menteur	Fort Wood	Defenses of New Orleans
Fort at Plaquemines Turn	Fort Jackson	Defenses of New Orleans
Fort at Fort Point	Fort Point	Defenses of San Francisco Bay
Fort at Foster's Bank	Fort McRee	Defenses of Pensacola Bay
Fort at Mobile Point	Fort Morgan	Defenses of Mobile Bay
Fort at Old Point Comfort	Fort Monroe	Defenses of Middle Atlantic Coast
Fort at Old Topsail Inlet	Fort Macon	Defenses of Southern Atlantic Coast
Fort at Plaquemines Bend	Fort Jackson	Defenses of New Orleans
Fort at Sandy Hook	Fort Hancock	Defenses of New York City

Fort at the Rigolets	Fort Pike	Defenses of New Orleans
Fort at the Rip Raps	Fort Calhoun	Defenses of Middle Atlantic Coast
Fort Barrancas	Fort Barrancas	Defenses of Pensacola Bay
Barrancas Redoubt	Advanced Redoubt	Defenses of Pensacola Bay
Fort Calhoun	Fort Calhoun	Defenses of Middle Atlantic Coast
Fort Carroll	Fort Carroll	Defenses of Middle Atlantic Coast
Fort Caswell	Fort Caswell	Defenses of Southern Atlantic Coast
Fort Clinch	Fort Clinch	Defenses of Southern Atlantic Coast
Fort Constitution	Fort Constitution	Defenses of Maine-New Hampshire Coast
Fort Delaware	Fort Delaware	Defenses of Middle Atlantic Coast
Fort Diamond	Fort Lafayette	Defenses of New York City
Fort Gaines	Fort Gaines	Defenses of Mobile Bay
Fort Gorges	Fort Gorges	Defenses of Maine-New Hampshire Coast
Fort Hamilton	Fort Hamilton	Defenses of New York City
Fort Hancock	Fort Hancock	Defenses of New York City
Fort Jackson	Fort Jackson	Defenses of New Orleans
Fort Jefferson	Fort Jefferson	Defenses of Florida Strait
Fort Knox	Fort Knox	Defenses of Maine-New Hampshire Coast
Fort Lafayette	Fort Lafayette	Defenses of New York City
Fort Livingston	Fort Livingston	Defenses of New Orleans
Fort Macomb	Fort Wood	Defenses of New Orleans
Fort Macon	Fort Macon	Defenses of Southern Atlantic Coast
Fort Massachusetts	Fort Massachusetts	Defenses of New Orleans
Fort McRae	Fort McRee	Defenses of Pensacola Bay
Fort McRee	Fort McRee	Defenses of Pensacola Bay
Fort Monroe	Fort Monroe	Defenses of Middle Atlantic Coast
Fort Morgan	Fort Morgan	Defenses of Mobile Bay
Fort on Alcatraces Island	Fort Alcatraz	Defenses of San Francisco Bay
Fort on Clark's Point	Fort Taber	Defenses of Southern New England Coast
Fort on Cockspur Island	Fort Pulaski	Defenses of Southern Atlantic Coast
Fort on Dauphin Island	Fort Gaines	Defenses of Mobile Bay
Fort on Garden Key	Fort Jefferson	Defenses of Florida Strait
Fort on Georges Island	Fort Warren	Defenses of Boston Harbor
Fort on Grand Terre Island	Fort Livingston	Defenses of New Orleans
Fort on House Island	Fort Scammel	Defenses of Maine-New Hampshire Coast
Fort on Key West	Fort Taylor	Defenses of Florida Strait
Fort on Oak Island	Fort Caswell	Defenses of Southern Atlantic Coast

218

Fort on Pea Patch Island	Fort Delaware	Defenses of Middle Atlantic Coast
Fort on Santa Rosa Island	Fort Pickens	Defenses of Pensacola Bay
Fort on Ship Island	Fort Massachusetts	Defenses of New Orleans
Fort on Soller's Point Flats	Fort Carroll	Defenses of Middle Atlantic Coast
Fort on Willett's Point	Fort Totten	Defenses of Defenses of New York City
Fort Pickens	Fort Pickens	Defenses of Pensacola Bay
Fort Pike	Fort Pike	Defenses of New Orleans
Fort Point	Fort Point	Defenses of San Francisco Bay
Fort Popham	Fort Popham	Defenses of Maine-New Hampshire Coast
Fort Preble	Fort Preble	Defenses of Maine-New Hampshire Coast
Fort Proctor	Proctor's Tower	Defenses of New Orleans
Fort Pulaski	Fort Pulaski	Defenses of Southern Atlantic Coast
Fort Redoubt	Advanced Redoubt	Defenses of Pensacola Bay
Fort Richmond	Fort Richmond	Defenses of New York City
Fort Rodman	Fort Taber	Defenses of Southern New England Coast
Fort Scammel	Fort Scammel	Defenses of Maine-New Hampshire Coast
Fort Schuyler	Fort Schuyler	Defenses of New York City
Fort Scott	Fort Point	Defenses of San Francisco Bay
Fort Sumter	Fort Sumter	Defenses of Southern Atlantic Coast
Fort Taber	Fort Taber	Defenses of Southern New England Coast
Fort Taylor	Fort Taylor	Defenses of Florida Strait
Fort Throgg's Neck	Fort Schuyler	Defenses of New York City
Fort Tompkins	Fort Tompkins	Defenses of New York City
Fort Totten	Fort Totten	Defenses of New York City
Fort Trumbull	Fort Trumbull	Defenses of Southern New England Coast
Fort Wadsworth	Fort Richmond	Defenses of New York City
Fort Warren	Fort Warren	Defenses of Boston Harbor
Fort Washington	Fort Washington	Defenses of Middle Atlantic Coast
Fort Weed	Fort Richmond	Defenses of New York City
Fort Winfield Scott	Fort Point	Defenses of San Francisco Bay
Fort Winthrop	Fort Winthrop	Defenses of Boston Harbor
Fort Wood	Fort Wood	Defenses of New Orleans
Fort Wool	Fort Calhoun	Defenses of Middle Atlantic Coast
Fortress Monroe	Fort Monroe	Defenses of Middle Atlantic Coast
Post on Alcatraces Island	Fort Alcatraz	Defenses of San Francisco Bay
Proctor's Tower	Proctor's Tower	Defenses of New Orleans
Tower Dupre	Tower Dupre	Defenses of New Orleans

Appendix C
Coastal Defenses of the Third System
by Location

The following chart lists the coastal defenses of the Third System, listed by the location they were designed to defend. The list includes new-construction forts, other new-construction structures, and older forts that were incorporated into the system.

The Defenses of the Maine-New Hampshire Coast

EASTPORT

Fort Sullivan	Second System blockhouse and battery

WISCASSET

Fort Edgecomb	Second System blockhouse and battery

PENOBSCOT RIVER

Fort Knox	New Construction fort

KENNEBEC RIVER

Fort Popham	New Construction fort

PORTLAND HARBOR

Fort Gorges	New Construction fort
Fort Scammel	New Construction fort, used portions of Second System fort in design
Fort Preble	New Construction fort, used portions of Second System fort intact

PORTSMOUTH HARBOR

Fort Constitution	New Construction fort, replaced Second System fort of same name
Fort McClary	New Construction fort, replaced Second System blockhouse of same name

The Defenses of Boston Harbor and the Massachusetts Bay

GLOUCESTER HARBOR

Fort at Gloucester	First System fort, repaired in Second System

SALEM HARBOR

Fort Pickering	First System fort, upgraded during War of 1812
Fort Lee	First System earthworks, upgraded in Third System

MARBLEHEAD

Fort Sewall	First System fort, upgraded in 1861 (local funding)

BOSTON HARBOR

Fort Warren	New Construction fort
Fort Winthrop	New Construction tower and batteries
Fort Independence	New Construction fort, replaced Second System fort of same name

The Defenses of the Southern New England Coast

NEW BEDFORD HARBOR

Fort Taber	New Construction fort
Fort Phoenix	New battery to supplement Second System fort

NARRAGANSETT BAY

Fort Adams	New Construction fort, replaced Second System fort of same name
Dutch Island Batteries	New Construction batteries
Fort Wolcott	First System fort, batteries upgraded in Third System
Fort Greene	First System fort, batteries upgraded in Third System
Bonnet Point Fort	Second System batteries, rebuilt in Third System
Fort Hamilton	Second System batteries

THAMES RIVER

Fort Trumbull	New Construction fort, replaced Second System fort of same name
Fort Griswold	New earthwork battery supplemented ruins of Second System fort

NEW HAVEN HARBOR

Fort Hale	Second System fort

The Defenses of New York City

NORTHERN APPROACHES

Fort Schuyler	New Construction fort
Fort Totten	New Construction fort

SOUTHERN APPROACHES

Fort Hancock	New Construction fort
Fort Hamilton	New Construction fort
Fort Lafayette	Transitional Fort 2→3
Fort Richmond	New Construction fort, replaced Second System fort of same name
Fort Tompkins	New Construction fort, replaced Second System fort of same name
Fort Wood	Second System fort
Castle Clinton	Second System fort
Castle Williams	Second System fort
Fort Columbus (Jay)	Second System fort
Fort Gibson	Second System fort
South Battery	First System fort
Battery Morton	Second System battery
Battery Hudson	Second System battery
Fort Ganesvoort	Second System fort
Hubert Island Battery	Second System battery

The Defenses of the Mid-Atlantic Coast

DELAWARE RIVER

Fort Delaware   New Construction fort, replaced a Transitional fort of the same name

Fort Mifflin   First System fort, additions during Second System

BALTIMORE HARBOR

Fort Carroll   New Construction fort

Fort McHenry   Second System fort

ANNAPOLIS, MARYLAND

Fort Severn   Second System fort

Fort Madison   New battery to replace Second System fort

WASHINGTON CITY

Fort Washington   Transitional Fort 2→3

HAMPTON ROADS

Fort Monroe   New Construction fort

Fort Calhoun   New Construction fort

Fort Norfolk   Second System fort

Fort Nelson   First System fort

The Defenses of the Southern Atlantic Coast

BEAUFORT HARBOR, NORTH CAROLINA

Fort Macon   New Construction fort

CAPE FEAR RIVER

Fort Caswell   New Construction fort

Fort Johnston   Second System fort

CHARLESTON HARBOR

Fort Sumter   New Construction fort

Fort Moultrie   Second System fort, modernized in Third System

Castle Pickney   Second System tower

BEAUFORT – PORT ROYAL, SOUTH CAROLINA

Beaufort Battery   First System battery, updated periodically

SAVANNAH RIVER

Fort Pulaski   New Construction fort

Fort Jackson   Second System fort

ST. MARY'S RIVER

Fort Clinch   New Construction fort

ST. AUGUSTINE, FLORIDA

Fort Marion   Battery added to supplement Colonial fort

The Defenses of the Florida Strait

Fort Taylor	New Construction fort
East Martello Tower	New Construction tower
West Martello Tower	New Construction tower
Fort Jefferson	New Construction fort

The Defenses of Pensacola Bay

Fort Pickens	New Construction fort
Fort Barrancas	New Construction fort, used Spanish water battery (modernized)
Advanced Redoubt	New Construction fort
Fort McRee	New Construction fort

The Defenses of Mobile Bay

Fort Morgan	New Construction fort
Fort Gaines	New Construction fort

The Defenses of New Orleans

Fort Massachusetts	New Construction fort
Fort Pike	New Construction fort
Fort Wood	New Construction fort
Battery Bienvenue	New Construction battery
Tower Dupré	New Construction tower
Fort Proctor	New Construction tower
Fort Jackson	New Construction fort
Fort St. Philip	Spanish Fort, modified in Third System
Fort Livingston	New Construction fort

The Defenses of San Francisco Bay

Fort Alcatraz	New Construction fort
Fort Point	New Construction fort
Lime Point Battery	New Construction battery
Point San Jose Bty	New Construction battery
Angel Island Battery	New Construction battery

The Defenses of Columbia River

Cape Disappointment	New Construction batteries (3)
Fort Stevens	New Construction battery

Appendix E:
Index

Bold type indicates a primary referene to the subject. *Italicized type* indicates a photograph.

Appendix F:
Bibliography

American State Papers, Military Affairs, (Washington, DC: Gales and Seaton)

Arthur, R., and Weinert, R., *Defender of the Chesapeake, The Story of Fort Monroe,* (Shippensburg, PA: White Mane Publishing Co., 1989)

Barnard, John Gross, *Eulogy on the Late Brevet Major-General Joseph G. Totten, Late Chief Engineer, United States Army,* (New York: D. Van Nostrand, 1866)

Bearss, Edwin, *Historic Resource Study: Fort Massachusetts,* (U. S. National Park Service)

Bearss, Edwinn C., *Historic Structure Report: Fort Point,* (U.S. National Park Service)

Bergeron, Arthur W., Jr., *Confederate Mobile,* (Jackson, MS: The University Press of Mississippi, 1991)

Bethel, Rodman, A Slumbering Giant of the Past, Fort Jefferson, USA, in the Dry Tortugas, (1989)

Branch, Paul, Jr., The Siege of Fort Macon, (Morehead City, NC, 1982)

Brice, Martin H., Forts and Fortresses: From the Hillforts of Prehistory to Modern Times – the Definitive Visual Account of the Science of Fortification (New York: Facts On File, Inc., 1990)

Brice, Martin H., Stronghold: A History of Military Architecture (London: B. T. Batsford, Ltd., 1984)

Browning, Robert S., III, Two if by Sea: The Development of American Coastal Defense Policy, (Westport, CT: Greenwood Press, 1983)

Burns, Zed H., Confederate Forts, (Natchez, MS: Southern Historical Publications, Inc., 1977)

Cartographic Branch, National Archives and Records Administration, Record Group 77 and others.

Coleman, James C. & Irene S., Pensacola Fortifications 1698-1980: Guardians on the Gulf, (Pensacola, FL: Pensacola Historical Society, 1982)

Coleman, James C., Fort McRee "A Castle Built on Sand," (Pensacola, FL: Pensacola Historical Society, 1988)

Corvisier, Andre, ed., *A Dictionary of Military History and the Art of War,* (Lymington, Hants: The Spartan Press, Ltd., 1994)

Davis, William C., *Weapons of the Civil War,* (New York: Mallard Press, 1991)

Delgado, James P., Alcatraz Island, The Story Behind the Scenery, (San Francisco: KC Publications, 1985)

Dibble, Ernest F., William Chase, *Gulf Coast Fort Builder*, (Wilmington, Delaware: Gulf Coast Collection)

Dibble, Ernest F., *Antebellum Pensacola and the Military Presence*, (Pensacola, FL, 1974)

Drury, Ian, and Gibbons, Tony, *The Civil War Military Machine*, (New York: Smithmark Publishers Inc., 1993)

England, Howard S., Barron, Ida, Fort Zachary Taylor, A New Call to Duty, (1977)

Final Report of the Board of Engineers for the Pacific Coast

Fort Pulaski and the Defense of Savannah, (Eastern Acorn Press, 1985)

Fort Sumter, Anvil of War, Harper's Ferry, VA:: U. S. National Park Service.

General Order No. 14, Army Adjutant General's Office, 16 March 1840

Gillmore, Q.A., *Official Report to the United States Engineer Department on the Siege and Reduction of Fort Pulaski*, (New York, 1862)

Gillmore, Russell S., *Guarding America's Front Door, Harbor Forts in the Defense of New York City*, New York: The Fort Hamilton Historical Society, 1983)

Groene, Bertram Hawthorne, *Pike: A Fortress in the Wetlands*, (Hammond, LA: Southeastern Louisiana University Press, 1988)

Haas. Irvin. Citadels, Ramparts, and Stockades: America's Historic Forts, (New York: Everest House Publishers, 1979)

Halleck, Henry Wager, Elements of Military Art and Science, (Westport, CT, 1846)

Hammond, John Martin, Quaint and Historic Forts of North America, (Philadelphia: J. B. Lippencott Co., 1915)

Harrison, Joseph H., Jr., The American Middle Period: Essays in Honor of Bernard Mayo, "Simon Bernard, The American System, and the Ghost of the French Alliance," (Charlottesville, VA: 1973)

Hart, Herbert M., Old Forts of the Far West, (New York: Bonanza Books, 1965)

Hinds, J.R., and Fitzgerald, E., Bulwark and Bastion: A Look at Musket Era Fortification With a Glance at Period Siegecraft, (Las Vegas, 1981)

Hinds, James R., "Stone Walls and Iron Guns: Effectiveness of Civil War Forts," in Bulwark and Bastion, by Hinds and Fitzgerald.

Hogg, Ian V., Fortress: A History of Military Defense, (New York: St. Martin's Press, 1975)

House Executive Document No. 5, 32nd Congress, 1st Session, Dec. 8, 1851

Hughes, Quentin, *Military Architecture*, (New York: St. Martin's Press, 1974)

Johnson, Robert U., and Clarence Buel, editors, *Battles and Leaders of the Civil War*, 4 volumes, (New York: Century Co., 1887-88)

Lattimore, Ralston B., *Fort Pulaski National Monument*, (Washington, DC: National Park Service, 1954)

Letters folder, New Bedford Public Library, New Bedford, Massachusetts

Lewis, E.R., *Seacoast Fortifications of the United States, An Introductory History*, (Presidio, 1970).

Martin, Benjamin Ellis, Eulogy on the late Brigadier General Joseph Gilbert Totten, (New York, 1866).

Martini, John A., Fortress Alcatraz, Guardian of the Golden Gate, (Kailua, HI: Pacific Monograph, 1990)

Martini, John A., Fort Point, Sentry at the Golden Gate, (San Francisco: Golden Gate National Park Association, 1991)

Miller, Francis T., The Photographic History of the Civil War – 10 Volumes, (New York: The Review of Reviews Co., 1911)

Moore, Jamie W., The Fortifications Board 1816-1828 and the Definition of National Security, (Charleston, SC: The Citadel, 1981)

Muir, Thomas, Jr., and Ogden, David P., The Fort Pickens Story, (Pensacola, FL: The Pensacola Historical Society, 1989)

National Archives, Cartographic Branch, various record groups

Odier, Pierre, *The Rock, A History of Alcatraz, The Fort/The Prison*, (Eagle Rock, CA: L'image Odier, 1982)

Parkerson, Codman, *New Orleans: America's Most Fortified City*, (New Orleans, LA: The Quest, 1990)

Parks, Virginia, and Johnson, Sandra, ed., *Civil War Views of Pensacola*, (Pensacola, FL: Pensacola Historical Society, 1993)

Parks, Virginia, Rick, Alan, and Simons, Norman, *Pensacola in the Civil War*, (Pensacola, FL: Pensacola Historical Society, 1978)

Peters, Richard, ed., *Pubic Statutes at Large of the United States of America*, (Boston, MA, 1850)

Peterson, Harold L., *Forts in America* (New York: Scribner's Sons, 1964)

Peterson, Harold L., *Round Shot and Rammers* (Harrisburg, PA: Stackpole Books, 1969)

Report of General J. G. Totten, Chief Engineer, on the Subject of National Defenses (Washington, DC: A. Boyd Hamilton, 1851)

Report of Lieutenant-Commander Williams, U. S. Navy, Roxbury, Mass., September 27, 1864, to Gideon Welles, Secretary of Navy. Available in *Official Records of the Union and Confederate Navies in the War of the Rebellion*

Report of the Secretary of War, November 1, 1851

Robinson, Willard B., *American Forts-Architectural Form and Function* (Urbana, IL: University of Illinois Press, 1977)

Sarty, Roger F., *Coast Artillery 1815-1914,* (Alexandria Bay, NY: Museum Restoration Service, 1988)

Simpson, Jeffrey, *Officers and Gentlemen, Historic West Point in Photographs,* (Tarrytown, NY: Sleepy Hollow Press, 1982)

Still Pictures Branch, National Archives and Records Administration, Record Group 77 and others

von Scheliha, Viktor E.K.R., A Treatise of Coast Defense: Based on the Experience Gained by Officers of the Corps of Engineers of the Army of the Confederate States, (London: UK, 1868)

Weigler, History of the United States Army, (1967)

Wilcox, Arthur M., and Ripley, Warren, The Civil War at Charleston, (Charleston, SC: Post-Courier, 1961)

About the Photographs and Drawings

The photogrphs used in this book were obtained from several sources, and are used with permission. The author is grateful for the generosity of those providing illustrations, they have greatly enhanced the quality of this book. Source credits are used in the caption of each photo.

Photographs obtained from these sources were published as received, with the possible exception of dust spotting and cropping.

Photographs taken by the author were often modified to depict the fortifications as they were in the nineteenth century. In many cases, this simply involved removing automobiles and landscaping equipment from the photographs. In other cases, it involved minor "rebuilding" of a fort, or the inverse. In a photograph of Fort Taber, for example, concrete blocks blocking the loopholes and howitzer embrasures were removed from the photograph. In certain cases, however, it involved the removal of significant structures that were added in later periods. The author was very sensitive in this operation to maintain the historical accuracy of the photographs, usually using NARA drawings as direction in the modifications.

All drawings were obtained from the National Archives and Records Administration (NARA), and are the original documentation of the forts. Some of these drawings were printed as recieved, others were used as a basis for the author's sketches. All labels in the drawings were added by the author.

Original drawings by the author wer not listed as to source. They were created by the author after study of drawings, existing structures, and textual references. All sites of Third System forts were visited and photographed by the author on numerous occaisions, and this documentation was used extensively in this process.

Key to the credits:
Photo courtesy of NARA indicates a photograph copied from the National Archives and Records Administration Still Pictures Branch, Archives II, College Park, Maryland.

Drawing courtesy of NARA indicates a drawing obtained from the National Archives and Records Administration Cartographic Branch, Archives II, College Park, Maryland.

Photo courtesy of MHI indicates a photograph obtained from the Military History Institute, Carlisle Barracks, Pennsylvania.

Photo courtesy Terrance McGovern or *photo courtesy Dale Manuel* are photographs taken by those noted historian/photographers and used with their permission.